P9-DDF-939

How I Gave Up My Glitzy Job in Television to Have the Time of My Life Teaching Amerasian Kids in Vietnam

SIMON & SCHUSTER

New York   London   Toronto   Sydney   Tokyo   Singapore

A YEAR

IN

SAIGON

Katie Kelly

SIMON & SCHUSTER
Simon & Schuster Building
Rockefeller Center
1230 Avenue of the Americas
New York, New York 10020

SIMON & SCHUSTER and colophon are registered trademarks
of Simon & Schuster Inc.

Designed by Nina D'Amario/Levavi & Levavi
Manufactured in the United States of America

1   3   5   7   9   10   8   6   4   2

Library of Congress Cataloging-in-Publication Data

Kelly, Katie.
  A year in Saigon : how I gave up my glitzy job in television to have
the time of my life teaching Amerasian kids in Vietnam / Katie Kelly.
      p.   cm.
   1. Kelly, Katie.   2. Volunteer workers in education—Vietnam—
Saigon—Biography.   3. Amerasians—Education—Vietnam—Saigon.
4. Amerasians—Vietnam—Saigon—Social conditions.   5. Children of
military personnel—Vietnam—Saigon.   6. Abandoned children—
Vietnam—Saigon.   I. Title.
LB2844.1.V6K45   1992
371.1'0092—dc20   92-5989
                                                          CIP

ISBN: 0-671-75090-9

ACKNOWLEDGMENTS

I would like to thank all my friends in Saigon—mothers, cyclo drivers, old soldiers, shopkeepers, strangers on the street—who helped me, encouraged me, kept me going during the year. The goodness and kindness and generosity—and humor—of the Vietnamese people are treasured moments in my life. And back home, my thanks to everyone who cheered me on in this endeavor, especially the Vietnam vets who expressed support. And, of course, many thanks to Marilyn Wagner, cat-sitter *extraordinaire*. Thanks also to my agent Barbara Lowenstein, to Loretta Barrett for her guidance, to Marilyn Abraham who edited with such sensitivity, and to copyeditor Margaret Cheney who lent her own gentle touch to the project.

To Kim. And Bryner and Jim and Pearl and Thanh. And all the other American children we left behind that day in 1975. And, of course, to Mr. Linh.

CONTENTS

REMEMBERING VIETNAM

It seemed insignificant at the time. I saw a pretty young girl in front of me. She had brown wavy hair, hazel eyes, and a scattering of freckles across her nose. She looked like a high school senior on her way to cheerleading practice or senior homeroom or, maybe, just to the local mall. I became puzzled and disoriented. Had we met before? Were we related? Then she asked if I wanted to buy some postcards and I was knocked back to reality. Intellectually, I knew where I was, but standing there and looking at that smiling all-American face in front of me confused me. Sent me into some deep-down part of myself that denied where *I* was if only to deny where *she* was, this lovely American girl. I was in Vietnam. And she was an Amerasian. Her name was Kim and little did I know that moment would change my life.

"What are you doing here?" I asked, still disoriented.

"I sell you postcards, O.K.?" She had a smile of such sweetness it took my breath away.

There are moments when the world seems to stop. Not with a bang or a crash. But with silence. I was standing on a battered sidewalk in downtown Saigon. I knew that. The venerable old Hotel Continental with its potted palms and ceiling fans—a remnant of Vietnam's French Colonial days—was off to my left. Behind me, at the far end of the street, was the old red brick cathedral. And all around me were vivid reminders of precisely where I was: women in cone hats, men pedaling cyclos, the bustle of everyday life in Saigon. But that day the edges of that world closed in on me, shutting out my surroundings. It was as if the camera eye began closing, blocking out everything that was unimportant until all that remained was that lovely American face in front of me.

"My name Kim. You buy postcards? You buy peanuts?" I blinked and peered at her, and as my vision cleared, the peripheral darkness diminished and I was once again in control of my senses. Kim was the first Amerasian I met in Saigon. And it was a shock to my soul, seeing that smiling American girl standing there on a street corner in Saigon, speaking broken English and selling postcards and peanuts. A sobering experience indeed.

Trying to recover, I bought some postcards and asked if I could take her picture, and she agreed. The light wasn't good but I took the picture anyway and then I started to walk away. But that didn't seem quite right: buy some postcards, take a picture, and then just walk away. So we strolled down to the river and sat on some tiny wooden stools in an outdoor stall and had a lemonade. Kim had taught herself some basic street English so we talked for a while. I managed to learn that she was eighteen years old, lived with her mother and her half sister in a distant suburb of Saigon, and came downtown every day with her armload of postcards and maps and peanuts to sell to the few Western tourists who came through Saigon. She told me that her mother's name was Nguyet and she sold cigarettes outside the Rex Hotel. She also told me that someday she would go to America and live with her GI father and have a wonderful life. I was swept with sadness at her ability to dream such dreams. We talked for a while and then I left.

I was busy being a tourist in Vietnam and spent the rest of my time there going off to see the sights. But from time to time I would catch a glimpse of Kim, smiling and holding her postcards out to tourists, mostly beefy Russians on packaged tours from their factories or work groups. She was so tiny next to them. Sometimes they stopped, turned the cards over in their hands, then shrugged and walked away. More often they didn't even stop, just pushed past her and continued down the street as if she didn't exist. I wanted to run after them and shake them for being so blind.

And then it was time to go. I gave Kim some gifts—a bar of soap, some toothpaste, a crisp $5 bill, a small American flag—and then I left, flying off to a life in America she could hardly imagine.

As my car pulled away from the hotel, I looked back and saw her standing there on the sidewalk, clutching her gifts and that little American flag. She looked so vulnerable. I felt my cheeks. They were covered with tears.

Vietnam had changed my life back in the sixties. I had come to New York in 1959, straight out of Boone County, Nebraska, by way of the University of Missouri School of Journalism. There was a brief break in 1961 when I left New York to get married and teach school in the Midwest and California. I spent four years teaching everything from one year of rural high school in Nebraska, to two years of fifth grade in suburban Chicago, and back to high school for a year in Alameda, California, a Navy town just outside San Francisco. There I had students whose fathers served on the aircraft carriers coming into port. Carriers going back and forth to a place called Vietnam. I must have had students in my senior homeroom who went off to Vietnam. I didn't know. And then, I guess I wasn't much interested. It was only 1965.

I had become a teacher by accident and I loved every minute of it, but by 1966 the marriage had gone bust and I was back in New York for good, this time working for *Time* magazine. And I was becoming dimly aware of a place called Vietnam. I might have been a big-city journalist by this time, but I was still a bumper-sticker kid from the Midwest: AMERICA—LOVE IT OR LEAVE IT! MY COUNTRY RIGHT OR WRONG! Indeed, I was a charter member of the Silent Generation that glided so quietly out of the 1950s. The noisiest thing in our lives was Elvis Presley. Acceptance was our operating philosophy. So when Vietnam came along, we accepted it. I was in New York, where political opinion swirled through the air like leaves before a storm, but I was untouched by those conflicting ideas and ideals. My country was at war. I accepted that.

Some of New York's activist spirit eventually got to me, however, and in 1967 I joined my first demonstration: I marched down Fifth Avenue to protest the antiwar activists who had burned their draft cards in front of the Selective Service office in downtown Manhattan. I even remember what I was wearing: a white blouse, red-white-and-blue-striped scarf, navy-blue miniskirt, white knee socks, and white patent-leather Mary Janes. All topped off by a geometrically precise Sassoon haircut. It was, after all, the Swinging Sixties. I shouted patriotic slogans and sang every verse of "God Bless America." Six months later, I was marching on Washington with an oddball assortment of hippies, yippies, mommies, daddies, and others in the antiwar movement. America would never be the same again. Nor would I. I had changed completely.

The six-month sea change that came over me in 1967 was gradual but steady. When I first went to work for *Time* in 1966, I was a researcher (the only job a "girl" could get in the mid-sixties) floating between the Nation and World sections. And I was still unabashedly gung-ho, very much a hawk on the war. Every week I would see the unedited copy coming in from our correspondents in the Saigon bureau. At first I read it because often I had nothing else to do. Late closings at *Time*—when the week's issue was finally written, edited, and ready to be shipped off to the printers—were legendary in those days, often due to last-minute, late-breaking stories on the war. Like the other Nation and World researchers, I had to stand by, in case a writer needed me to dig up any material or check any facts at the last minute. And if you were in the Nation or World section the normal Saturday-night closing often stretched well into Sunday. So I would occupy myself by reading all the files sent in from our overseas correspondents. It was quite an education. Especially the copy filed from Vietnam.

Periodically, the correspondents, stringers, and photographers would stagger home for a little stateside R & R, and invariably we would end up at Hurley's Bar on Forty-ninth Street and Sixth Avenue. This was the old, scruffy Hurley's Bar that slopped gallons of beer and booze into an assortment of *Time, Life,* and *Sports Illustrated* types. As opposed to the new and improved Hurley's (read: gentrified) that stands there now, serving up designer water and wine spritzers to the hoity toity types from NBC. But back then, in the dark and sudsy comfort of the old Hurley's, those veterans of the war of the words would regale us rear-echelon troops with their front-line dispatches from that faraway place called Vietnam.

I remember one particularly boozy night, which had sloshed over into dawn of the next day. As usual, the discussion became heated, with the on-scene correspondent accusing *Time*'s then-conservative editors of avoiding the reality of our presence in Vietnam. The fired-up reporter believed that it was the wrong war in the wrong place at the wrong time with thousands of people on all sides dying because of it. That while body bags were being filled with American GIs, corrupt South Vietnamese officials were filling their pockets with profits. War was big business in South Vietnam.

"Those fucking editors!" the correspondent railed. "The only way to get a decent Vietnam story in the magazine is to plant it in the *New York Times* first!"

Shortly after that, a zinc table went sailing through the front window and out onto Sixth Avenue. It was followed swiftly by all of us, tossed out by the fed-up night manager. He was a decent sort, though: he sent us out through the swinging doors.

As time passed, I saw more and more correspondents come home in a daze. I met photographers who couldn't sleep at night. One quiet New York night some of us were strolling down the street with Tim Page, that legendary *Time-Life* photographer who would have part of his head blown away in Vietnam in 1969. But this was only 1967, long before his encounter with the booby-trapped 105-mm shell that tore through his skull. Page was back from Vietnam, taking a break from Vietnam with some stateside shooting assignments. As we all walked down that silent street, our footsteps echoing through the silence, someone behind us kicked over a metal garbage can. The lid went rolling and banging across the concrete. Page went flat out on the sidewalk. It was that kind of war. And it changed my life. Because for the first time in my no-questions-asked existence I was forced to confront my own upbringing. "America Right or Wrong" was now open to serious debate. It was a shattering experience for someone who knew all the verses to "God Bless America."

Yet even then I was conflicted by Vietnam, and probably I still am. I turned thirty in 1966, about the same time the world was told not to trust anyone over thirty. So there I was, caught flat-footed in the Generation Gap. Old enough to have known about independent countries like Tibet, Latvia, Lithuania, and Estonia, not to mention the entire Eastern Bloc, China, and Cuba before they were eaten alive by Communism. I was in high school during the Korean "police action." It even figured prominently in the speech I gave at my 1954 graduation. So the threat of international Communism was very real to a mid-century, Midwestern kid like me. On the other hand, I was young enough to have gnawing doubts not only about what Vietnam might be facing (Communism) but what it was already experiencing (a pathetically inept and hideously corrupt regime).

Living in New York—in America—in the late sixties and early seventies was a political education, an exercise in political involvement. On the issue of the Vietnam War, it was impossible to be neutral. There were moratoriums, marches, sit-ins, teach-ins, write-ins. For many the catalyst was the 1968 Democratic Convention in Chicago, with its chaos and hatred. Everything that had been smoldering for years finally broke loose and exploded over America like a fragmentation bomb, showering the whole country with reality.

There was indeed no place to run, no place to hide. You simply could not stand on the sidelines any longer. In 1969 I rode a chartered school bus to Washington, D.C., for the Moratorium to End the War. Wrote letters for "Another Mother for Peace." Wore my VIVA (Voices in Vital America) bracelet every day until 1973, when I learned that the MIA whose name was etched on it—an Air Force helicopter pilot missing since November 6, 1965—had been released from his North Vietnamese prison and had come home.

Of course, we eventually got out of Vietnam and I joined everyone else in America in heaving a sigh of relief and going on to other things. That war, which had changed me so significantly, receded into the background like an old song. Instead of marching and picketing and writing letters to end the war, I directed any residual activist energies I might have had to the women's movement and various environmental causes. But mostly I was reveling in finally having a "career" instead of just a "job" because by then I had become a full-time, full-fledged writer (and, for a time, the only woman writer) for *Time* magazine. My specialty: show business.

By 1972 I had been a *Time* writer for five years. I guess it went to my head: I quit to freelance. That turned out to be a shocking experience, quickly teaching me that even after publishing two books (*The Wonderful World of Women's Wear Daily* in 1972 and *GARBAGE: The History and Future of Garbage in America* in 1973) freelancing, for me at least, was just a fancy word for "unemployment." In 1977 I was rescued from that state by becoming the television columnist for the Rupert Murdoch version of the *New York Post* ("Headless Body Found in Topless Bar!" "Torture Teens Find Happiness at Last"), which led to the ultimate surprise: from writing *about* television, I landed a job *on* television. In 1978 I became the on-air entertainment critic for WNBC-TV, the local NBC affiliate in New York. No one was more shocked than I.

By this time it was 1978 and Vietnam was long gone, yesterday's news safely buried for me and, indeed, for most of the rest of the country; a part of our collective past that had been put in a box and stored in the national attic along with fading campaign ribbons, uniforms that no longer fit, and old ideas that didn't wear so well either.

And so I plunged into the eighties. I had a glamour job and an agent who negotiated television deals for me. As NBC's theatre and movie critic, I was on the aisle with a pair of coveted opening-night tickets for every Broadway show. Ditto for every blockbuster Hollywood movie. I flew to Tinsel Town two or three times a year, stayed in a bungalow at the Beverly Hills Hotel, interviewed the stars, and put it all on my expense account. There was even a brief stint as the television critic for the *Today* show, sharing the set with Jane Pauley and Tom Brokaw. And I loved every minute of it.

I had grown up without indoor plumbing in a house heated by a kerosene stove. The closest telephone was in the rooming house next door and it was primarily used to place and receive calls about terminal illness or death. We hadn't even heard of television. My winter coats were sewn from hand-me-downs by my resourceful mother but periodically I would stick my nose in the air and sail off to school wearing the latest castoffs from a cousin in California. I was jubilant on those occasions when "the box" from California arrived in the mail. It was always full of store-bought clothes. For years after arriving in New York I sewed my own clothes, shopped at the Salvation Army, bought discount "designer" clothes with the labels slashed out of them, and lived in a fifth-floor walk-up on the Lower East Side with the bathtub in the kitchen and the toilet in the hall. But with television that all changed. I ended up with a landmark Victorian brownstone in the Chelsea section of Manhattan, a Gold Card, and new clothes with the labels still firmly in place. I told myself I deserved all this, that it made up for that outdoor privy and the fact that I didn't have a date to the senior prom.

Then in 1985 something significant happened: New York had a parade.

Now, New York is always having a parade, everything from the St. Patrick's Day colossus to Gay Pride and the Macy's Thanksgiving Day Parade. But this one was different. Unique. In 1985 there was a grass-roots movement that turned into a groundswell of emotion: our first Vietnam parade.

There they were, ten years after we pulled out of Vietnam: Vietnam vets, marching through the canyons of downtown Manhattan to the roaring thunder of laughing, crying, and cheering New Yorkers. Lower Manhattan became a massive small town filled with confetti and tears and American flags. To this day, it remains one of the most emotional moments this city has ever seen. Millions of New Yorkers turned out to honor those men and women, who were marching, walking, limping, being pushed in wheelchairs.

I was back in the newsroom, watching the parade on a monitor. It was overwhelming. I saw reporters break down and start to cry. We had to cut to another shot when one of our cameramen suddenly stopped shooting and ran into the parade itself. He had spotted some of his buddies from Vietnam. None of us knew he had even been there. I was scheduled to review a movie that day but somehow I knew I could not do that.

Fortunately, my producer agreed, and with no firm idea in mind I was given a crew and dispatched downtown to the parade's end: New York's own Vietnam Memorial, a green frosted glass wall on which letters written home from Vietnam had been etched. My on-air piece that night was simple: veterans reading excerpts from those letters. And it was then the emotion of Vietnam flooded back. I cried all the way through the editing of that piece. And then I realized I had done what so many others had done: I had pushed Vietnam away. Stuffed it in some far-off and forgotten corner of my mind where it had stayed, remote and untroubling for all those years. But now, here it was. Back again. Nudging me. Haunting me. And I knew where all this emotion was leading me.

How could I have forgotten about Vietnam and all it had once meant to me? Was I now so caught up in the 1980s that I couldn't even remember that personal transformation of mine and its significance? Gradually, the books on Vietnam began accumulating in my living room. Was it my imagination or were newspapers and magazines now devoting a lot more space to Vietnam? Finally the message got through to me: whether I knew it or not, I was planning a trip. A pilgrimage. To Vietnam.

My first visit to Vietnam was in December of 1988. I went as a tourist. It was as if I were drawn there, pulled by some invisible thread that reached all the way back to the sixties, tugging at my conscience. While it was historically and personally interesting to visit all those familiar names and places: Hanoi, Danang, Hue, China Beach, it was in Saigon that the final chapter of that war came home to me: I saw all those Amerasians.

To this day, Vietnam and our involvement in it remain a place and time of terrible statistics: 58,022 Americans dead; some 300,000 wounded; 2,303 missing in action. But on April 30, 1975, when that final helicopter lifted off the roof of the American Embassy in Saigon, over 30,000 other Americans were also left behind. They were children, the sons and daughters of Vietnamese mothers and American fathers. Our children. Amerasians.

Kim was the first one I met and she shocked my sensibilities. But I met dozens more there. Some of them were a delicate mix of Vietnamese and American. Others were more obvious: the girl with blond hair and blue eyes selling cigarettes across from the cathedral.

The kid in the park I called Kellogg because he had bright red hair and freckles and looked as if he had just fallen off a cornflakes box. Black kids, Hispanic kids. American kids. Some of them had mothers and families. Hundreds of others were homeless, living on the streets of Saigon.

Because of the lack of diplomatic relations between Vietnam and the United States, Americans were a rare sight in Vietnam. Tourists there were mainly Russians and Eastern Bloc Communists, so the sight of an American in Saigon brought the Amerasians out in droves. They were thrilled to see a real, live American. A walking, talking, flesh-and-blood representative from the land of their fathers.

I bought their postcards, took them to lunch, sat in the park and talked to them for hours. Like Kim, some—with the help of their mothers—had taught themselves a few words of English. They were eager to learn more, so often our talks would turn into vocabulary lessons. And I learned that with eager, curious students anything is a teaching tool.

For some reason, I had stuck a calendar in my purse. It was nothing special. A giveaway gift from the insurance company that wrote the policy on my New York brownstone. It was a picture calendar entitled "Scenic America," and each month featured a beautiful full-color picture of the American landscape: Yosemite Falls (March), a lighthouse in Maine (April), the Golden Gate Bridge (July). The kids marveled at "The Grand Tetons, Wyoming" (September), sucked in their breath at the snow-covered landscape of "Redfish Creek, Idaho" (December). But their hands-down favorite bit of "Scenic America" was October: "Albany, Vermont." It was a portrait of a quiet country road running through an avenue of trees brilliant with fall foliage, a scene washed with peacefulness and gentleness. The calendar was passed from one end of the park to the other. It took nearly an hour for it to make its way back to me. By that time we had turned our attention to the United Airlines route map I had taken from the seat pocket in front of me on the flight over. They were curious about every aspect of that map and seemed very proud of America's position in the world. Most had never seen a map before. I felt a great sadness come over me, partly as a former teacher but mostly as a human being.

And then I left. I gave away the scenic calendar and the route map and came back to America and that cushy television job at NBC. Home to the land of indoor plumbing and bank accounts and occasional fancy parties and limousine rides. To a lifestyle that enabled me to spend more money on medical care for my cats than most Vietnamese will see in a lifetime. And I put Vietnam and those Amerasians out of my mind. Or so I thought.

In reality, I was haunted by those young people—people with tragic pasts and no future. Finally, I couldn't stand it any longer. (Actually I couldn't stand *myself* any longer. Flushing a toilet filled me with guilt.) I'd been extremely lucky. And I knew it. Instead of a midlife crisis, I'd been lucky enough to have a midlife career—a career that had given me enough financial security to be able now, perhaps, to put a little bit of my good fortune where it might do some good. It was not so much a matter of how could I leave all that big-city glamour and excitement but, rather, how could I not do a little something for these young people? I had forgotten about them—and now I couldn't forget them.

After I got back from that vacation trip to Vietnam, I made a file folder and stuck it in a drawer in my desk at NBC. It was marked "Volunteer Activities" and from time to time I would toss articles, clippings, and notes into it. I looked at it recently and it contained everything from a *New York Times* article on volunteer doctors in West Africa to volunteer teachers in Central America. There was also a hand-scrawled note to myself about a GI who had gone back to Vietnam to visit and had then gone on to establish a halfway house in Saigon for those homeless Amerasians he had seen there. The piece of paper about the halfway house worked its way to the top of the pile and stayed there. That was the first signal that I was becoming increasingly restless, and Vietnam was moving not only to the top of my list but to the forefront of my thoughts. Gradually, it became more and more apparent that what I really wanted to do was go back to Vietnam and work with Amerasians. I didn't want to think about reviewing television movies or inter-viewing celebrities because I couldn't stop thinking about those Amerasian kids. I would find myself taking out their pictures and looking at them. I began rereading the letters I received from them. Eventually I contacted some of the groups that had been working in Vietnam before 1975—the Mennonites, the Catholics, the Pearl Buck Foundation, and others—to find out if they had reestablished any projects back in Vietnam or if they were planning any for the near future and, if so, did they need any volunteers? Just asking, you understand. Just asking. They were all enthusiastic and encouraging but none had gotten permission from either the Vietnamese or the American government to go back in and set up any projects or programs. It all seemed hopeless until the day I dug out that hand-written note about that GI and his project.

I called him and we talked back and forth for a few weeks. His project seemed perfect for me: he told me he had rented a house in Saigon to provide the basics—a place to sleep at night and a small food program—for a hundred or so homeless Amerasians. And he was very enthusiastic when I mentioned my idea of setting up and running a tutoring program to help these kids learn English. Best yet, he told me he had permission from the authorities in Saigon as well as from the United States government to operate his facility.

Now, periodically I had dipped my toe in the mainstream of do-goodism, participating in an assortment of safe and, I suppose, politically correct activities. This consisted mainly of writing letters for Amnesty International and writing a lot of checks everywhere else. On Thanksgiving I volunteered to serve meals to senior citizens at St. Malachy's Catholic Church in Times Square. And at Christmas and Easter I would go and do likewise at a center for homeless women. But I was still just a dabbler. Not much more than my big toe ever got wet. But that trip to Vietnam kept gnawing at me, nudging my guilt feelings. And finally it got to me. I was ready to jump in feet first. Those Amerasians had so captured my attention that I realized that here, at least and at last, was something I could focus on. Something I could concentrate on.

Meanwhile, there had been some very important activity in Washington concerning the Amerasians in Vietnam: Congressman Robert Mrazek of Long Island, who had visited Vietnam and had likewise been emotionally bowled over by the sight of all these Amerasian youngsters he kept seeing on the streets, had authored the Amerasian Homecoming Act. This mandated the establishment of a cooperative effort between the Vietnamese government and the American government to locate and process every Amerasian in Vietnam and bring them and any immediate family members—mothers, stepfathers, siblings—to America as part of the State Department's Orderly Departure Program for refugees. The Amerasian Homecoming Act was passed in December of 1987, and although these young people and their families were now being processed by the thousands, it would still take years to get them all through the labyrinthian bureaucracies of both countries.

Thus, that vet's idea to shelter as many of these homeless Amerasians as he could and my idea to start teaching them English in preparation for their eventual relocation to the United States seemed a perfect match. So I threw my lot in with him and his project, and with a great deal of confidence, I quit that cushy job of mine and announced to family and friends alike that I was leaving NBC, leaving New York, leaving the country to go to Vietnam to teach school. It was the easiest decision I have ever made. Corny but true: I had to follow my heart before it broke altogether. Beyond that, there's really no explaining it. I just did it.

I suppose, though, that decision was ultimately made for the simplest of reasons: gratitude. And guilt. I had been so lucky in life. I not only had the luck of the Irish but the luck of the draw to have been born in the right place at the right time: the U.S. of A. Before the war. The Big One. I had a simple life in the simplest of times. Despite my Depression beginnings, my life really was the American Dream. My mom really did bake apple pies. From scratch. She wore hair nets and sensible shoes and housedresses. My dad worked hard and played catch with me and gave me a dog for my first birthday. I had a red tricycle that I rode up and down the sidewalk in front of my white frame house with its green screen door. I learned to ride my Schwinn two-wheeler on a gravel street in a small town in Nebraska where nobody locked their doors and everybody knew your first name. My backyard really had a picket fence.

And that made me feel guilty. Unlike many of us and our fortunate kids, those Amerasians we left behind in Vietnam had so little. And, in Vietnam at least, even less to look forward to. They were uneducated and underprivileged, some with no homes and no hope. As for me, I had nothing to hold me back. My husband and I were long divorced and I had no children of my own to worry about. So I announced my plans to my friends in New York and my family back in Nebraska—my brother and sister and an assortment of nieces, nephews, and cousins.

As usual they simply accepted this announcement of mine, having long ago gotten used to unusual behavior on my part. ("Well, she is from New York," observed one of my nieces by way of explanation when I told them I was celebrating my fiftieth birthday by taking a 120-mile hike through the Atlas Mountains of Morocco. I guess to them this decision of mine to pack it all in and go to Vietnam was just another 120-mile hike.)

As for me, I suppose there was also a good deal of curiosity involved in this decision of mine. As a journalist, a writer, a human being, I was certainly curious about that country that had so involved us all—including me for so many years. Curious about the people we had left behind, about those children, by now teenagers and young adults. The big question was: how would I react to being plucked from my la-de-da lifestyle in New York and plunked down in the middle of a strange country, a strange culture, thinking about someone besides myself for a change.

Professionally, it wasn't such a far-out decision either. I had worked in television longer than I had worked at any other job. And after twelve years I had done just about everything there was to do in television—local, network, syndication—and I was beginning to get restless. Finally, I had to admit I was approaching my limit of reviewing movies and TV shows and interviewing celebrities. (Face it: how many times can you ask about some star's stay at the Betty Ford Clinic and still be interested in the reply?) I figured I'd better leave before restlessness turned into full-blown boredom. Meanwhile, during the twelve years I had worked in television, it too had changed. Dramatically. By the time I left, all three networks had been sold to other larger corporations and had thus become just another order of business at annual shareholders' meetings. The venerable RCA, NBC's parent company, had been gobbled up by General Electric. We were now just part of a company that made refrigerators and light bulbs. Television news was just part of a business and was itself turning into business-as-usual. So very few of my colleagues were too surprised at my decision to leave and go off to Vietnam. They were intrigued, however. There was a flurry of headlines and news stories in the local New York press. The Associated Press put a story on the wire. Obviously it was a very slow news day in December. Jane Pauley even interviewed me for an NBC special she was working on. Six months later it was old news and NBC promptly lost interest.

So I organized my life and took off for Saigon. My self-appointed mission was simple. I would do the only other thing I could do besides review movies: teach English to any Amerasian I could find who wanted to learn.

I couldn't wait.

RETURN TO SAIGON

I was making my last public ap-
pearance representing NBC, and the crowd was enormous. The
cheers and shouts could be heard for miles, echoing through the
cold winter air, and I was absolutely exhilarated, enveloped in the
waves of warm good cheer. I couldn't stop grinning. I gave the
crowd a big smile and waved heartily as I leaned over the railing.
Then I turned and faced forward. I was looking squarely into an
enormous rear end. It was positively pneumatic: two large, rosy
cheeks staring me smack in the face.

Perhaps it was appropriate that my last appearance on behalf
of NBC was on the NBC float in the Macy's Thanksgiving Day
Parade. And I was located directly behind Snuggle the Bear. It was
Snuggle they were cheering for. And it was Snuggle's huge, inflated
rubber buns—dipping and swooping in front of me—that blocked
my otherwise perfect view of the parade as it made its joyful way
down Central Park West and then onto Broadway, past the millions
of people who lined the 2.5-mile route all the way to Macy's in
Herald Square. But I'm no fool: I basked in Snuggle's reflected glory
and waved madly at the crowd.

My appearance in the parade was a complete fluke. They
couldn't find anybody else. The producers had gone around and hit

up all the local anchors—the hotshots who can sometimes be seen on the network in the middle of the day, sandwiched in between *Days of Our Lives* and *Another World,* doing news updates—and spent hours begging and whining and pleading with them to get up at the crack of dawn, stand for five hours in the bone-breaking cold, all the while trying to smile, wave, and wipe their runny noses at the same time. I couldn't believe they all said no. But that was my big break: I got it by default. (P.S. I have never had so much fun in my life. And it was good to know that nose wiping is not such an art form that I couldn't get it mastered within a couple of blocks of our kickoff point.)

My moment of real, never-to-be-forgotten glory came a bit further on when we hit Herald Square: Deborah Norville and Willard Scott were waiting for us. Later in the day, when my family in Nebraska recovered from the shock of it all, they reported that both Deborah and Willard had actually mentioned me by name.

Once we were past Deborah and Willard we turned and went slowly and triumphantly across Thirty-fourth Street, past the Macy's reviewing stand and a few stragglers shivering in the icy cold, and then on to the end of the parade. We slid to a halt across the street from Macy's and I climbed off the float, frozen stiff. It was exactly noon and oddly silent there at parade's end. The limousine that had picked me up five hours earlier was nowhere in sight. The keeper assigned to me—who had picked me up at my house in that toasty warm limousine to make sure I actually ended up in the right place at the right time on the right float—had likewise disappeared. Meanwhile, the entire area at parade's end had been blocked off, which meant no buses or cabs were available, so I began hobbling up Seventh Avenue on my frozen feet. In the distance I could hear the crowds cheering for someone else. Then I looked over and saw something vaguely familiar lying alone in the cold snow and slush on a side street. I stopped to stare, icy cold-induced tears scratching down my face. It was Snuggle the Bear. He lay there on West Thirty-seventh Street, abandoned for the moment, his once pink and chubby buns now wrinkled and deflated in the snow and ice on the dirty pavement. I looked at him, that once-proud star of the Macy's Thanksgiving Day Parade. Only moments before, millions had been cheering his progress down Broadway. Now, here he was—flat and forgotten, sprawled like a bum in the middle of the street.

"Get a life!" I suggested. Then I wiped my nose and struggled up Seventh Avenue. I had to go to work.

*   *   *

That Thanksgiving Day Parade only served to remind me that my time at NBC was winding down. By Friday, December 29, it was indeed all over. Just before my last on-air appearance there were cake and champagne in the newsroom. For various reasons, four of us were leaving on the same day, so the top of the cake was a little crowded, what with all our names inscribed on it. The fourth person was obviously a surprise to management: that name had to be put on a three-by-five file card and attached to the cake with a glob of frosting. The cake was a cheerful-looking, store-bought confection covered with gooey flowers, which someone sliced into mismatched pieces with the handle of a plastic fork from someone's Chinese takeout lunch. It ran out just as they got to me. Was it an omen? No matter. It just meant I didn't have to brush my teeth again before I went on the air. I collected some hugs and kisses and well-wishes from the gang in the newsroom and then went down to makeup and had my face done for the last time, had my hair combed for the last time.

The David Letterman show was done in Studio 6A, right across the hall from the studio where my show was broadcast. So I walked over and stuck my head in to say goodbye to Dave and Paul Schafer, the musical director. I don't know if they saw me or not. I waved anyway. Then I walked back across the hall to Studio 6B and reviewed something called *Chameleons,* a TV movie starring Stewart Granger as a crime-fighting millionaire grandfather. (I called it a "dippy, dopey mind-numbing movie." It aired on NBC.) My show's producers had put together a blessedly funny on-air goodbye piece to me—little bits and pieces of things I had done over the past few years—so I didn't cry too much. There were a few tears, however, and some hugs and then my twelve-year career in television was over. I stood up, unhooked my microphone, and as the commercials between the five and six o'clock news were running, I said my goodbyes to the six-o'clock news crowd. I spent a few minutes in my office upstairs picking up the last of my belongings, turning out the light, and locking the door. A few of the reporters grabbed me and we went downstairs and hit Hurley's Bar for a few final beers.

As usual, the crowd was friendly and familiar and the din was enormous. But as I stood there at the bar, I had an intense and overpowering case of déjà vu. It was practically physical. I could barely breathe. For a moment, it was as if I had never left that bar. It was the sixties. The reporters were from *Time* magazine, not NBC-TV. The war was raging in Vietnam. I steadied myself on the bar, took a deep breath, kissed everybody in sight, and got out of there fast.

The sunshine caught up with me just outside of Bangkok, breaking through the cementlike pollution that covers that city most of the time. It followed me all the way to Ho Chi Minh City, glancing off the silvery skin of the plane. Back home in New York it was midwinter. It had taken me a few weeks to button things up enough to be able to leave with a clear conscience. But finally I had dovetailed all the arrangements—flights, visas, shots, and malaria medication—not to mention the life I was leaving behind. That included getting both a house sitter and a cat sitter and stashing enough cat food and kitty litter in the house to get them through a nuclear winter. I had also scoured New York for books and supplies for my tutoring project, but with a forty-four-pound weight limit in Asia I couldn't take much. So I settled for writing my own curriculum and taking one copy in with me, planning to rely on photocopying the necessary copies for my students. Beyond that I concentrated on extras like flashcards, a picture dictionary, and a jigsaw map of the United States, plus dozens of ballpoint pens donated by a bank in Scribner, Nebraska, where my brother still lives. And for those extra-special occasions: I had hustled up a few dozen team caps from the New York Giants and the New York Mets.

My plan was first just to get to Saigon, which was difficult enough since I needed a visa. And because Vietnam and America didn't have diplomatic relations, I couldn't get one in the United States. I had to go to a third country—one that did have diplomatic relations—to get that precious visa. Most people going to Vietnam have to stop off in Bangkok, go to a travel agent there, and get all the paperwork done. This can take days. I have known people who have spent over a week sitting in hot, humid Bangkok waiting for their paperwork to be processed. I was lucky. I used the same Asian travel agency I had used before so I was in and out of Bangkok in about twenty-four sleep-deprived hours.

From that point on, I was taking it one step at a time. I had no hotel reservations, figuring I could just go back to the hotel I had stayed in before and get a room, temporarily, until I got my bearings, found the halfway house, and had a better idea of what was available to me—what my options were. At one point in one of my many conversations with that Vietnam vet, he had indicated that I, too, could stay at the halfway house. He said that, although it was an old villa and wasn't in the greatest of shape, perhaps I could fix up something suitable for myself. I had gone to Hawaii in early February to participate in a fundraiser he had organized—a rock concert in a park near Waikiki Beach—and he had shown me some videos he had shot of the halfway house in Saigon, actually an old French-style villa. I remember being struck first by what a lousy cameraman he was (I seriously doubted that Saigon, despite being a tropical country, was that green), then by the fact that the house was big and bare and had a lot of mildew.

He didn't seem to have a specific address but that didn't bother me. Street names and numbers seemed to change at will in Saigon. Some people are still using the old French addresses, some use the addresses from the American time, while others use those imposed by the Communists after 1975. To the outsider, it all gets very confusing after awhile. Fortunately, the Vietnamese know exactly what you're talking about and where you're going. I was just told to ask around.

So now here I was—finally—in Vietnamese air space, preparing to land in Saigon. Part of me was in a jet-lagged twilight zone that had me partially numb after that twenty-four-hour flight across time zones and a date line, first to Bangkok and now into Saigon. The rest of me was wired tight and plugged into Tomorrow Land. I was ready to go, so electrified I was practically coming out of my skin. I'd really done it. I felt like Dr. Frankenstein: I had really taken my life apart and put it back together. I could only hope I hadn't created a monster. As I sat there, watching Saigon rush toward me, I nearly choked on excitement, anticipation. God, I was happy.

I noticed immediately that my arrival this year was somewhat different from my arrival the year before. Then I had come into Vietnam by way of Hanoi, where the landscape was a carpet of green, but shrouded in mist and rain. Outside Hanoi, we had banked toward a spine of low mountains. For the American pilots on bombing runs during the Vietnam War, that ridge of mountains pointed directly down the Red River and straight into Hanoi. Those pilots called it Thud Ridge after "The Thud," their nickname for the F105 Thunderchief. And below me, through the mist, I could see decades-old bomb craters filled with water. Vietnamese farmers raise fish in them these days. Nothing goes to waste in Vietnam, not even old bomb craters. We had dropped through the mist, and beneath the plane I could see small figures bent over the green rice fields. It looked like a postcard or an old photograph from *National Geographic*.

But today was different. Today I was arriving in Vietnam by way of Saigon. The sun was bright, the sky was blue, and I could see tropical palm trees bending in the breeze. As we taxied down the runway I could see dozens of old military helicopters, their olive-drab paint dull and faded, their blades drooping uselessly in the hot sun. This was Tan Son Nhut Airport, once the busiest air base in the world when those millions of American troops poured in and out of Vietnam during the late sixties and early seventies. Then, dozens of runways accommodated the almost constant activity surrounding that massive, hard-fought war. Now, there was only one runway. And there was not a single other plane on it besides the one I was in.

Inside the terminal, I was handed a customs form announcing I was in the Socialist Republic of Vietnam, home of "Independence-Freedom-Happiness." I started to fill it out and I immediately knew I was in terrible trouble. I had figured out how to answer Questions 1 through 9 (Name, Age, Address, and so on) but Question Ten stopped me cold:

> Objects must be declared. If there isn't any object mark "X" only at the quantity "Yes" column and if there are any objects, cross out letter "No" and at the same row write exact amount of weight of these objects in words or in figures.

Now, I had worked my way through college and emerged with a B+ average. I have even finished the Sunday *New York Times* crossword puzzle. Once. None of that helped me with Question 10. Further, the form warned me sternly against "giving false declaration or having the action of tricking." That did it. I took it personally. I was in a state of despair, totally unable to tell my objects from my quantities not to mention my "Yes" from my "No." It was *Heart of Darkness* come to life. Only instead of being stuck on the Congo River, forced to read Dickens over and over and over again, I would be stuck in Tan Son Nhut Airport in Saigon, forced to fill out customs forms over and over and over again. Customs forms I couldn't understand. Customs forms that were threatening to suffocate me.

Meanwhile, the heat was building, pressing in around me. My armpits turned soggy. I could feel my upper lip bead up and my hair start to frizz. The customs forms started sopping up the moisture from my sweating hands. Then they stuck to my palms. I looked down and discovered to my horror that those by-now soaking-wet customs forms were printed on paper so cheesy it was disintegrating right before my eyes. Soggy bits of wet paper were stuck haphazardly to my fingers and hands. I headed toward a customs official, the forms decorating my hands like wet toilet paper on a shoe. I was prepared to beg for help when she reached over and peeled the forms off my hands, and without a second glance, stamped them a zillion times. I watched the official red ink soak in, then spread out. Then she held one limp, runny form toward me, shook it expertly from her hand, and threw the other on a soggy pile. I grabbed my bags and ran like hell before she could change her mind.

I shared a van into the city with some other arriving visitors. They were staying at the Caravelle Hotel in downtown Saigon so, as they unloaded, I got out and looked around and saw some familiar landmarks: the old Continental Hotel was directly opposite the Caravelle, across a wide expanse of boulevard. The Continental holds a special place in the hearts of old Saigon hands, since most of the news operations were headquartered nearby and the terrace bar of the Continental was a favorite watering hole. In *The Quiet American,* Graham Greene set some of his key scenes at the Continental. When I had last seen it—could it really have been an entire year ago?—it had been undergoing a face lift and renovation and had been covered completely with scaffolding. It was now finished and reopened and gleaming in the sunlight. For purists, however, it had been ruined. That old outdoor terrace bar—the so-called "Continental Shelf"—had been enclosed and was now an upscale restaurant charging exorbitant prices and catering to the international business crowd.

I was standing there getting my bearings when suddenly I heard someone yell:

"Hey! American woman! You Kim's friend!"

I looked over and saw a young Amerasian running toward me. He was clutching the usual load of tourist postcards and maps. I had never seen him before in my life but he obviously knew who I was. He ran up to me, a big smile on his face.

"You Kim's friend," he repeated.

"Yes," I said. "How did you know?"

"I see pictures. You, Kim, Li-Ly, Mai. American flags. You Kim's friend!" He kept repeating this excitedly referring to a photo

I had someone take of me and Kim and her friends Li-Ly and Mai. They were all holding the small American flags I had given them.

I was amazed and somewhat flabbergasted. But it felt pretty good to have this welcoming committee of one mark my return to Saigon. It was also oddly touching to realize that a few snapshots—taken by a tourist who had wandered briefly through their lives—were so important. It was just one of many reminders of how much those things we take for granted—like full-color photos on demand—are so scarce and therefore so personally valuable in a country like Vietnam.

I had written to Kim faithfully during the past year and even had a few replies from her. But I had no way of knowing exactly how many of my letters had actually gotten delivered to her. I had told her I wanted to come back to Vietnam but I hadn't been specific about either my plans or my exact arrival, since both were so hard to nail down, thanks to the vagaries of visa approvals and airline schedules. There was also probably a bit of a guilty conscience at work there, too: I thought of how many times these people had been disappointed by promises made by Americans. I didn't want to add to that or be a part of it. But I had written and sent copies of the pictures I had taken. And Kim had obviously gotten them because here was this Amerasian—a stranger to me—who recognized me immediately.

Getting mail in and out of Vietnam was a roll of the dice, and only later did I realize both the sacrifice and the ingenuity it took to get a letter out of that country. To mail a letter out of Vietnam costs $1 per letter. This was cruelly expensive for the average Vietnamese, who made only 50 cents a day. So letters were handed off to foreigners to mail from their next stops, which meant that any letters I had received from Vietnam invariably came with a variety of strange and exotic stamps on them, mailed from Bangkok or Paris or Cairo or, in one case, West Seventy-ninth Street in Manhattan.

"Where you go now?" the Amerasian was asking me.

The Caravelle Hotel was too expensive for me, so I explained that I was heading off to the hotel where I had stayed before, the Que Huong. I figured I'd stay there just long enough to get my bearings and then find something cheaper. It was only $24 a night, but for an extended stay that would be prohibitive.

"O.K., Mama. See you later." And with that, the Amerasian disappeared down the street.

I took the van on over to the Que Huong and checked in. After I had stashed my bags, I went back outside and found that nothing

much had changed. Hung, my cyclo driver from a year ago, was still
there, as dusty and disheveled as ever. (The cyclo, a bicycle-powered
rickshaw, is the main means of transportation around Vietnam. The
passenger sits in an open seat in the front while the driver pedals
from behind.) Hung worked hard—and it was hard work—and had
a perpetually sad and bewildered look on his face. He gave a shout
of recognition when he saw me and loped over, leaving a trail of
dust and debris in his wake. His hat fell off, a thong slipped off his
foot, his shirt flapped in the air. He was followed by the rest of the
drivers, who had likewise staked out the area around the hotel,
hoping for fares.

"Good to see you, Kelly!" Hung said, grabbing my hand. (I was
called a number of different things in Saigon. After many attempts
to master my first name, the cyclo crowd at the Que Huong simply
gave up and settled for calling me by my last name, which they
probably thought was my first name anyway since name order is
reversed in Vietnam. Most of the Amerasians came to refer to me as
"Teacher" or "Mama." At first this was a little disconcerting, but
then I realized "Mama" was used much the same way youngsters in
American families might call close friends of their parents "Aunt"
or "Uncle," implying no blood relationship but indicating there is
genuine affection and warmth nonetheless.)

So I stood there, catching up on the Que Huong gossip: Anh
had taken over the cigarette spot in front of the hotel from Hyuyen,
who had gotten the side entrance, which was also the entrance to
the disco. Hyuyen was also pregnant. And Hung—whose wife had
abandoned him and their three children years ago because he was so
poor—had gotten married.

He reached down into some hidden compartment in his cyclo,
hauled out a photo album, and showed me pictures of the wedding.
I was astonished. I had only seen Hung in his ratty old cyclo-driving
clothes, dirty and sweat-stained items that had long ago given up
any resemblance to what they had originally been. But there he was,
captured in photographs, in all his polished wedding glory: he was
actually wearing a suit. Like a lot of us, he cleaned up real nice.

"Wow! Mr. Hung! You look great!" I enthused.

"Yes," he agreed solemnly. "Nice suit," he pointed out, just in
case I had missed it. "And look," he said, pointing to his feet.
"Shoes."

The bride was picture-perfect, too, a pretty young thing with a
sweet, shy face. She was wearing a long, frilly white Western-style
wedding dress and veil. There were pictures of them leaving for the

wedding, pictures at the church (Hung was a Catholic), pictures at a Buddhist temple (just for good measure, I guessed), pictures at a restaurant, with a lavish photographic record of the food.

"That's a great-looking suit, Mr. Hung," I told him.

"Yeah. I rent."

"You rented your suit?" I asked, just to make sure I had it right.

"Oh, sure, Kelly. I very poor. I no have money buy suit." He shrugged.

"What about your wife? Where did she get her beautiful dress?"

"She rent, too."

"She rented her gown?"

"Her what?"

"Her gown. Her dress," I clarified.

"How you spell?"

"G-O-W-N."

"Thanking you, Kelly." He meticulously wrote the word "gown" in a notebook he had produced from somewhere. Then he smiled a big smile. "Last year you tell me: Learn English! Good for business." He shook the notebook under my nose. "I learning." He paused to locate the thread of our conversation. "Yes, sure. Rent gown, too. Why buy—what you say?" He looked at his notebook.

"Gown," I prompted.

"Right. Thanking you. Why buy gown? Wear one time." He looked at me. "You married, Kelly?"

"Well, I was. Once."

"You buy new dress? He buy new suit?"

"Well, let me think now." It had been quite awhile. I made myself a new dress but my husband wore an old suit. An expensive old Brooks Brothers suit, as I recall.

"You wear dress again?" Hung asked. I was beginning to get his well-made economic point. Then I thought of all those useless wedding dresses hanging in garment bags in closets all over America. A few years ago, my own came out of the closet and saw the light of day in front of my young married nieces. I had just closed up my mother's house and we were unloading a pickup truck full of boxes at a U-Store-It shed on Highway 275 in Nebraska. A box spilled open and there it was. They fell apart laughing at the sight of my short homemade wedding dress.

All of this went lazily through my head as I stood there on a side street in Saigon, looking at snapshots of a cyclo driver's wedding with all its rented finery. The faces of Hung and his bride looking back at me from the photographs were the universal wedding faces: young, hopeful, fairly bursting with pride and happiness. So what if they had to take the suit and dress back the next day. I was mulling all this over when I felt a stirring near me. I looked up. It was Kim.

"You come back," she said in a near whisper.

Oh, Kim. You found me. "Yes, I came back," I said, giving her a big hug and starting to cry.

"Oh, Mama! Why you cry?" A look of concern and horror crossed her face. "What I do wrong? I so glad to see you. I make you sad? What wrong?"

I assured her she had done absolutely nothing wrong. "I'm just glad to see you, Kim. Sometimes Americans cry when they're happy," I explained, mopping my face and blowing my nose.

"I glad, too. You come back. I think you no come back. I think I never see you again. I very sad. But you come back!" She kept repeating it over and over again while I sopped up my face and blew my nose over and over again. I looked at Kim and noticed little things about her. Her hair had gotten longer. She seemed to have gotten a bit taller. Her English was better.

"I find my father," she said without preamble.

"What?" I couldn't believe I had heard her correctly. "What did you say?"

"I have father. I see him. I go America soon."

I was stunned. I remembered the conversation we had had a year earlier, standing on Dong Khoi Street. She had told me that someday she would go to America and live with her American father and have a wonderful life. I had chalked that up to sheer fantasizing, the kind of wishful thinking that just about all the Amerasian kids in Vietnam indulged in from time to time: the fantasy of finding their American fathers and being whisked off to America to have all their hopes and dreams come true.

"Yes. It true." She nodded her head up and down for emphasis. "I have father. Him name Ron. He come see me." She reached into her bag and pulled out a photograph and handed it to me. It was taken at Tan Son Nhut Airport, and there she was, standing with a tall, handsome man.

"He go back America. I cry all day," she said.

Kim's father had been a young GI in Vietnam during the war. He had met Kim's mother in Vung Tau, where she worked. They had a relationship and he left the country not knowing she was pregnant. By the time he found out, he was back in the States and it was too late for either of them to do anything about it. They exchanged a few letters but then the politics of war and its awful aftermath interfered and all contact was severed. But he had never forgotten about that daughter he had never seen. And as soon as relations between the two countries eased up enough for him to get back into Vietnam, he went back and began his search in Saigon. He hit the streets armed only with her name and her birthday. Fortunately Kim and her mother had been relocated to Saigon. And he found her. It was one of the very few success stories of that terrible time.

"I leave soon," Kim said, without preamble, breaking into my thoughts. "I leave tomorrow."

This was blow number one. I was stunned. Kim! You can't do this to me! I wanted to yowl in spoiled, selfish pain. Remind her, Hey! What about me? I just got here! I want to teach you English and do all those good things I have been dreaming of. For a moment or two I clicked over into spoiled-brat mode and concentrated on myself and my feelings. I mean, after all, whenever I thought about those Amerasians, it was Kim's face that would lead the parade. Fortunately, I snapped out of that little bit of self-importance almost immediately. Of course I was thrilled for Kim. I was just sorry that I would see so little of her. I could feel my eyes filling up all over again.

"Don't worry, Miss Katie," she said, patting my hand. "I see you America. That even better, don't you think?"

I agreed. She kept patting my hand, comforting me. "You know, Miss Katie, I never think my father find me. I never think I see you again. And soon I will see my father. And now I see you." She looked at me with her green eyes, her brown hair falling in soft waves around her face. "You know, Miss Katie, I am very lucky. I think God must love me very much. He let my father find me. I very lucky." What a wise child this was, this child of war standing on a street corner in Saigon talking to an American about good fortune. I pondered the serendipity of it all.

As I was marveling over seeing Kim again and reeling over the news about her father and the fact that she would be leaving Vietnam tomorrow, I saw a cyclo pull up and a tiny Vietnamese woman get out. She was absolutely lovely, with warm eyes and a big smile. But I was struck by her feet: they were the smallest feet I had ever seen. They were the size of flower petals. She paid the cyclo driver, then took off her cone hat and started walking toward our little group.

Kim pulled away and ran over to the woman, calling back to me. "This my mother. She come see you."

That delicate Vietnamese woman stunned me as I would continue to be stunned and surprised no matter how many mothers I met. I would always feel stupid about it but nonetheless I was always startled whenever I saw these kids' Vietnamese mothers or grandmothers. These very American-looking kids—freckles, sunburns, green eyes, curly hair, some black, some white, some with big American feet and big American noses—introducing me to their Vietnamese mothers, grandmothers, brothers, sisters.

"Oh, Miss Katie. How you do. I Kim's mother. I name Nguyet. I glad to see you. When you come my house for dinner?" She ran rapidly through her repertoire of leftover English, then, obviously exhausted by the effort, gave a big sigh, and grabbed my hand as if to hold on for dear life. We made a date for the next Sunday. Hung would bring me out in the cyclo and I would come for dinner. It would turn out to be the first of many such evenings, thus beginning the most incredible year I have ever had, centering around the gracious and unstinting hospitality of the Vietnamese people, particularly those remarkable mothers.

Nguyet was certainly one of those. She and thousands of mothers like her in Vietnam had constantly been called upon to make at first life-threatening decisions about even keeping their American children, and now, in Nguyet's case, a life-changing decision.

We went across the street to a little outdoor refreshment café and ordered some iced coffee. As we talked, I learned that Nguyet had another Amerasian daughter named Roan-na.

"She also my American child," Nguyet said proudly. "She not child of Ron. She half sister of Kim. Her name Roan-na. She my black American child. Roan-na stay home today but she want meet you very soon." Then she sat back, sighed, and smiled again. Kim then went on to help Nguyet explain that, during one of the many medical examinations required under the Orderly Departure Program, Roan-na had been judged to be mentally retarded and was denied permission to leave the country by the Vietnamese government. This obviously threw an enormous monkey wrench into the entire family's plans, and for months now their departure date had been held up by this decision. Finally, Nguyet made a decision of her own: she would send Kim and her Vietnamese brothers out of Vietnam. Nguyet would stay behind with Roan-na to continue pressing her case, trying to get someone somewhere to decide to let this family be reunited. It was one of the more heartbreaking decisions she would have to make, but as I learned, for Nguyet it was no decision at all. It was good for Kim, who could leave the country and start her new life. And Nguyet would just continue what she had been doing her whole life: fighting furiously for her American children.

"I love my children," Nguyet said, grabbing Kim's hand. "I love my American children. I want what right for them." She stroked Kim's pale arm as if it were made of silk. "I want my Kim go her father in America. I want her have future. I stay and help Roan-na. Someday—we go America, too."

I was so choked up I could only nod.

The Rex Hotel was one of the best—and best-known—hotels in Saigon. It dated back to the French Colonial period of the 1920s and had started life as a small, two-story Art Deco structure, although over the years it had lost much of that character. During the Vietnam War it had been a billet for U.S. Army forces, and extra floors had been slid onto it like layers on a cake until now it was five new but fairly nondescript stories high. Ordinary as it might have seemed from the outside, however, it was topped with one of the best outdoor terrace bars in all the world. Big, sprawling, comfortable, and quiet, it was loaded with greenery—trees, plants, flowers—and cages of delicately singing birds. You could spend hours undisturbed there, relaxing in a rattan chair, drinking coffee, and listening to the birds sing. I had discovered the Rex and its rooftop terrace on my last trip to Saigon. It quickly became a welcome respite from the Que Huong and its killer cockroaches, and I had vowed that the next time I came to Saigon I would stay at the Rex. Unfortunately, even at only $40 a night for a single, it was now out of my price range. What I needed was something infinitely cheaper than either the Rex or even the Que Huong.

I had spent the morning at a police station having my papers stamped—again—and was aiming for the terrace of the Rex and a glass of *café da*, delicious iced Vietnamese coffee. I wanted to sit quietly, relax, and work my way through whatever residual jet lag I might be suffering from. I also wanted to think about some more affordable living arrangements, so I could check out the halfway house and its facilities in a more leisurely fashion. But before I could make it inside the Rex and up to the terrace, I got distracted by some kids in front of the hotel selling postcards. Out of habit I was about to ask if Kim was around. I had spent so many months thinking about her and associating her with her postcards and the

Rex Hotel that it was hard for me to realize that she was really gone. While I was sitting in the police station getting my papers stamped to stay in Vietnam, she was out at the airport fulfilling a dream: to get out of Vietnam. To fly off to America and her new life. (Even though Kim had an American father ready and waiting for her in Fayetteville, North Carolina, she and her brothers still had to spend six months in a refugee camp being processed and prepared for entry into the U.S., the theory being that this way things like showers and time clocks wouldn't come as a complete shock.)

The Rex still had its regulars, among them, Linh. He was eighteen years old, Vietnamese, and spoke fairly decent English, so we sat and talked for awhile in the little vest-pocket park that fronts the Rex Hotel. At night that little park is crowded with families out strolling and socializing, but during the day it is quiet and fairly empty. I figured if Linh hung out around the hotels selling his postcards, he might know of something cheaper than the Que Huong and the Rex. So I asked if he knew of a cheap hotel nearby.

"Sure, Kelly. How much you pay?" I mumbled something about $10 a night.

"No problem. You want hot water?"

"That would be nice."

"No problem. You need an elevator?" I shrugged.

"I got the place for you. You stay Kim Do Hotel. Let's go, Kelly." He led me down Nguyen Hue Street, a broad boulevard punctuated by twin malls that run from the Rex Hotel down to the Saigon River. The malls are tree-shaded with a parade of little one-story kiosks on them. Linh and I were walking down a wide sidewalk that ran alongside Nguyen Hue Street, although in reality sidewalks in Saigon have almost nothing to do with walking. They are actually there to hold as many small stalls as possible, with vendors of every possible description. Women with *panniers* (pole baskets) had hunkered down, opened up their baskets, and were selling every imaginable kind of food: soup, chicken, beef, pork, innards, rice, and things I couldn't even identify. There were cigarette sellers with their typical flat hinged boxes opened to display a dazzling array of cigarettes from around the world. The most popular brands were American: Marlboro and Winston. There were people selling clothing, new and used. There were pushcarts with colorful fruits and vegetables artfully carved and displayed. Down on the sidewalk a woman had an old scale on which you could weigh yourself for a few Vietnamese dong. All this economic activity was a recent development as the government began slowly loos-

ening up its tight control on the economy. And the Vietnamese—
ever the entrepreneurs—were taking full advantage of it.

Somewhere in the middle of this crush, Linh had turned in to
a doorway almost lost in the clutter of sidewalk stalls. I followed
him in but for a minute I wasn't sure he had gotten the right place.
It was pitch dark, there was loud rock music (Phil Collins singing
"Sussudio," if I remember correctly), and the next thing I knew I
had tripped over a motorbike and sat right down on my butt.
Suddenly that darkness exploded with an orderly series of crashes
and bangs. I sat there, mesmerized by the sight of dozens of Hondas
falling over one by one, each taking the next one with it, until finally
there was one last crash, then a bang, and then—silence. As the dust
cleared, I could see a few dozen motorbikes, all laid out as efficiently
as corpses at an Irish wake.

All my middle-class sensibilities were offended. I was horrified
at what I had done. I was also very embarrassed. All that noise. All
that confusion. Then, through the strange and shocking silence that
now surrounded me, I could hear Linh calling out: "Hey! Mama
Kelly! Where you?" Suddenly, all around me there was a great
commotion as people scrambled over the felled Hondas to find me.

"Oh, my God! She gone! She lost! Where is she? American
woman! Where are you?" The voices seemed truly concerned. But
to make matters worse, I began to laugh at the goofiness of it all. I
mean, here I was, a grown woman, sitting on her behind, gaping at
the chaos she has caused. Unfortunately, I laugh the way I sneeze:
I make a lot of noise. By this time, tears were rolling down my
cheeks and I'm sure they thought I was screaming in agony. Little
did they know I was in the death throes of humiliation. In the
darkness I could see dozens of hands reaching out and getting me
back on my feet. I felt like an earthquake victim being rescued by
the Red Cross.

Meanwhile, I was beginning to question Linh's knowledge of
the neighborhood, because we had obviously blundered into a parking lot of some sort. But when I righted myself I noticed some
stern-looking chairs against the wall, and at the end of the room
was a desk with a handwritten card propped on an empty Coca-
Cola can. It was a card announcing the room rates. Then I looked
at the absolute chaos around me. Dozens of downed Hondas that
had once been neatly parked handlebar to handlebar were now
lying on their sides. Dust and debris floated through the disarray as
people scrambled around to put me and all those Hondas back on
their feet. This was the lobby of the Kim Do Hotel.

And that wasn't all. I looked around and discovered I was not only in a parking lot and a hotel lobby, I was also in a clock store. The walls were covered top to bottom with clocks. Clocks with awful, sentimental pictures on their faces: fuzzy kittens playing with balls of yarn, fluffy dogs with ribbons around their necks, blond-haired Western children holding stuffed animals. And the strangest of all: an American tract house in some anonymous suburban setting. And they were all chiming and gonging and banging at once.

It seemed to take a long time to announce that it was noon, but once twelve o'clock had come and gone and all the bonging and chiming had stopped, I crawled over the remaining downed Hondas and checked in with Linh up at the Coke can. The front desk was populated with some hotel workers who were obviously still in the beginning stages of a long battle with the English language. (I should talk: they were light-years ahead of me and my Vietnamese.)

"You want a rheum?" This was asked by a very serious young woman wearing a stern expression and glasses that kept slipping down on her tiny nose. She sounded like Inspector Clouseau. I told her I wanted something inexpensive.

"You want chip?" she asked, peering at me.

"Chip?"

"Chip. You know: chip. No money."

"Oh, yes. Cheap. Very cheap."

"Well, we have very much chip room back there." She gestured back to a six-story building that had been stuck on a tiny handkerchief of space right behind the main hotel. "It have elevator but you no stay there. For Vietnamese only. Too dirty. No toilet seats. Elevator break all time. People stuck inside. Oh, get very mad. You stay up there. Top floor. Chip." She motioned behind me to a flight of worn wooden steps in the original front part of the building.

"How much?"

"Ten American do-lah."

Sounded good to me, but first I wanted to see the room. She handed me the key and pointed toward the stairs. I looked at the old elevator shaft that had once served the original building. It was a ghost now, its filigree cage sheltering only vacant space. As I spiraled up the twisting wooden staircase, I could see the few screws and pulleys and gears that remained were covered with cobwebs so filthy it looked like greasy moss dripping down.

I heaved and panted my way up to the top floor, trying to convince myself that if I did this a few times a day it would be just like having joined a health club only cheaper. Room 34 was cavernous, obviously a tired remnant from some grander days in the past. I paced it off and it measured about eighteen feet by thirty feet. It had a ceiling fan, an overhead fluorescent light, a badly tiled bathroom with a hand shower and a toilet, which did indeed have a toilet seat, although it was so cruddy it should have been declared a national health hazard. There were some electrical outlets, all of which had been yanked out of the walls and left to dangle and die. There were two single beds, each with a rock-hard mattress and matching foam pillow, and two chairs covered with what appeared to be yellow linoleum. The room also came equipped with a family of geckos that sped quietly across the walls, doing their jobs well and efficiently: there was never a mosquito in Room 34 on the top floor of the Kim Do Hotel.

I went back downstairs and signed up with the serious young woman at the front desk. I would later join with other guests in calling her "Miss Congeniality" for her abrupt handling of guests, particularly her fellow Vietnamese. She was also very good at disciplining any beggar who might have the misfortune to wander in looking for a donation.

Linh was hovering outside, so I took him down the street to a café for a glass of milk to celebrate my new home.

Linh was Vietnamese. He was eighteen years old when I met him and had been homeless most of his life. But the first thing I noticed about him, standing there in front of the Rex Hotel holding his postcards and maps, was his crooked smile: it could light up a room. He was born in 1971 and was stricken with polio when he was only a few months old. He didn't know much about his mother, only that she was a secretary for the Americans up in Pleiku and she would leave him in an orphanage in Pleiku during the week and would visit him only on the weekends. Then, one weekend, as best he knew, she just didn't come at all.

"I remember my father," he told me. "He was in Vietnamese army. He would come visit me in the orphanage, too. He would bring me food to eat. One day he even brought me a cake. He was very tall and very handsome."

Linh was rescued from the orphanage by his grandmother, but even that refuge ended in 1978 when his grandmother died and Linh was alone again. Linh knew he had an Amerasian half-sister but in 1978 he didn't know where she was. So he got on the train and came to Saigon. "I get here at night. I very frightened. I have some money so I buy bread but still I am very hungry." He was only seven years old.

After he got to Saigon, he somehow made his way to the Majestic Hotel (now the Cuu Long) down by the Saigon River. "I have some dong and I buy some bread but you know, Mama—I still very hungry." He slept on the street, across from the Majestic Hotel, in front of a barbershop that was closed for the night.

"My God, Linh! Weren't you scared!" I couldn't get it through my head that a seven-year-old kid was all alone in a strange city, sleeping on the street.

He shook his head. "No, I not scared. Many people there with me."

I would soon discover that, after the vigor and energy of daytime, downtown Saigon would completely change character along about seven o'clock. The day crowd would pack up their boxes and pole baskets and tote bags and pushcarts and whatever else they were peddling their wares from and they would just seem to disappear. Dematerialize. Fade away. Then the night people would take over. And like the day people, they would just seem to appear, materializing like ghosts along the downtown streets and sidewalks. Going out in the evening I could see them opening up tattered folding chairs and bedding down babies, toddlers, grandparents. Tiny little kerosene lights winked around the area like fireflies.

I came home late one night—along about midnight—and the sidewalk approach to the Kim Do seemed deserted. Most of the vendors had packed up and gone, but the area was in fact still alive with people. They quietly populated the nooks and crannies of every building and doorway along the streets of downtown Saigon, wraiths and ghosts whose sleeping sighs would periodically rise up and fill the air with a sad, mournful chorus. Nearby, the Rex Hotel glowed and sparkled, its rooftop crown illuminated like a jewel. It was only across the street, but as those shadows stirred around me, it was glimmering in a whole other world.

As Linh and I sat there in the café, I looked over at him and tried to picture him as a tiny little seven-year-old ghost, sleeping in the shadow of a barbershop across the street from the Majestic Hotel. The Majestic had an outdoor bar on a sidewalk terrace looking out over the Saigon River. I wondered if the laughter from the Majestic Bar carried across the street to him while he slept.

"Sometimes the police come and arrest me," he said matter-of-factly.

"Why?"

"Because I have no home."

"What did they do to you? Where did they take you?"

"Oh, sometimes they take to prison. But when I real little they take me to Orphanage No. 5. I stay for a while, then I run away. Until they catch me again."

"Did you spend much time in prison?" I asked him.

He shook his head. "Except in 1985. Then it very bad."

I would soon learn that 1985 was a very bad year indeed. By 1985, the ten-year anniversary of the "Liberation" of South Vietnam from the American imperialists, some Americans were starting to drift back into Vietnam. Some were journalists, a few were veterans, but most were fairly well-heeled American tourists, who could get to the fabled Angkor Wat temple complex in Cambodia only by coming to Saigon first and then going on into Cambodia, then under the military control of Vietnam. Linh was caught talking to some of these Americans and was hauled away by the cops. I asked him what happened.

"Oh, Mama. They beat me up. They kick me in the head and chest. They hurt me so much." Then they took him away to prison for six months. He was fourteen years old at the time.

"I don't talk about this much, Mama," he said. His eyes had filled with tears. So had mine. "It hurts my heart very much."

"What was the worst thing about being in prison?"

He looked at me, this teenager with his sunshine smile, this kid who had been stricken with polio and abandoned. "I could not see the moon. I stay there day after day after day, Mama. I am kept in one room. All life is going on outside: cars, cyclos, people. I can hear it but I cannot see it. I cannot feel the sun or see the trees."

Linh and I talked for hours during my stay in Saigon. Most of the time it was trivial, wonderful talk. He had a great sense of humor and we would laugh a lot. But over the weeks and months his sad story came out in bits and pieces. We got caught one night during the rainy season, swept up in one of those driving rainstorms that wash over the Southeast Asian tropics during monsoon season. We had gone to a noodle shop for dinner, squatting on those typical little Vietnamese stools that get your butt up off the floor only about six inches. We had big bowls of steaming noodle soup and I ate four or five sticks of fried bread. It was a cheery, friendly place presided over by three substantial young women with red cheeks and huge smiles that never seemed to leave their faces. As we were leaving that particular night, it started to sprinkle lightly. We were only two blocks from the Kim Do, but by the time we got to the corner the rain was coming down in sheets so thick you couldn't even see to the other side of the street. All around us people were breaking camp, moving back into doorways or just packing up and moving on altogether. Within seconds the sidewalk was bare and the streets almost deserted. Occasionally a Honda would putt past, a cheap plastic poncho covering its passengers.

Linh and I dashed down the sidewalk, then joined a dozen or so others taking refuge in a video rental shop on the corner. I fished in my tote bag and passed Linh a tissue to mop his face with. "Oh, Mama—you are too good to me," he said, laughing. Then he paused and said seriously, "But I think all Americans are good."

"Yeah? Come on, Linh—what do you *really* think of Americans?" I was joking, but he wasn't.

"I think Americans are the most wonderful people in the world. I think America is kind and has a good heart. I will go to America, Mama, and I will work hard and get a job. Americans will like me and help me."

"Did you ever work here, Linh? I mean besides selling post-cards."

"No. Here I am lazy. But what can I do?" It was a lament, the cry of a generation of young men and women with no futures in a country as desperately poor and economically starved as Vietnam. "I have dreams. I have dreams in the daytime. I dream of America and my future. I dream of my mother. I dream of my life."

At that, Linh was one of the lucky ones. He had somehow found his Amerasian half sister, Thanh. She was qualified to go to America under the Orderly Departure Program and, as her half brother, Linh could accompany her. His paperwork hadn't even gotten started, so he wasn't due to leave any time soon. I asked him what he thought America would be like when he finally got there.

He sighed, the rainwater still running down his face. "I think America will be so wonderful. I will have a good life. I will go to school. Maybe even a university. It will not be difficult because I will work hard. And I will study. I think if I study it will be easy."

"What do you think you want to do, Linh? What kind of job do you want?" I bit my tongue as soon as I said it because what could he say? I thought. He couldn't even dream about a real job: they just didn't exist in Vietnam, not for homeless kids like Linh.

But Linh had an answer. Without hesitating, he looked at me and said: "I want to be a friend to children. I want to help all the children in the world. I will earn money and give it away."

Outside the rain was falling more gently, so we got up and prepared to leave. "If I have lots of money I will go around the world, Mama. But first I will come back to Vietnam." He wiped his face. This time it wasn't rain on his face. "I will come back to Vietnam in five years and be a friend to poor children. I will give them money and shirts to wear." He paused. "You know, this is my mother's homeland."

3

IT ALL BEGINS

My mission now was to find that halfway house and introduce myself to whoever was in charge and get going with my tutoring program. Linh assured me he knew all about the halfway house. He wasn't exactly sure where it was but he agreed to put out the word, locate the house, and take me there. Meanwhile, I continued my leisurely settling-in process at the Kim Do. It took a few days to get over that lingering case of transpacific jet lag but after a couple of days—when I could actually sit down without falling asleep in my chair—I figured I had it licked, so I chanced a late-afternoon stroll.

The rainy season was approaching and the city was hot and humid and absolutely stifling during midday. In addition to that, I had quickly learned that three days a week the authorities cut the power, so even buildings in downtown Saigon were plunged into a soporific, heat-soaked darkness as the electricity went off and even the wonderful old-fashioned paddle fans stopped turning. Half the population of Saigon took this as just another indication of the inefficiency of the Hanoi government: the Communists couldn't even provide enough electricity to keep the city going. The other half believed just as firmly that it had nothing to do with efficiency but was merely another way of punishing the people of Saigon for being on the wrong side during the war: deliberately turning off the power during the hot season. I figured there was probably a little truth in both theories.

I had waited until the heat had died down from a broil to a boil before going out for my constitutional. I had been wandering longer than usual, and as I headed back toward the hotel the street lights came on, casting weak puddles of light at irregular intervals down the street. Then I saw them: three very American-looking young men standing under a street light. And I couldn't help myself: I had the same reaction I had had with Kim the first time I saw her. For a moment, I simply couldn't figure out who these American kids were in front of me. These three looked completely American right down to their sunburns. And although I was getting better at this, it still took me a few seconds to realize that they were not American kids in Vietnam on vacation with their families. They were Amerasians. These particular Amerasians were Bryner and Jim and Pearl. Each had taken his father's name or, in the case of Pearl, the name his father had chosen for him. And each knew at least something about his American father.

The Rex Hotel was right around the corner, so I suggested we go to the little park in front of it. They all trailed after me and we sat for a while talking, mostly about them and their American fathers. Pearl knew his father was from Texas and his name was Theodore. "When I born he name me," he said proudly. The name he had chosen for his son was "Chau," which means Pearl. A few weeks later I visited Pearl and his mother. They lived in a corrugated shack attached to a small house in a far-off section of Saigon. There they made sticks of incense to sell at Buddhist temples. Pearl was an American-looking kid complete with a rather typical American nose, which he was none too happy with until one day, a few weeks later, he made a very important discovery.

"Mama!" he enthused. "You know Bruce Princeton?" I confessed I didn't, but Pearl insisted. "Yes! Yes! You do!" Then he launched into his version of "Born in the U.S.A."

"Bruce *Springsteen!*" I cried.

"Yes! Yes! I hear! I like!" Then Pearl began pointing madly at his nose. Seems he had not only heard Bruce Springsteen but he had also seen a picture of The Boss—with his equally assertive American nose—and everybody, but *everybody,* saw the amazing similarities between Pearl and Bruce Springsteen and their noses. Pearl became instantly content with his nose.

Then there was Jim. Jim lived a few blocks away with his

mother and an assortment of Vietnamese brothers and sisters, and he actually knew his father's name and address. "He from Sparks, Nevada," Jim told me. "Someday I find him."

The third young man standing in that puddle of light that night was Phuong. He called himself Bryner, which was his American father's last name. And he not only knew his father's name and address but they had actually had contact with each other over the years. As we sat there talking, he reached into a pocket and pulled out a plastic packet from which he extracted some tattered letters. He thrust them into my hand. They were letters from his father in California, which he carried with him everywhere. Letters rejecting him. When I met him, Bryner was homeless and drifting from one place to another, staying with friends and trying to keep his life together.

Pearl spoke very little English when I first met him; however, Jim and Bryner had taught themselves a little rough street English over the years and by Saigon standards were fairly fluent. When they discovered I was a teacher, the three of them promptly recruited themselves for English lessons. I was more anxious than ever to get going out at the halfway house, and if the kids there were as educationally eager as these three, this would be a breeze.

Despite four years of teaching, I had somehow never really thought of myself as a teacher, possibly because that career had come so accidentally. I was married, I couldn't get a job on a newspaper, my husband was a teacher, so: I became a teacher, too. I taught one year in a small high school in rural Nebraska, then followed my husband to his teaching job in Illinois (it was 1961 after all; we did things like that back then), where I taught for two years in an elementary school south of Chicago. Although I had a degree in journalism plus enough hours for majors in history and in literature, I didn't have a single educational credit to my name, so I taught under so-called "emergency certification." But in my own defense, I managed. My students were great and I couldn't find too much fault with a fifth-grade class whose IQs ranged from 65 to 140 and whose favorite subjects were reading, science, and history. And who wouldn't love a class whose favorite occupation was dramatizing important events in American history?

Costumes generally consisted of old bridesmaids' dresses their mothers wanted to get rid of and men's suit jackets whose pants had worn out. They wrote so many historical plays we were finally forced to put on a public performance called—what else?—*Five*

Historical Dramas. My favorite was "Colonizing the New World." There was Queen Elizabeth (elegant in a pink frothy number), who waved goodbye to Sir Walter Raleigh (dashing in a suit of armor that wiped out South Chicago's supply of Reynolds Wrap) as he set sail to colonize the New World. His vessel was a large Kotex carton. In our version, however, the queen obviously figured she would be missing out on one swell time in the New World because during the performance she hoisted two handfuls of pink net, yelled: "Hey! Wait for me!" and jumped into the Kotex box with Walt. I liked to think that in our revisionist version of American history Queen Elizabeth I actually made it to the colonies circa 1961. That experience ruined me for life, though. I came out of that two-year stint in fifth grade convinced the world would be a far better place if everyone in it was ten years old. I still feel that way.

I rounded out my four-year teaching career at Encinal High School in Alameda, California, teaching English and journalism to the class of 1966. My marriage—which had been rocky for a number of years—broke up for good that year, and I left California and teaching and headed right straight back to New York City. Which, I suppose, is how I came to be sitting in a small park in downtown Saigon with a handful of Amerasians smugly thinking about how exciting it was going to be to teach school again. Why, I couldn't wait to get to that halfway house and get going. The schoolmarm in me was taking over. I was a woman possessed. The chalk dust was fairly raging through my veins.

One problem: there was no halfway house.

"What?!" I think I screamed. I was sitting on a concrete bench in the little park in front of the Rex Hotel. I was with Linh and some of the Amerasians I had met over the past few days. First I jumped off that concrete bench. Then I sat down. Then I jumped up again. I paced. I sat down.

"That right, Kelly. House not there." Linh was back with news of the halfway house. And it wasn't good.

"O.K., now. Let me get this straight," I said. I felt panic rising in my throat like bad seafood. "There was a house." They nodded their heads. Then I mentioned the man's name.

"Right. Him have house. But no more. No more house."

I sat there, stunned. "No more house?" I asked once again. They were all looking at me. It was a very solemn moment. Then slowly they all shook their heads at once.

"Mama. Listen: NO MORE HOUSE."

If it hadn't been so awful it would have been funny. They spoke almost in unison, slowly and loudly, like people the world over trying to get other people to understand a strange language. Talk about role reversal. Since the invention of the travel agent, Americans have roamed the world wearing clothes that would frighten dogs, and when confronted with a language other than our own (which can include regional variations of English, too: have you ever heard someone from, say, Omaha trying to speak to someone in New Orleans?), we all do the same thing: our speech slows to the speed of an LP played at 45 rpm and we articulate until it looks like a facial disability. And now here were all these kids doing likewise to me. Then they paused, waiting—hoping—it would soak in.

It had. I sat there for a moment, then I jumped up and said something truly profound. "Oh, SHIT!" I think I even struck my forehead with the heel of my hand. If I had been auditioning for a Hollywood movie I would have lost the part. I was an acting cliché.

I had not only run up horrendous telephone bills with that guy in Hawaii, but early in 1990—just weeks before I headed off to Saigon—he had actually talked me into flying to Honolulu to do some press interviews and to participate in a fundraiser he had put together. Now I might not be smart enough to do my taxes every year, but I did have enough brainpower to get myself through a New York City real-estate closing, so I couldn't exactly be considered brain dead. I had done my homework. After all, I was a paranoid, suspicious New Yorker, so I checked him out. From top to bottom. And he was indeed a legally constituted, nonprofit group with a board of directors that met regularly in Honolulu. I flew there. I met them. I spoke with the law firm handling his nonprofit status, the same one that had gotten his permit from the U.S. government to operate that facility in Vietnam. They provided me with copies of all the paperwork involved, which I had my lawyer check out. Everything was legal and buttoned up tight. Just because he wore white shoes and decorated his house in crushed velvet was no reason for me not to trust him.

So why, then, was I sitting halfway around the world with nothing to do? This was terrible. I was devastated. I was also furious and scared to death. And embarrassed. What in God's name have I done to myself? I have just given up the best job I ever had, accepted all the praise and back patting that goes with other people's idea of self-sacrifice. *Jane Pauley had interviewed me, for God's sake!* And then I flew off like some Goody Two-Shoes about to be recast as Lady Bountiful. This was awful. Goody Two-Shoes was barefoot.

By this time I was pacing like a crazy woman. This called for drastic measures. So I hauled all the kids up to the terrace of the Rex Hotel and bought a round of Coca-Colas. They were a dollar apiece but I was in a weakened state. As we sat there, I tried to get the story of "the house" from them. It was a story I would have to piece together over the year but basically yes, there had indeed been a house. I took a cyclo out to it one day, and sure enough, there it was, that old villa I had seen in that green-hued video at the vet's house back in Hawaii. It was all chipped and peeling, but I could see how it would be spacious and comforting to a kid who didn't have a home. And for a time some of the homeless Amerasians had indeed stayed there. But since the GI didn't stay around to keep tabs on things, I gather it had been improperly supervised and it simply fell apart.

Meanwhile, I later learned, the authorities in Hanoi had gotten in on the act. As best I could figure, the GI had gotten authorization for his halfway house only from someone in Saigon. An official? A private entrepreneur? I never found out. Either he had been suckered by some smart operator in Saigon or he had gotten permission from the proper authorities in Saigon (when in fact he should have gotten authorization from Hanoi) and then got caught in a power struggle between Saigon and Hanoi, something that has been going on ever since the North came south in 1975. All I know is that nobody in either place—Saigon or Hanoi—gave a damn about the Amerasians, much less that GI's sincere effort to help them. So the house had been closed down—shortly before I arrived, as it turned out—and the Amerasians were once again left to fend for themselves.

Meanwhile, the gang had been very quiet through all of this, eying me with curiosity. I wasn't paying too much attention to them (after all, I was too busy feeling very sorry for myself) when Linh interrupted my mental whining.

"Mama—what this?"

He was pointing to his glass.

"That's a glass, Linh." I tried to ignore him.

"What this?" He stuck his finger in the milk.

"That's milk." I tuned him out again.

"What this?" Since there isn't any fresh milk in Vietnam, all the milk is canned and served with ice. He was pointing to an ice cube.

"That's ice, Linh." God, wouldn't he ever shut up.

"What I doing?" He took a swig of his milk.

"You are drinking milk."

Then it hit me: improvise. I looked around the table. There were five or six kids sitting there looking at me looking at them. In the middle of all their Vietnamese I could hear words like "glass" and "milk" and "ice" floating around like ideas. That did it. We spent the rest of the afternoon there at the bar in the Rex Hotel, and by the end of the day they had the present tense of the verb "to be" down pat, singular and plural. By the end of the day they could combine it with such verbs as "sit," "stand," "walk," and "drink" to form the high-falutin present-tense structure "I am sitting" and the like. I gave them each a piece of paper and a pen and they wrote their first essays: "I am sitting. I am drinking milk. You are sitting. You are drinking milk. We are sitting. We are drinking milk. They are standing. They are drinking beer." Three Australian business-men standing at the bar provided that perfect third person plural change of pace for the gang.

My bar bill for the afternoon—one Coke apiece for each of the kids followed by countless glasses of milk—came to about $20. I considered it an investment in education.

We convened at the Rex for a few more mornings (milk for them, iced coffee for me) until I mapped out a plan of attack. Finally, I was ready to make my move on the bureaucracy. I had arrived in Saigon with a notebook full of names and addresses culled from dozens of discussions with various people—doctors, scientists, aid workers, Vietnam veterans—all of whom had been quietly traveling back and forth to Vietnam attempting to get some humanitarian projects underway. I had also picked a few brains at Operation Smile, a group of American plastic surgeons who roam the Third World as volunteers doing facial reconstruction, and came away with what I was assured was the name of The Person to talk to in Saigon, along with the telephone number. He was the head of the Foreign Ministry office in Saigon. A full-fledged important person.

"This guy runs Saigon," I had been told. "He makes everything happen in South Vietnam. Mention my name. Talk to him and you'll get anything you want."

Great. I was completely confident I could talk to this man and tell him what I wanted to do: set up an English tutoring program for Amerasians who were going to be leaving the country anyway.

Down in the Kim Do lobby someone was overhauling a Honda, and thick clouds of blue-gray exhaust smoke had completely en-gulfed the desk. I could barely see Miss Congeniality, but gradually

she materialized through the fumes, her eyes running and a handkerchief clamped tightly to her mouth. She looked absolutely miserable.

"Oh, Miss Kelly. What I do for you?"

"I need a telephone."

Blank look. Her nose was running by this time.

"Telephone?" I think I even did something helpful like making
dialing motions in the air. More blank air passed between us. "I
need a telephone." Pause. "Do you have a telephone?"

"Yes."

"May I use it?"

"No." She mopped her eyes and face, then her nose. "No can't
use. Have phone. No work." She gestured to an old telephone col-
lecting dust on the desk. The Americans had left a fairly efficient
telephone system in Saigon when they pulled out, but like so many
things it had completely fallen apart.

Since it was obvious I couldn't call the minister I wanted to see
and set up an appointment, I packed up all my credentials and pro-
posals and important papers and went off to see him. When I had
switched hotels, I also had switched cyclo drivers, trading in Hung
for Minh. Minh and the rest of the cyclo drivers outside the Kim Do
were very distressed when I told them where I wanted to go.

"You in trouble, Kelly?" Minh asked.

"No. Why do you ask?"

He eyed me keenly. "Government office. May never see you
again." He made it sound like a Roach Motel. I reassured him I'd be
fine and off we went. Two other cyclo drivers were so curious they
tagged along just in case. The three of them parked across the street
from the Foreign Ministry and settled in to await my fate. Their
faces were serious and drawn with concern. They looked like the
Three Stooges. At the gate to the Foreign Ministry, I showed the
guards the magic key that opens any door in Vietnam—my American passport—and was allowed inside the building.

There should have been a revolving door, I was spun in and out
so fast. I was ushered into a waiting room and sat down, joining a
family of very large mice who were grouped in a corner chowing
down on a glob of rice. A few minutes later an officious young man
entered the room, followed by a young woman who translated for
him.

"He wants to know what you want," she said, smiling.

I introduced myself, presented my folder of credentials (a very
old transcript from the University of Missouri and some letters of

introduction and recommendations from my old teaching days),
and explained that I was a teacher interested in teaching English. I
told him that I brought greetings from their friends at Operation
Smile, who had suggested I see Minister Bong. Then, as instructed,
I dropped the name of the American doctor and waited for the
doors to swing open in welcome. As they examined my papers I felt
something on my foot. I looked down. A gigantic mouse had gotten
tangled in my shoelaces.

Now I am a rather calm individual in tense situations, having
had extensive experience in facing down everyone from licensed
plumbers to celebrities so stoned they couldn't stay upright in a
chair during a live interview. I was mugged on Ninth Avenue one
night after a Broadway opening (and you wonder how I could give
up a glamour job like that?) and gave the guy such a tongue lashing
he apologized and settled for an autograph and a subway token. On
this occasion in Saigon, however, I screamed. Nobody paid the
slightest bit of attention to me. It was as if strange American women
wandered in off the streets of Saigon every day, sat down in a chair,
and began to scream. Finally the mouse left and I was about to be
invited to do likewise. The young man closed the folder, said something to the young woman, who repeated it in English to me.

"You are a tourist." I nodded since I had indeed come in on a
tourist visa. "Why do you want to teach English?"

"Because I am an English teacher," I replied. Then I launched
into a spiel about friendship between our two countries, coopera-
tion among people, how I wished to volunteer my services, but
mostly how *I wished to speak directly to Minister Bong* about my
desires.

The young man closed my folder and looked at me. "I think
you would like the museums here," he said through the interpreter.
Then, by passing the translator altogether, he leaned forward and
whispered to me: "Go visit a pagoda, lady." I think I actually
gasped. The little creep: he spoke perfect English. I felt like someone
who has just lost a round in the principal's office. When he got to
the door he turned and asked me: "Do you know the Bronx?"

"Why?" I was very sullen by this time.

"I have relatives there," he said.

Note: I never did hear from Minister Bong.

Weeks later, during a dash to Hanoi for some serious sightseeing, I happened to run into someone from the Ministry of Foreign
Affairs in Hanoi. Purely by chance we ended up at the same table in

a crowded Hanoi restaurant and, like most Vietnamese, he wanted to practice his English. So we started talking and he mentioned that he not only worked for the Foreign Ministry but was assigned to the North America Department and his special area of interest was—Amerasians. I tried to press the point, hoping to discuss my pathetic idea of tutoring Amerasians, when he cut me short.

"You should forget about Amerasians," he snapped. It was as if someone had unrolled a safety gate and slammed it down over his face. His expression was absolutely rigid.

"Why?" I asked.

"They are all bad. They are no good." He went on to tell me, at great length, about the recent murder of an Amerasian in Saigon. The day before he was scheduled to leave under the Orderly Departure Program, he had been stabbed to death during a fight with another Amerasian, just the proof this midlevel Communist bureaucrat needed to back up his argument that they are "all bad." Later I learned that an Amerasian had indeed been killed just before he was finally escaping the country—murdered by a Vietnamese kitchen worker, not another Amerasian. "Besides," the young bureaucrat said smugly, "they are all so stupid. They don't want to learn anything."

I was stunned. I looked at that face. There was such iciness there I decided to shut up. I had to bite my tongue to keep from reminding him that if any Amerasians are indeed bad and stupid it just might be because—in addition to having been abandoned by both the American government and, in most cases, their American fathers as well—they have been discriminated against, ostracized, imprisoned, beaten, and deprived of an education by the policies of his Communist government in Hanoi. However, at that time, I was hanging on by a thread down in Saigon, living from one visa renewal to another, so I knew that giving this junior official a load of my very big lip wouldn't help matters at all. So I chickened out and buttoned up. Believe me, as someone who has spent most of her life earning a living by having opinions and expressing them as forcefully as possible, it broke my heart to keep my mouth shut.

Well, when I got back to the Kim Do after my worthless visit to the Foreign Ministry, they were all there waiting for me—Jim, Pearl, Bryner, Linh, and a gaggle of others I knew by this time. And thanks to the efficiency of the Saigon gossip machine, they not only knew I had been to the Foreign Ministry but they also knew it had been a total disaster. They looked very serious, so I hauled them all down the street to an outdoor stall for some lunch. I was caught somewhere between depression and anger. I was furious at being so summarily dismissed by that bureaucratic little pipsqueak. On the other hand, I was devastated that my idea of teaching English to these kids was still a pipe dream.

By this time an Amerasian named Raymond had wandered up, ordered something that looked like snake, and sat down to join us. Now Raymond was an interesting guy. He was a black Amerasian, older than the rest of the kids. He had grown up on various U.S. bases down around Vung Tau, a seaside town about two hours outside Saigon. According to Raymond, his father left the country after his tour of duty, then his mother died, and Raymond became the adopted "mascot" of various U.S. Army units, where he learned to speak flawless English without a trace of an accent. Talking to Raymond was like talking to another American until you realized there were certain cultural gaps: try explaining a Big Mac attack to someone. It was Raymond who came up with the solution to my problem.

FIRST DAY OF SCHOOL

The Amerasian Transit Center is a sprawling complex on the outskirts of Saigon. It had been built by the U.S. government to serve as a transit point for those Amerasians and their families lucky enough to slog through the red tape imposed on them by two governments and get permission to leave Vietnam and emigrate to the United States under the Orderly Departure Program. Sometimes their stays were brief—just a few days while they waited for their planes to leave; sometimes the stays stretched into weeks as various snags in their paperwork were unraveled.

As we pulled up in our various cyclos, I was astonished at the place. It was brand-new, indeed it had just opened the month before, and although it was a little dusty it was neatly arranged and orderly and people were out busily planting trees and flowers. The compound consisted of a series of solid, two-story concrete dormitories, which housed Amerasians and their family members. From the outside, it looked like a low-rise suburban motel complex. Inside, the rooms were spacious and airy. Each had a bed (for adults—any children scattered themselves around on the floor), a small table, a wardrobe, and lovely Vietnamese tiled floors. There was also a mess hall, an administration building, and a building that had a snack bar and what appeared to be a section set aside for recreation, although at the time it contained only a Ping-Pong table and a punching bag. A desk stuck in a corner of that building turned out to be the medical station, and my on-the-spot donation of some aspirin provided its entire inventory.

We sat in the snack bar having orange drinks while Raymond went off to find the director and try to set up an appointment for me to see him. Jim and Bryner and Pearl and the rest of the gang seemed to know everybody in the place, and as the word went forth that an American was actually in the compound, we were soon surrounded. I was getting acquainted when Raymond came rushing in.

"Come on, Kelly. He'll see you now."

The director was a good Communist who spoke not a word of English, but with Raymond's expert help, I broached my idea to him: as long as those kids were at the Transit Center with nothing to do, why not set up some tutoring sessions so they could at least work on their English? This would keep them busy and out of harm's way (good for him) and get them started with their new language (good for them). He seemed interested but not enthusiastic.

"He'll think about it," Raymond told me. Then the director stood up and signaled our interview was over.

Figuring this was my best shot at doing what I wanted to do, I wasn't about to let this ready-made opportunity disappear, so two days later, with Raymond and the rest of my delegation in tow, I went back out to the Transit Center. This time I was armed with a picture dictionary and two dozen ballpoint pens. The director relented, and I taught my first class five minutes later.

I stood facing the class. I spoke almost no Vietnamese. They spoke almost no English. They ranged in age from five years old (someone's little brother) to fifty-five years (someone's mother, who had slipped into the class with her Amerasian son). Her son spoke no English and her English ranged from "You want starch?" to "Clean out pockets, please." Seems she'd been a laundry worker at the base at Vung Tau during the war. She never stopped smiling.

Obviously the director had been thinking about my proposal because here was a proper classroom. Almost. It was long and skinny, with a middle aisle and tables and benches for desks. It had a blackboard but no chalk and no textbooks. Fortunately, I had a box of Woolworth's chalk in my tote bag, so I got to work. And with Raymond acting as my educational recruiter, the room quickly filled up.

The heat was extreme and I was soon slippery with sweat. It was slow going that first day, but somehow we muddled through, although I could have written off the first ten or fifteen minutes of that initial class. The students were all too busy staring at this honest-to-goodness oddity in their midst: me. They were clearly overwhelmed, suffering from great culture shock because there were so many things for them to absorb. My white hair bowled them over, and they had no sooner recovered from that than they had to deal with the fact that it was curly. Then my glasses became the center of attention and finally the hair on my arms. It was hard to say what intrigued them the most. I wondered what would happen if I neglected to shave my legs for a few days. A complete shutdown, no doubt.

At the sound of my voice spouting American sounds, a dead silence gripped the room, followed by an explosion of excited conversation. My strange American name written on the blackboard for all to see silenced them completely. The day ended on yet another high note when I exchanged my reading glasses for a pair of prescription sunglasses. Imagine. Two pairs of glasses.

They worked diligently that first day, and by the end of the day half of them were able to say, "Hello, how are you? I am fine," and then go on and get up close and personal by asking, "What is your name?" and "How old are you?" Meanwhile, Pearl and Jim and Bryner had taken up positions around the room, and every time I got stuck one of them would swing into action. No teacher in the history of the profession ever had more enthusiastic and dedicated assistants than I did with the three of them, especially Pearl. I could hear him sounding out words, helping students make the difference between those tricky "p" and "f" sounds, so that when they discussed living arrangements in New York City it didn't come out "afartment."

A routine quickly developed. Classes were held very early in the mornings, before the heat became so oppressive that even learning English was a chore. Minh would load me into his cyclo and pedal me out to the Transit Center around seven-thirty. I would be ready to meet my students at eight o'clock. And they were always there, waiting eagerly. We would work diligently for about ninety minutes, then take a break. Since I wouldn't allow smoking in the classroom, there would be the usual mad dash outside for cigarettes. Then we would all sit around in the shade and "talk," which generally consisted of all of them showing off their newfound vocabulary by having very serious discussions over what they were doing (verbs) or wearing (clothing). I had brought some vocabulary flashcards along with me, and these went over like gangbusters. Likewise the mathematics cards, which kept the kids occupied for hours. Then we would go back in and review for a half hour or so. By late morning—what with the heat building and stomachs growling—we were all more than ready to call it quits.

It was during one of these "talks" of ours, squatting under a tree outside the classroom trying to avoid the hot sun, that I learned one of the most distressing things about post-Liberation Vietnam: The educational system was a shambles. Just for conversation I had asked some of the Amerasians how many years they had gone to school. Most had gone only four or five years. I was appalled.

"It very hard, teacher." Jim and Bryner were squatting down outside with all the rest of them.

"How many years did you two go to school?" I asked them.

Each of them had gone only five years.

"It very difficult," they repeated. "School no like Amerasians. Call us bad. Call us Americans. Call us spies." It was even worse for black Amerasians. In some cases, they were physically attacked. Beyond the verbal abuse and the physical abuse, money was a problem. There was no such thing as free education in liberated Vietnam. Because of the fluctuation of the dong it was difficult to pin down the exact cost, but it was roughly a dollar a month. And while that doesn't sound exorbitant, if you make little or no money (the average income when I was there was 50 cents a day, $15 a month) and you have three or four kids, $3 or $4 a month for education is steep. Factor in years of discrimination and, in some cases, physical abuse for Amerasians and it became easier to see why these young people were so educationally deprived. What a pity. What a waste.

I was slowly realizing that Vietnam was a country where sadness piled upon sadness. This had been a well-educated country that revered and respected learning. Unfortunately, the educational system—along with just about everything else—had gone into a near collapse since 1975. School buildings had fallen apart, then fallen down altogether. As the economy worsened, there was no money for school buildings. No money for books. No money for teachers who earned only $6 a month. Most preferred working in the new fish cannery in Saigon for $20 a month. Worse, the teachers were now rebelling. I met one young woman—a member of the Young Communist League no less—who had finished her teacher training.

Then, when told she would be shipped off to some obscure village to teach, she refused.

"Why should I go there to some stinky little village?" this Saigon beauty sniffed. "It would be so boring." So she simply thumbed her tiny nose at the bureaucracy and began teaching in one of the hundreds of private schools that had begun to spring up in Saigon to teach English to adults. Obviously someone in her family had enough clout to protect her when she thumbed her nose at the Party. (The Communist Party in Vietnam isn't dumb: with the Socialist sun setting in the Soviet Union, they could see they were fast becoming the Little Orphan Annie of Communism. They also knew the sun would come up tomorrow and it wouldn't be in Moscow. Like dollars in the international wallet, English was likewise the language of choice.) As sad and as frustrating as it was to see this educationally needy generation sitting in front of me, it was also great to see such desire fighting its way out of that need. Motivation was no problem with these students. No teacher in the world was as lucky as I was at that point in time.

As for that curriculum of mine, most of what we were doing was in the realm of the concrete. If you couldn't point to it, it didn't exist. Ideas and concepts had no place in my curriculum. My sister-in-law had given me an old seed catalog, which was perfect for studying American fruits and vegetables. Clothing and colors were easy: We just used what we were wearing (red shirt, white shoes) or what we could see outside the window (blue sky, green tree).

Verbs presented a bit more of a problem, but it was then that I discovered my twelve years on the fringes of show business—going to movies, going to the theatre, watching television—began to pay off. I simply acted things out. I had no trouble with "sit," "stand," and "walk." No problem with "Open the door," "Close your book," "Take off your shoes, uh—thongs," "Put on your thongs." "Lie down" involved doing just that, although the first time I threw myself down on the floor it threw a panic into the class.

"Teacher! You sick?" Bryner asked, bending over and peering at me.

"She die?" another suggested.

"I lie down!" I kept insisting. "I lie down!" I was beginning to feel like a dog in obedience class, when one of the younger kids threw himself on the floor.

"I lie down?"

"Yes! Yes!" Two more joined in. Pretty soon the entire class had tossed themselves down on the floor and were shouting at the top of their lungs: "I lie down! I lie down!"

And, since one thing just naturally leads to another, we spent another ten minutes shouting, "I get up! I get up!" at each other.

But it was the little things that kept stopping me in my tracks. Windows turned out to be nearly impossible. Most of the people in my class were from small towns and villages outside Saigon, and a window as we know it—a piece of glass stuck in a house—was a totally alien concept to them. There was not a single window in the entire center. As in most Vietnamese buildings, the windows there were simply framed openings covered with decorative metal grates or heavy mesh screening to keep the bad guys out. Wooden shutters kept the rain and the bugs at bay. Only a small area in downtown Saigon had actual windows with real glass: hotels, government offices, and some of the newer shops. Most stores in Saigon still relied on solid metal accordion doors, which were simply pulled shut at night to cover the front of the shop. My picture dictionary was of no help because it spent most of its time up in the administration building being pored over by everyone who worked there.

I borrowed a glass from the snack bar one day and tried to indicate that in America a "house" had a "window" with "glass" in it. They stared suspiciously at me. Actually, I had first tried that "window-glass" connection with my glasses and half the class walked out of the room. They stood outside debating the issue among themselves. They argued back and forth, then came back into the room and told me I was crazy.

"Teacher, I think I no right," I was told firmly. (Obviously, we hadn't nailed down personal pronouns. It took a long time to demonstrate the difference between "I" and "you." Try it sometime. It's a challenge.) As new English was learned or old English was remembered, a spokesperson would rise through the ranks to help out my teaching assistants (Bryner, Jim, and Pearl). And what she was telling me was that they thought I was wrong. How could those little bitty pieces of glass I wore on my nose possibly fit into an entire window? And, more important, why? Why in the world would anyone want them to? I was desperate until I remembered I had an old *Time* magazine stuck in my tote bag. I hauled it out and riffled through the pages until I found a picture of a building. I stuck it out for them to look at.

"There. See." I sounded like a spoiled preschooler. They gathered around the picture I was holding out to them. There was more discussion, and finally the spokesperson confronted me again.

"I no crazy," she said, pointing to herself. "I crazy." She pointed at me. Then she held the magazine out so I could see the photograph. It was a picture of a resort hotel, its façade a curtain of windows glistening in the sunlight. Unfortunately, a huge airplane was flying in front of the hotel. What I had shown them was an advertisement for Singapore Airlines, and all they could focus on was the enormous airplane taking off from some country they had never heard of bound for yet another country they could only dream of. Flying off with its tiny little airplane windows, which, in a photograph, look as if they are about the size of fingernail clippings.

"I crazy," she said, pointing at me again.

Then I remembered something and I knew I could pull this out of the fire. I had with me a photograph taken years ago at a Kelly family reunion. I'm holding my nephew Tom's new baby, surrounded by about a dozen other kids. In the background is my brother's house—*with windows!* And off in one corner is their neighbor's house—*with windows!* My reputation was saved. That one small photograph became the teaching tool of the day as I improvised an entire lesson using it.

From the very first day, a desperate race to stay ahead of my enthusiastic students began. We slowly and methodically progressed from "Hello, how are you?" (Unit 1) to "Yesterday I sat in the chair" (Unit 11) to "Tomorrow we will go to the market" (Unit 20). Every afternoon I would dash back to the Kim Do and upgrade the next day's lesson if necessary. Then, before class the next day, I would run to a nearby copy shop and duplicate the day's work. After that I would jump in a cyclo and be pedaled out to the Transit Center, where I would conduct the lesson, sometimes still warm from the copy machine.

As for those classes—well, let me put it to you this way: How many classrooms have you ever seen where students were clamoring to get in and reluctant to leave? Partly it was the oddity of it all: an honest-to-goodness American standing there teaching the class. Partly it was the opportunity: to learn English. The room could hold only twenty-five students at a time, but as word spread after that first improvised day dozens of kids stood, packed shoulder to shoulder, in the back of the room. Through the heavy mesh screening that served as windows there must have been two or three hundred more watching the proceedings during those first days. I felt like *Wheel of Fortune* on location. As someone who worked in television and reviewed Broadway theatre productions, I knew the meaning of ratings. Of an audience. And let me tell you, I was hotter than *Dallas* at its peak. If my classes had been a Broadway show they would have been standing room only. As for me, I had forgotten how much I really liked teaching. How exciting it was to introduce something completely new and strange—the English language!— and then, suddenly, to have it start to make sense. To watch kids struggle through frustration and bewilderment and then suddenly have that breakthrough when a word or a sentence becomes something other than just a jumble of sounds and letters. Watching a face explode with pure joy at being able to say, "Hello. How are you?" and then understand the answer: "Fine, thanks. How are you?" For a teacher—for a human being—this was exciting beyond belief. Every day I would stand there, covered in sweat and coated with chalk dust, marveling at how happy I was. Could Madonna have been any happier? I sincerely doubt it.

Through all this, my smiling mother from the laundry was still ecstatic over her newfound good fortune: studying English in a real classroom with a real American. To her, life could be no better. "I love you, Americans," she would say to me, over and over. Whenever I would pass her in class, as I patrolled the room checking on vocabulary progress and listening for misplaced sounds, she would grab my hands and stroke them. "You very good womans. You very good womans. Like very much. Thank you. Thank you." It was a litany. Then she would smile, pat my hand, and go back to the challenge of trying to figure out the difference between a floor and a ceiling.

Now, for better or for worse, when you work in television you get used to people telling you you're wonderful: your agent, your accountant, people out on the street. Sometimes even your friends and, occasionally, even members of your own family. I had two babies and a dog named after me, although I think the parents were probably leaning in the direction of "Katie" long before I came on their scene. The dog, however, might have been more deliberate. No matter. Shortly before it goes right straight to your head, it makes you feel real good.

But this. This was different. This was so real and sincere and heartfelt it was unreal. I knew that a lot of it was not so much *who* I was as *what* I was not: not so much that I was an American as the fact that I was not Russian. Not from the country just about every Vietnamese loves to hate. In one sense, I loved it. Why not? Everybody wants to be loved. But this devotion directed at me simply because I was an American made me feel strange, bewildered, uncomfortable. After all, we did fight a war here. Right or wrong, good or bad, we bombed these people. We coated them with napalm and washed their countryside with chemicals. We carpeted their country, and our own, with death and destruction and birth defects, and fatherless children—a human trail that was still following us all the way back to America.

One day I couldn't stand it any longer. I leaned down and asked the woman why she was so happy. Why she liked me so much. Why she liked Americans so much. She thought for a moment. "Well, American woman, you very funny." (We were hard at work on food names—pork, I believe—and I had just oinked.) "You also very nice. I think all Americans very nice." Then she paused and touched the handsome young Amerasian sitting next to her. "Besides—you the father of my child."

The Great Kim Do Upgrade: I came back one day to discover an army of men swarming through my room. They smiled politely and then ran out. I looked around to see what they had been doing but I could see no conclusive evidence of any productive work. The Kim Do obviously had a modernization plan, apparently someone's desperate attempt to turn it into something other than a glorified Honda parking lot–clock store. When it rained the next day there was the usual decorative pond in the corner of my room, so I knew they hadn't been fixing the roof, much less my ceiling. A cockroach the size of an M1-A1 tank rumbled across the floor, so I knew they hadn't been engaged in any sort of jungle warfare with those beasts.

Then a few days later I noticed small wires coming through another part of the ceiling, running down the wall and dangling over the head of my bed. And a few days after that, the mystery was cleared up. A telephone had been installed. There it was, sitting right there on my night table: a real telephone. A real *old* telephone covered with equally old dust and dirt. It was an old-fashioned rotary phone with a brown cord, squared-off sides, and a receiver that swooped to fit the configuration of a real hand. I figured it was at least thirty years old. I turned it over and saw the words "Western Electric" printed on the bottom. It must have been here during the war. I became so excited I actually tried to use it. I guess I just got carried away.

"No can do," I was told cheerfully by Miss Congeniality when I reported this little lapse to her. "You call me, that all."

From somewhere, retrieved from some far-off and forgotten storeroom, someone in the Kim Do had dug up a switchboard. I truly believe it was older than I was. And for weeks that switchboard remained both a shrine and a mystery to all concerned. But eventually someone put the pieces of the puzzle together and residents of the Kim Do could actually talk to the switchboard and vice versa. Although they never mastered the art of room-to-room calls, they did figure out a way to allow a conversation to take place. If you wanted to talk to someone in another room, you simply called down to the switchboard. That call was received on a phone at the desk. Then they dialed up to the other room via the switchboard and held the desk phone close to the switchboard receiver and both parties shouted as loud as they could. Sometimes a caller could even be understood. But that was all. No outgoing calls, no incoming calls. Nonetheless, the staff of the Kim Do was mighty proud of that switchboard. They could be seen patting it and stroking it. Hitting it soundly. Slamming their fists into it. Sometimes they even climbed up on the desk and honored it with a swift kick on its backside.

Actually, the discovery of those phones in the Kim Do paled in comparison to another discovery I made. It was early one evening. I had been out for dinner with some Americans I had met earlier that day, and after dinner we had repaired to the Rex for a beer. We were sitting there in the cool of the evening watching the swallows wheel through the air. I remember remarking how delightful it was to be in such a setting: the terrace bar was beautiful, the beer was cold, and right there in the middle of downtown Saigon you could sit and watch the swallows fly through the air. And way down at the end of the street the sun was setting over the Saigon River, turning everything pale pink, then rosy, and finally a deep, dark blue as night finally tumbled and fell over Saigon.

I got back to the Kim Do and made it to the top floor, headed to my room, when what to my wondering eyes should appear in that top-floor hallway: swallows. Wheeling delicately through the air over my head. The stairwell at the Kim Do had huge old shuttered windows and, of course, there was no glass in them. The shutters were kept open to let the breezes blow in. I assumed that is how the swallows that were now swooping and diving toward me got in.

I noticed there were a few swallows that seemed to be aiming directly for me, so I ducked my head as I reached the top of the stairs. I was also surprised to see that these swallows had an interesting webbed quality to their wings. Then I observed a few of them slamming onto the plaster walls. That's odd. I didn't know swallows actually flew into walls. And then stuck there. Then, as the dive bombers got closer and closer to me, I suddenly wised up: These weren't swallows. *These were bats!* Fortunately, as a seasoned world traveler I was philosophical about the presence of those bats: "Oh, shit!"

As I have said before: I'm not much of a screamer but I pierced the air that night. The rush of my footsteps and the sound of my door slamming must have echoed halfway to Hanoi. From that point on I took steps to protect myself whenever I ventured up the stairs. Every night, to get up to my top-floor room, I would slip into serious protective gear: a cone hat and a broom left on the second-floor landing by the cleaning people. I would wave the broom over my head, all the while swatting the air and making loud noises as I made my way up the stairs. I was in full gear and full voice and full flight one night, when I asked myself: Would Jane Pauley do this? Of course not. Ask a stupid question, get a stupid answer. At least I had the decency to feel like a fool.

Note: Discovering those bats solved a mystery that had been bothering me for weeks at the Kim Do. Every morning when I went down to find breakfast for the day, there were tiny little black pellets all over the floor. They were like miniature BBs and all of us top-floor types would have to slip and slide through them to get to the stairs. Now, finally, I knew what that stuff was: bat shit. And that godawful smell that went with it? Bat pee, of course. Until I spent time on the top floor of the Kim Do Hotel, I had no idea anything in this world could smell so bad. I am here to tell you, pigpens in Nebraska smell far sweeter than bat piss in a downtown Saigon hotel.

APPOINTED ROUNDS

I was making this up as I went along. Result: Things just sort of happened that year in Saigon. I had gone over to spread the words of the English language to a bunch of Amerasians but, like Topsy, it just grew. When there were constant complaints of headaches and vague references to "sore stomachs," I finally figured out what was wrong: These kids were hungry. So I fed them. Vietnam was poor. These kids were poor. Period. After all, as a well-fed Midwesterner I grew up thinking the four major food groups were breakfast, lunch, supper, and bedtime snack. Thus began the so-called Downtown Saigon Breakfast Club, which consisted of all the milk they could drink and as many loaves of fresh bread (another legacy of the French: delicious baguettes, fresh-baked every day in old wood-fired brick ovens) as there were kids.

The Lunch Bunch was formed later as was the Supper Club. These were free-form, floating affairs that just meant whoever was hanging out in my vicinity when I got hungry also got scooped up and fed. The rules were simple: if there were a lot of kids (more than ten), we headed for a sidewalk stall and carbo-loaded on rice and chicken for about fifty cents a head. If there were fewer than ten kids we actually went to a restaurant and sat down on real chairs and ordered from real menus. This was a treat because meals in a restaurant generally hit a dollar or more, and it also meant they could order what the menu referred to as "American beefsteak." It bore not the slightest resemblance to an American steak, but just the fact that it had the word "American" in front of it was enough for them. I think if the menu had offered American Floor Tiles they would have ordered them.

It was at one of these sit-down extravaganzas that I discovered something else was wrong with a lot of these kids: Bryner had skipped his usual order of American beefsteak and opted for soup instead. Not that Vietnamese soup is anything to scoff at. Indeed it is not. Vietnamese soup redefines the word "hearty." Whole vegetable gardens seem to be involved in a bowl of Vietnamese soup. Likewise, entire schools of fish. I sat in wonder watching what appeared to be the entire bean-sprout reserve of Southeast Asia disappear into Bryner's mouth. Still, it wasn't American beefsteak.

"What's wrong?" I asked, figuring something was up if he was choosing soup instead of steak.

"My teeth gone," he confessed. Then he opened his mouth to show me the gaping hole where his front teeth used to be.

"My God!" I cried. "What happened?"

"I take them out. They broke." Seems he had lost his teeth years ago. Some replacements had been hooked up but now even they had broken off.

"Anybody else?" I asked, pointing to my teeth. "Sore teeth? Raise your hands." Every hand went up. Then I kicked myself for not being more aware. After all, some of the problems were pretty noticeable: Pearl's front teeth had rotted away, so obviously he was none too comfortable. And with those badly rotted teeth, he also thought he was ugly and always smiled behind his hand. Bryner, who cheered up enough to show me he could actually whistle an entire Bee Gees medley through the vacant hole in the front of his mouth where two teeth had once been, was still uncomfortable. Other kids complained of an assortment of toothaches, so after lunch off we went.

I wasn't looking for a high-priced specialist. No peridontist. No orthodontist. No oral surgeon. Just someone who could look into a kid's mouth and say something all-knowing, like "Hmm-m-m." Bryner thought he had a line on one over near the Central Market. So we headed over to where he thought he had seen the dentist's office.

"Well, it used to be here," he said, looking down at a pile of bicycle parts. Seems the dentist had decamped and a bicycle-repair shop was now in full operation. At least I hoped that pile of twisted stuff had nothing to do with dental work. (Old retainers? Old braces?) We finally found a dentist and she seemed not only pleased to see us but startled as well. I guess not many patients arrived by the dozen headed up by a woman whose own mouth was the History of American Dentistry, circa 1936–1990.

Her office was a tiny cubicle carved out of the front hall of a building. Around the work area was a partition that didn't quite reach to the ceiling. Inside there was just enough room for a chair and some thirty-year-old equipment: a drill and a porcelain rinse basin. (Rinsing was actually done by the dentist squirting water into the patient's mouth with a large hypodermic needle. The basin, instead of being continuously cleaned by running water, was cleaned out at the end of each patient's session by pouring water into it.)

"*Xin muoi ngoi.*" Please sit down. She smiled at me, motioning me to sit in a chair that looked to be just slightly younger than I was.

"Oh, no—it's not for me," I said, smiling back. I indicated the army of cavities and vacancies behind me. She persisted, taking my arm and finally easing me down in the chair.

"It's O.K., teacher," Bryner reassured me. "She just want to see."

She turned on the light (a ratty, rusted gooseneck lamp more often associated with illegal abortions), put on thick glasses, and peered into my mouth. She twisted my head this way and that. Pulled my cheeks out of the way and periodically gave a knowing thump on a particularly interesting specimen. This was all to the accompaniment of a series of grunts and sighs. Finally she sat down, took off her glasses, cradled her head in one hand, and shook her head slowly back and forth. She looked as if she were going to cry.

"What's the matter?" I was alarmed. I sat upright with a start.

"Wonderful, wonderful," she sighed in English, looking up at the ceiling with a dreamy, slightly dazed look on her face. "Truly wonderful." She sighed again and shook her head. "Never have I seen anything so wonderful." Then she got up and went through a bamboo curtain decorated with a rendition of the "Mona Lisa." I thought she had gone to compose herself, but she returned in a few minutes with a glass of lemonade for me and then settled down for a little dentist talk before she began her real work.

Seems Dr. Vo was very appreciative of the dental break-throughs evident in my mouth: the Maryland bridge on my lower jaw that replaced two missing teeth. My caps and crowns. My various fillings, most of which actually matched the color of the surrounding teeth. But what impressed her most: the cosmetic bonding that graced my four front teeth. Never had she seen such work, much less been in such close proximity to it. She sighed again at the wonder of it all, then pulled herself together enough to make appointments for us to come back the next morning so she could start working on more mundane things, like cavities and tooth replacements. When we left, she was still shaking her head in amazement at having had such dental wonders walk in right off the street.

As for me, I couldn't understand why it was so difficult to find a dentist in Ho Chi Minh City. Even a nonprofessional like me, a person whose closest encounter with a dentist was being on the wrong end of a root canal, could make a quick diagnosis: Vietnam is a dental disaster. A combination of poor diet, bad water, and no dental hygiene have conspired to make Vietnam a nation of rotting teeth. Bryner's dental problem, however, was somewhat more unusual: he had lost his front teeth in 1985 when he had been beaten up by a policeman.

Bryner was twenty-two years old when I met him and extremely bright, a self-taught artist. I remember sitting in an outdoor café one hot Sunday afternoon. It was a slow, quiet day in Saigon. Nothing much was moving, most especially me. Even the cyclo drivers, generally desperate for customers, were taking it easy. The few that were out drifted by silently, as if floating on the clouds of heat that would settle down on Saigon during the midday hours. Somewhere during our lazy stay at that little café, I had passed out some gum (note: in this Communist country it was Big Red, an ironic but welcome change from the ubiquitous Doublemint available on every cigarette stand). Then I noticed Bryner was bent over a small scrap of paper doing some casual sketching. What he was drawing was unimportant (Bon Jovi, I think; or maybe it was Michael Jackson), but what struck me was that he had opened up a discarded gum wrapper, smoothed it out, and was using it to draw on.

"Why are you using that gum wrapper?" I asked him, fishing around in my tote bag for a notebook.

He looked at me as if I were as thick as a tree. "It's paper," he said, shrugging. I was ashamed of myself for forgetting just how precious things are in a country like Vietnam—especially paper for drawing. And to think I grew up in a family of Depression-era string savers. I was in grave danger of forgetting my roots.

Bryner was always drawing and sketching. Cats with long whiskers, rabbits eating carrots, John Lennon playing his guitar. Adolf Hitler next to a swastika. Even Charlie Chaplin brandishing his cane.

"How do you know these guys?" I asked him one day, pointing to Adolf Hitler and Charlie Chaplin.

"My grandfather," he said, explaining that when he was a small child he had lived with his grandparents. And through his grandfather, an officer in the South Vietnamese Army, Bryner knew about World War II, Nazis, Hitler, the rise of Communism in Eastern Europe and China, not to mention Charlie Chaplin and The Beatles. Indeed, Bryner's knowledge and appreciation of John Lennon came directly from his grandfather: He grew up listening to his grandfather's Beatles records. And his grandfather, who died in 1989, had obviously passed on a lasting interest in world affairs in his grandson; of all the young people it was Bryner who was the most interested in the Iraqi invasion of Kuwait that August and what it might mean to the world. He listened to the BBC Vietnamese-language broadcasts, read the news in the Vietnamese newspapers, and would then want more information and clarification from me.

Whenever Bryner couldn't get a word or a description out, he would automatically reach for a pen and start to draw it. One day I watched him doodling in my notebook. Gradually a soldier appeared holding a rifle and wearing a helmet, a watch, and some insignia on his uniform. As a final flourish, an American flag waved in the background. Above the sketch he wrote "USA ARMY" and the date, 1966. It was the year his father came to Vietnam.

Even more impressive than his drawing and sketching, however, was the fact that in 1985 Bryner had started teaching himself English, picking up a word or two from old South Vietnamese soldiers who spoke English, along with every English-speaking visitor he could find in Saigon. Which is how he came to lose his two front teeth, because unfortunately one of the first English-speaking people he met was a reporter from *Newsweek* magazine.

In 1985, to celebrate those ten fabulous years of Liberation, the Communist regime threw open its borders and invited the world press into Vietnam for the big celebration. Reporters from around the world came flooding in, converging on Ho Chi Minh City. Among them was Ron Moreau, a *Newsweek* correspondent who had been assigned to Vietnam during the war and who was fluent in Vietnamese. Bryner ran into him in front of the old American Em-

bassy, where he was also interviewed by him. Everything was fine—
until Moreau left the scene. Then the security police moved in and
Bryner was promptly arrested, bashed in the face, and thrown in
prison. Result: a smashed-up jaw and a lot of loosened teeth, including his two front ones, which eventually broke off altogether.
He was eighteen years old when this happened. Somewhere along
the way he had been fitted with two false teeth to cover the gap in
the front of his mouth, but they kept slipping and sliding and falling
out.

"Why did they arrest you?" I asked him.

"I talk to American. They say I CIA," he said with a laugh and
a shrug. Despite having invited the world press into the country and
despite all the pomp and parades and fireworks and speeches, in
1985 the Vietnamese government was obviously still wary of al-
lowing its citizens free access to foreigners. And vice versa. Especially foreigners from the media.

Now, it must be noted that going to the dentist in Vietnam is
a very social affair. If you are lucky enough to be able to go to a
dentist, you are not expected to go it alone. Everyone who happens
to be with you on the appointed day goes with you. So the next day,
when Bryner and Pearl and the others were scheduled to get their
teeth fixed, nearly a dozen assembled for the excursion to the dentist's office. Everyone was terribly excited. This was an event! A
great break in the routine. To celebrate, we took a bus.

Now, I had seen—and heard and smelled—those belching be-
hemoths lurching down the streets of Saigon. They are the dino-
saurs of the bus world. The great hairy mammoths of public
transportation. In any civilized country they would have been declared extinct and packed off to the Bus Museum. Made in Czecho-
slovakia, they are the last word in public discomfort and, to my
mind, yet another ringing argument against international Communism. Given a choice, I do not think any nation would freely choose
to have as their only friends countries that make buses such as these.
For starters, they are painted in what appears to be two colors of
vomit. Closer inspection reveals it is really cream and green paint.
The doors stick, the windows are broken, the floors—which look
like presplintered wood—give out from under you without warn-
ing. (I should talk: after a long, hard winter in New York—thanks
to snow, potholes, and salt—I have sat in many a high-priced New
York City cab being driven at breakneck speed by some maniac who

has only a passing interest in speaking my native language. All this for the privilege of sitting there and watching Tenth Avenue rush by through the rust holes under my feet).

Well, we all packed onto the bus, which then stayed exactly where it was, moored in the blazing sun, for a good fifteen minutes while we all baked inside. Our gang did provide a great deal of free entertainment for the rest of the passengers. A whisper, which turned into a roar, swept through the bus. Imagine, marveled the rest of the passengers—a real honest-to-goodness American. Sitting right here next to us. Then some of the kids started to laugh and poke one another.

"What's so funny?" I asked.

"They think we Americans," Jim said, pointing to himself, Pearl, and Bryner. "So we tell them you our mother." They laughed again. And the fact that they were passing themselves off as that most precious thing of all—Americans—made it even better in their eyes. I looked back at them, these all-American-looking kids with their rotten and broken teeth, and a cloud of sadness settled down around me. What a disaster, I thought to myself. These kids growing up without their fathers and fathers halfway around the world without their children. Young people who have spent their lives chasing down the dream of an American father who may or may not even know of their existence, much less care. Or, perhaps even worse, the fathers—like Kim's father—who knew they had children caught there and were tortured by that knowledge. The waste was almost overwhelming. Fortunately, I was wearing very dark glasses. They couldn't see how my eyes had suddenly gotten red and puffy.

We eventually got going, lumbered two blocks, and stopped right next to a pile of moldering garbage that pumped a load of methane gas into the bus. It was there the first of an army of hawkers and sellers got on the bus. Now, if we have street theatre in America, Vietnam has what can only be dubbed "bus theatre." And if it isn't an art form, it should be because it is not only terribly informative but immensely entertaining. The passengers on the bus are quite respectful of it and, in some cases, responsive to it. This was my first encounter with this activity and I must admit I was impressed.

First up was Razor Blade Man, deftly whisking single-edge razors out of their little cardboard coats and brandishing them skillfully under our noses, all the while shouting their praises. I wasn't so worried about those tiny little Vietnamese noses, but the closer he came to me and my all-American nose, the more fearful I became. Fortunately, we escaped with our nasal passages intact. Razor Blade Man made a couple of sales and got off the bus. Then Literary Man got on. He was selling paperback novels that appeared to be printed on paper designed to test the outer limits of recycling. The paper was brown, thick, and crunchy to the feel. It looked as if it had whole-grain oats in it. Who knows? Eating it might solve Vietnam's severe nutrition problems. Anyway, he gave a rousing, no-holds-barred book review filled with drama and emotion. He appeared to be acting out all the parts of an obviously dramatic work of fiction. It paid off: he sold out his armload of paperback books. Then came a parade of beggars, lepers, blind children, and cripples, who got on at various stops and begged for money at the top of their lungs.

But the best was last: Catheter Man. He climbed aboard, his ragged cotton shirt completely unbuttoned and flapping in the hot Saigon air. The better to see his heavy-duty catheter bag, which had been inserted right smack in the middle of his chest. A thick wad of scar tissue the color of boiled liver had grown up around it. Obviously the procedure had been wildly successful, too: The bag was filled with fresh, golden urine that sloshed back and forth as the bus lurched down the street. I was simply mesmerized. I tried not to stare but I simply could not take my eyes off it. I was both horrified and admiring. I have friends who have had exactly the same operation, and their surgery is sleek and discreet. Nobody knows. And for their emotional concerns there are support groups and newsletters and hot lines. On the other hand, here was this man wearing his problem openly and obviously right in the middle of his chest—and nobody gave him a second glance. He didn't need discretion or support groups because to the people around him he didn't have anything to be discreet about. Maybe there was a lesson here. As for me, I kept staring open-mouthed at that urine sloshing around in the front of his chest. Then I became embarrassed at what I was doing and shifted my gaze and only then did I realize that everyone was staring at *me*. Just as I was intrigued with that man and his catheter bag, the rest of the passengers on the bus were equally intrigued with me, an American woman, sitting right there in their midst. To them, I was just as exotic as a plastic bag of urine.

Finally it was time to say goodbye to Razor Blade Man and Literary Man and Catheter Man and proceed to the dentist's office. She was ready and waiting for us. Indeed, the entire neighborhood appeared to have turned out. We filled the tiny room and spilled over onto the sidewalk.

I was perfectly content to sit outside, where it was cooler, but the dentist cleared a path in the crowd and beckoned for me to come in. From somewhere she produced a fan, found a severely overloaded electrical socket, and jammed the fan plug into it, sending a shower of sparks out over the floor. I jumped out of harm's way, the fan came to life, and I figured if I did die in an electrical fire at least I would go out cool. Bryner had stuck his old bridge back in for the occasion, so I settled down, joining the crowd around Bryner watching the dentist as she peered into his mouth.

While I was up there I figured I might as well sneak a peek, so I bent over and looked into Bryner's mouth. It was disgusting. I had never seen such a mess. His mouth was a network of old-fashioned metal clamps holding most of his back teeth in. Things were so bad even I could see the cavities that decorated his teeth like tiny brown polka dots. She poked around at them and they seemed to spring back like flecks of sponge. There wasn't an X-ray machine in sight (nor, the dentist told me later, was there any X-ray film much less the means to develop it and read it properly). Turns out most dental work in Vietnam is much more basic. The dentist simply eyeballs it: if you can see it—fill it. Or pull it.

Meanwhile, we all ogled the now-toothless and grinning Bryner, while the dentist went through the bamboo curtain with the "Mona Lisa" painted on it to the back of her office. I could hear her moving around back there, and presently she came out and refitted Bryner's old false teeth.

"Come back two days," she instructed me. "New teeth."

Bryner breathed a sigh of relief and turned the chair over to Pearl. After gazing at Pearl's two badly rotted front teeth she nodded knowingly. This was obviously going to be a serious procedure, because she reached over to a small table, dropped a cassette into a ghetto blaster, and pumped up the volume. It was *Barry Manilow's Greatest Hits*. Then she turned her attention to Pearl and, without a single shot of novocaine, she revved up the drill and set about reducing Pearl's front teeth to small, sharp points.

I was horrified. I think I groaned out loud.

She looked over at me, and with a look of concern mixed with panic on her face, she put down the drill and once more ran into the back. She came out moments later brandishing a newspaper clipping, which she shoved into my quaking hands. It took me a few moments to focus my fear-ridden eyes, and when I did I realized I was reading her cousin's wedding announcement. In a Connecticut newspaper. I was dimly aware of the drill again, heard Pearl let out a small squeak, and looked over to see his white knuckles gripping the arms of the chair. Around me, gasps from his stricken-looking friends, most of whom had never been near a dentist before.

"Done," she said, putting down her weapon. "Come back two days."

Cocky, silly, good-looking Pearl was limp in the chair, his head in his hands. She had drilled away his front teeth in preparation for what appeared to be the beginning of a double root canal treatment without even a hint of novocaine.

"No drugs?" I whispered to her, as if she might for some reason be oblivious of the fact that she had forgotten to give him a shot.

"No drugs," she agreed. "No drugs since 1975." She made a face and rolled her eyes. I walked out of there like a zombie. No drugs!

For two days, Pearl was a shadow of his former self. Even his hero, Bruce Springsteen, couldn't cheer him up. Two days later we all headed back to the dentist. By this time we were a much more subdued crowd, with Pearl and Bryner dragging along behind. Once again, the dentist was on the sidewalk to greet us, once again surrounded by curious neighbors. This time she had dressed for the occasion: She was wearing a spanking white silk blouse and black silk trousers.

"Hello. You come back. You come in." She bustled around and within minutes Bryner had spanking-white front teeth. Two more visits and so did Pearl.

"You like?" she asked, admiring her handiwork. How did she do that? Pearl and Bryner were grinning like idiots, their new teeth seeming to send off sparks of gleaming brilliance. The damned things actually fit. And they actually stayed in. The total bill for both sets of front teeth: $28. I paid the bill, and while everyone was admiring Pearl's new front teeth, I asked the dentist why people in Vietnam had such terrible teeth. She sighed and looked at me the way you look at a child who has just asked where babies come from.

"Why bad teeth? Easy: no dentists."

Actually, there are a few dentists. But the problems are daunting, what with no preventive dentistry and poor nutrition. Add to that a populace that, when forced to choose between paying for food and paying to have the teeth to chew that food with, would, obviously, choose eating every time—and you have a mouthful of problems. And then there is what I call (as George Bush might put it) That Sugar Thing. The Vietnamese put sugar in everything and then drink it. Tablespoons of sugar in coffee. Sugar in liquified red beans. One day I saw a glass filled with something that was a lovely green color. I tasted it. It was very sweet and I thought there was something familiar about it but was still surprised to discover it was avocados, mashed up with milk and sugar. They even put sugar in milk. I couldn't quite figure the reason for that until I realized: All the milk in Vietnam is canned and probably tastes so awful people feel compelled to load it with sugar just to kill that canned taste.

As for the dentistry that has to deal with these terrible problems, nothing is available. Forget advanced technology. Dr. Vo could barely scrounge up the materials necessary to make replacement teeth much less find enough cement to hold them in should anyone even want them. Besides, who would want to be a dentist these days? she asked. A dentist usually works for the government and makes only $8 or $10 a month. People can work in shops or factories and make more money than that. I asked if she was a government dentist.

"Of course not!" She laughed out loud at the silliness of my question. "I no want starve." She was a private dentist, operating out of her home. At least this way she was on her own and sometimes making more than those paltry government wages.

"So why are you even a dentist?" I asked. "Why not earn big bucks? Work in a factory?"

She shrugged. "I am forty-five years old. This is what I know how to do. Besides, I like this."

I asked her where she went to school and a soft smile crossed her face. "I went to school in Baltimore." She held the word in her mouth like a pearl. "That is in Maryland. Do you know Baltimore? Do you know Maryland?"

I admitted I had been to Baltimore once and had liked it very much.

"I love Baltimore," she said. "I would like very much to return to Baltimore." Then she reached up and opened my mouth. "I would like to know how to do that," she sighed, pointing to my four bonded teeth. "That is very wonderful."

Jim didn't need new teeth but he did need glasses. Back at the Transit Center, we were speeding along through my homemade English-language curriculum. Just this week we had arrived at what turned out to be one of their favorite units: "Ordering from a Menu." I had drawn up a "menu" with various food items on it, and the students would take turns playing the waiter and the customer, adding to their ever-increasing vocabulary by having to choose between chicken and steak and then selecting corn or green beans. They loved it. Through it all, though, I had noticed Jim squinting over the menu and asked what was wrong.

"Can't see, teacher," he replied firmly and matter-of-factly. "Can't see the menu." So I asked him if there was a place we could go for glasses. Of course there was, and it turned out to be much easier to organize than the Going to the Dentist expedition. One afternoon, after lunch and after class, we headed off to the Central Market, a sprawling indoor market near downtown Saigon with shops and stalls spilling out for blocks on the surrounding streets and sidewalks. We were headed for Eyeglass Street, an endless row of small shops and stalls outside the Central Market with every imaginable kind of eyeglass frame. We were about to embark on the ritual I like to call "The Finding of the Frames." It was an event fraught with great importance.

Jim, who had recently discovered The Beatles ("Have you heard them, teacher? They are wonderful!"), was looking for a specific kind of frame, and it took almost an hour of trudging through the oppressive afternoon heat to locate it. There were a lot of false starts and stops as Jim made his way down Eyeglass Street. Periodically he would stop abruptly, which would send the rest of us crashing and banging into one another on the crowded sidewalks. But Jim was not to be deterred in this, a most important quest, and he tried on dozens of pairs of frames, rejecting them all. Meanwhile, I was dripping with sweat and getting more bad-tempered by the minute. It was March and Vietnam's rainy season was late. Every day the temperature and humidity would climb and climb and climb and I would sweat and sweat and sweat. If I needed any convincing, days like these would reassure me that I am truly Irish: Anything over fifty-five degrees is hot to me. I was able to take some perverse pleasure in the fact that I wasn't the only person sweating and complaining. Even the Vietnamese would soak through their shirts. Everyone except those few Vietnamese women who were wearing the *ao dai,* the traditional garment of Vietnam—a long dress with a high neck and long sleeves, split up the sides to the waist and worn over long pants. For some reason they appeared to float beyond the suffocating temperatures, cool and delicate like flowers shimmering in the sunlight.

"Can't you find anything you like?" I began to whine after a while. "Don't you like these?" I tried to push a pair of aviator shades on him. "How about these?" I held up a pair of yuppie horn-rims. He had the decency not to pay the slightest bit of attention to me. Finally we had the breakthrough I was looking for.

"Yes!" Jim cried, pointing to the perfect pair of frames. They were round granny glasses with metal frames, just the kind John Lennon wore in the late sixties.

Like the dentist, the eye doctor operated out of a public hallway. But while the dentist's hall was about eight feet wide (which meant she could fit in a cubicle about five feet square for herself and her equipment), this was your basic hallway: narrow. Oh, it may have started out being about four feet wide, but within just a few feet it narrowed sharply to about twenty-eight inches. No matter. We all crowded in for the show, with Jim sitting on a small stool. It took a few minutes for the examination to get underway because the doctor had to run down the street and find a stool for me. He was finally successful, and I squatted down directly behind Jim, near the doorway.

Jim began reading from a metal eye chart bolted permanently into the wall, high enough so it would not decapitate or otherwise permanently disfigure anyone passing down the hall underneath it. And like everything else in Vietnam, that eye chart was interesting: it had letters for the more literate among us. For those less fortunate there were symbols: a man in a conical hat, a guy on a bicycle, a water buffalo.

Just beyond the sign, two women were huddled over a small kerosene stove cooking up mountains of steaming noodles. My glasses started to fog over. My clothes were soaked. Meanwhile, a constant parade of people trudged down the hall during the exam: people armed with bicycles, baskets, children, and—in one case—a woman with an armload of live chickens, one of which flapped out of the pack and landed with a loud *squa-a-awk!* in my lap. I leapt up and flipped the bird back to the woman but not before it had pooped all over my leg and I had fallen on the floor with a loud clatter and an appropriate Americanism: *"Shit!"*

This eruption on my part emptied out the hairdressing parlor next door, where an operator was involved in giving a young woman a haircut chosen from the latest "Hot Styles from Bangkok Hair Cutting Competition" poster hanging on the wall.

"Shit!" They laughed, pointing at me. "GI talk!"

They helped me up and cleaned off my legs. Then they all stayed in the hallway with us, obviously figuring this was much more fun than watching hair being cut and styled. Meanwhile the eye exam had continued uninterrupted throughout this dramatic display of mine and the doctor was now sitting on a low stool in that narrow hall grinding the lenses in his tiny little "laboratory," which was actually more of a suitcase about the size of a salesman's sample case. Finally they were ready and with a flourish he handed them to Jim. Total elapsed time: twelve minutes, and $16.

Now, I must admit that for a time I couldn't figure out why people didn't just go to the dentist or to the eye doctor and get themselves outfitted with false teeth or glasses or whatever they needed. Twenty-eight dollars for a series of fillings, false teeth, and root canals didn't seem such a bad deal. Sixteen dollars for an eye exam and a pair of glasses sounded good to me. Until I reminded myself once again: the average per capita income of just fifty cents a day didn't allow for such frivolity as trips to the dentist or the eye doctor. I felt chastened and a little guilty over my mouthful of cosmetic dentistry, the bifocals that meant I didn't have to take my glasses off to read a book. The luxury of a pair of prescription sunglasses (also bifocals—in case I wanted to read on a beach) in my tote bag felt like a bad conscience. I was beginning to realize, in these small ways, just how lucky I really was.

The final installment of all this cleanup, fix-up involved rounding up the usual suspects and heading off to yet another important professional appointment: the barber. Linh, along with Hung and Vuong—two newcomers to my entourage—had promoted this particular field trip when their hair got so long they couldn't see their English lessons. I made it through the haircut, had a teensy bit of trouble with the dry shave that followed, but I'll admit I nearly lost it in the final lap. That was when the Demon Barber of Le Loi Street hauled out a battered metal tray containing a series of sharp instruments, which he began shoving into Hung's ears. Periodically from the depths of Hung's ears this Saigon Sweeney Todd would hit pay dirt and he would haul out a load of ear wax and hold it aloft before wiping it on Hung's shirt. I was quite green by this time and finally had to leave the barbershop altogether.

Lesson Learned: sometimes it is not good to pay such close attention to native customs.

I was learning something else from being with these Amerasians. And it wasn't all ear wax. I was fast learning to think about someone else for a change. A single person tends to get a little self-directed after a while. Factor in a little TV-celebrity quotient—especially in a place like New York—and you also tend to get a little self-centered. Visitors from Long Island City really do want to have their picture taken with you in front of the Rockefeller Center Christmas tree. Round that out with living in New York for nearly thirty years, and I was dangerously close to coming down with a terminal case of attitude. I confess: I could actually be caught standing in my local supermarket back home sputtering: "What! You're out of Rain Forest Crunch ice cream!" There was an unmistakable how-dare-you quality to my voice.

But here it was different. There was such need—everything from education to dental cavities and dirty ears—that my petty problems not only faded into the background but hung around and embarrassed me. In the whole scheme of things, being deprived of Rain Forest Crunch ice cream became just the insignificant detail it deserved to be.

Oh, not that I gave up my old ways completely. I mean, there I was standing in the photo shop on Nguyen Hue Street one morning having a fit because my film wasn't ready yet, as promised.

"What kind of a place is this?" I mumbled to myself. I like to think I was just being rhetorical.

"This is my country," a small voice behind me said.

I turned and saw a young woman standing behind me, quiet fire in her eyes. I had the grace to feel like a total jerk. My behavior was inexcusable, but mostly it was simply childish. I had acted like a spoiled brat. An old spoiled American brat.

"I am so sorry," I said, my face flaming. "Please forgive me."

"Yes, of course," she said, smiling. And why not. They have been forgiving us for years.

Months later, after I got back to New York—home of such high-tech dental care as ultrasonic plaque removal and New Age pain therapy—I had a note from Pearl. It read: "Mother Kelly I have tooth still. I very happy. Very love them. Thanks to you."

BRYNER

Later people would ask me: how did you meet all those Amerasians? As if they were some sort of a scarce commodity. It was easy. There was no missing them. They were all over the place, right out in plain sight, like Bryner, who appeared that night under the street light as dusk was settling in around Saigon.

His name was Phuong Tuan Le but he called himself Bryner after his American father. Bryner was a skinny kid who carried his worldly possessions around in a backpack—everything from clothes to family pictures. And no wonder: he barely had a home. Bryner had spent almost his whole life on the move, on the run, drifting from one hoped-for safe haven to another. He wandered into Saigon from the countryside in 1988 and then spent months living in Amerasian Park with other likewise homeless and drifting Amerasians. But from time to time he would find shelter in one place or another, living like Blanche DuBois: off the kindness of strangers. When I met him, early in that winter of 1990, he was temporarily bunking with Linh, sharing the half a room that Linh rented from an elderly lady. And among the things he carried with him in that backpack was an old photo.

"This my father," he said to me one day after class, holding out a snapshot. The photograph he held out to me was a faded picture of a young GI taken in 1966. He is holding a gun, his face turned tentatively to the camera. I caught my breath. Tears stung my eyes. It was Bryner's face staring back at me from that old photograph. A small, delicate face with pale skin, high cheekbones, and a straight, slender nose and sharp jawline. I wondered what color his father's eyes were. Bryner had hazel eyes, the little flashes of green dancing behind the brown.

Then he dug around in his backpack again and came up with something else. "And this my mother," he said, holding out an old black-and-white photograph. I saw a little girl standing on a street corner with her parents. She is about eight or ten years old wearing a plaid cotton dress and little white shoes. Her parents are standing behind her, smiling for the camera's eye. The mother is wearing a traditional *ao dai*. The father, a handsome man with heavy eyebrows and a warm smile, is elegantly turned out in white flannels. They look so prosperous. So elegant. So European. So secure.

I looked at the two photographs, the picture of the little girl and her parents standing together on that peaceful street corner in Dalat and the picture of the American soldier. Looked from the face of that privileged little girl to the face of that young soldier to the face of the young Amerasian squatting in front of me. It was the recent sad history of Vietnam. It was the journey Vietnam itself had taken from Colonial privilege to war to despair.

Periodically more old photographs would surface from the depths of Bryner's backpack. Another picture showed his grandmother and her children—five of them, including his mother—sitting in a backyard. "This their house Dalat," Bryner explained. "They go Dalat in hot weather." They were sitting on French-style chaises longues, a scattering of children's toys beside them. They were obviously part of the Vietnamese upper class, educated and cultured. "You know S.O.?" Bryner asked, enunciating the two letters. "Before this war, my grandfather work for them in their office in Saigon." Ah, yes. Esso, the big oil company. "He speak French and English for them."

One day he showed me one of a group of Vietnamese men sitting around a table. It looked like a meeting or a conference of some sort. There were bottles of mineral water, glasses, cigarettes, ashtrays. It was a small group of military men. "This my grandfather," Bryner said with pride, pointing to one of the men. I recognized the handsome man with the sparkling eyes and the assertive eyebrows. "He good friend with Nguyen Van Thieu. You hear about him? You know him?" I nodded to show that yes, indeed, I had heard of the man who was President of South Vietnam from 1967 until 1975.

Bryner was born in 1967 in Dalat, a cool oasis high in the mountains north of Saigon. An escape for the French and the Vietnamese elite, Dalat was an off-limits sanctuary of gracious homes and villas, golf courses, tennis courts. Throughout most of the war, it was the one safe haven in all of South Vietnam. Bryner's grandfather, a lieutenant colonel in the South Vietnamese Army during the war and obviously a man of stature and means, had a villa there. He also had a villa in Saigon and one in the family's ancestral home, Can Tho, southwest of Saigon.

"My father there when I born," Bryner told me proudly. "He there in Dalat with my mother." Bryner's father and his mother, Thu, had met in Saigon in an English class where the young soldier was the tutor and she was a student. "My grandfather like my father very much. Every Sunday they go to Cholon and eat Chinese food. And my father—he want to marry my mother. He love her. I think he love her very much." I asked him what happened. I could see him struggling with the words.

"I born 1967," he repeated, as if for emphasis, to make sure I would get it all straight. "Then come 1968. Tet. You know Tet? Vietnamese New Year." He waited until he was sure it had soaked in. "My mother and father live together in Saigon." At this point he picked up a pen and a piece of paper and drew a large, ornate villa surrounded by a high wall. "This my grandfather's house in Saigon." Then he sketched in a smaller house within the confines of the family compound. "They live here in this small house. They will get married and my father will take us to America. His father say that is O.K." He nodded his head to emphasize this permission from his father's American family. "So my father tell my mother: Go visit her relatives. You know—to say goodbye. She leave with me and go to Dalat but then . . ." He struggled with the words. "Guns. Bombs. Explosions. All over there is danger and then the road is gone. You understand?" I nodded. Sadly, I understood.

Bryner's father and mother were separated by the 1968 Tet Offensive, a series of the most shocking and bloody encounters of the war. On the night of January 30, 1968, nearly 70,000 Communist soldiers launched a series of attacks in more than one hundred cities and towns in South Vietnam, including Saigon. They exploded through the South in a series of carefully coordinated and orchestrated raids and attacks that seemed to light up South Vietnam from the Demilitarized Zone to the very southern tip of the country. Even Dalat, always off limits by tacit agreement of both sides, was hit.

But the most audacious attack was saved for Saigon. And the main target was the ugly American Embassy that squatted like a huge wart behind high, thick walls in the very heart of Saigon. It was assaulted in the early-morning hours of January 31 and militarily it didn't amount to a hill of beans. Nineteen Communist commandos pulled up to the embassy at 3 A.M. They blew a hole in one of the walls and rushed in, automatic weapons blazing. When it was all over, five American GIs had been killed and all the commandos were dead. By ten o'clock in the morning, the embassy was secure again and it was generally agreed that the Tet Offensive was a complete military failure. Except for one thing: it stunned the world.

Some have said that the 1968 Tet Offensive was the beginning of the end of American involvement in Vietnam—the day America started going home from Vietnam. And lost in all the numbers and statistics and troop deployments and movements and encounters and, finally, withdrawals was a small Amerasian child. It was the beginning of the end for him as well.

As the war closed in around them, Bryner's mother, by this time trapped in Dalat, and his father, still in Saigon, were separated. In all the resultant confusion of war and politics, they were never reunited. His father was shipped out of the country, and then even Bryner and his mother were somehow separated. Two years later, she married a Vietnamese man and started another family. And, like so many Amerasian children, Bryner ended up living with his grandparents in the town of Can Tho.

Can Tho was an ancient Khmer market town on a branch of the Mekong River near Cambodia; it fell to the French in the nineteenth century and became a base for huge Colonial plantations in that area. By the twentieth century it was a small cosmopolitan city with elegant villas, botanical gardens, parks, and broad boulevards. By the 1960s, however, all that had changed and Can Tho was a full-blown American military town, headquarters for the U.S. Army, Air Force, Navy, the CIA, and the Green Berets. By 1967, the U.S. military had completely taken over that pleasant little city and sprawled far out into the countryside. The gracious fountains on the grand boulevards were drained, filled with sandbags, and mounted with machine guns. But the Le family maintained their family villa.

"I remember that house," Bryner told me. "It was very beautiful. It was French. A villa. I am very happy there."

But after the 1972 pullout of American troops from Vietnam, even that area of the countryside—fortified as it was—became increasingly more vulnerable and volatile as the government in Saigon grew weaker and weaker. By 1974 the attacks came more often and were more severe. "The Communists, they attack us all the time then," Bryner told me one night. We were sitting quietly, just the two of us. "When the attacks came, my grandfather would put rice and aspirin in my clothing." He held out his shirt front and demonstrated how he would roll the food and the aspirin in the front of his shirt or stuff it in the pockets of his shirt and pants. "That way, if I must run away I will have something to eat. And if I am hurt, I will have some medicine."

By this time I was beginning to feel a sad affinity for Bryner. He was a bright, curious person, comfortable and at ease with his friends. But he was also quiet and sensitive, a person who could withdraw so deep within himself—even in a noisy crowd of Amerasians—he could make himself almost invisible. Nonexistent. Maybe that was the way he survived: by making himself disappear. And there was a melancholy quality to him that I was finally, gradually beginning to understand. Sitting there with him that night, I could only think of a small, silent American child—Bryner was seven years old at the time—scurrying through a countryside by now completely ravaged by civil war with only rice and aspirin to ward off hunger and pain.

"In 1974, the Viet Cong attack Can Tho many times. My grandfather tell me they are shooting 105 [millimeter] shells at us. He make our family crawl on the floor and go close up against the wall, so if the shell hit, the roof and the wall would not fall on us and kill us." He threw himself down on the floor and showed me how his grandfather had taught him to crawl on his stomach. Then he huddled against the wall. "Oh, those sounds. I can still remember the sound of a 105-millimeter shell." He made a sharp whistling sound that grew louder and louder, then died away. "My house is never hit but one day I go out and I see the farmer next door. He is dead. His dog, too. I see them. It is terrible." He twists his face and body into a contortion of agony. "They are all black and horrible. I never forget that."

"One day, I hear my grandmother and my grandfather. They talk very loud. They fight. Fight about me. I am very scared. I do not know why they fight. What did I do?" In fact, it was early 1975 and what his grandparents were doing was arguing about their American grandson's safety. By then, it was becoming quite clear that the government of the South was crumbling and falling apart. And the North Vietnamese Army would be sweeping down from the North to join up with the Viet Cong at any time. Bryner's grandfather was arguing that Bryner should be sent further off into the countryside to be hidden with sympathetic friends in some distant hamlet where the Communists wouldn't find him. The grandmother was arguing fiercely that Bryner should be kept with them, with her.

"I love my grandfather very much," Bryner would tell me. "He was very good to me, very kind to me. I remember that he take me to school. Every day he drive me in his Jeep to my school." In his own unfortunate way, Bryner was one of the lucky Amerasians: he at least went to school. He had been able to go to school for four years before things fell apart for him in 1975.

One day a few months after the fall of Saigon, a Jeep pulled into the yard of their villa in Can Tho. Armed soldiers jumped out, pulled out their guns, and broke into the house. "They are Communists," Bryner said. "They have come to arrest my grandfather. They point guns at him." He couldn't find the next word so he made a motion with his hands, knocking his wrists together. I nodded my head. I understood. The Communist soldiers handcuffed his grandfather, threw him in the Jeep, and hauled him away. He spent the next eight years in the North in a reeducation camp. Bryner was eight years old when he stood in his house and saw the Communists shackle his grandfather and haul him off.

"When the Communists come, they arrest all my teachers and put them in prison. Then my new teachers are Communists. Only, you know, they are not like you." He nodded in my direction. "They are not real teachers. They do not teach us anything. They only tell us about Communism." His face was flushed with anger and disdain at the thought of them.

"And what about you?" I asked. "How did they treat you?"

"Oh, they hate me. They call me names. Then my classmates, they call me names too. They point to my face and call me 'My lai! My lai!' Half-American! Half-breed! And the Communist teachers, sometimes they hit me." He picked up his dictionary and found the word, then he held out the palms of his hands. "They hit me with the ruler on my hands.

"Then the Communists take our house. We must live here." Bryner made a dive for his dictionary and his ballpoint pen. He sketched a small house with a palm tree next to it. "The house, it is made of grass." When the Communists came to Can Tho they threw out the owners and confiscated the villas. Bryner and his grandmother ended up in a thatched hut in the countryside.

"When they arrest my grandfather, they take him to Hanoi by train. When they get to Hanoi, they take him off the train and make him walk in the street." It was the familiar walk the American POWs took through the streets of Hanoi during the late 1960s and early 1970s. "The people, they stand in the street and when he walk by they shout at him and spit at him. Then they all throw things at him." He fled to the dictionary for the proper word. "They throw rocks at my grandfather. I am very sad for my grandfather when I hear this. He come home 1983. I see him and I do not know him. I do not know that man is my grandfather. He is so thin. And I think he has gone mad." Within two years, Bryner's grandfather was dead.

As for Bryner, after his grandfather's arrest in 1975 he spent the next few years drifting and wandering through Vietnam's chaos and sadness. He joined an army of lost souls that swept like a sorrowful wind over Vietnam. In 1975 his grandmother sent him to Saigon to his relatives, who wanted no part of this obviously American child with his pale skin and pronounced American features. They threw him out after two weeks. He caught a bus to a village where they had told him his mother was, but he couldn't find her. He met some people who fed him and let him stay with them. "I ask around and then someone say she lived over there. So I go to her house and I find her."

I asked Bryner what his mother's reaction was to finally seeing her American son. He shrugged. "She look at me and she say, 'What are you doing here? Why are you here?' I say I come to see her. I come to see my mother." He makes a cradle out of his elbow. "She has her new baby." He laughs. "She let me come in but the next day she left. She say she must go to Saigon and she tell me to stay there. So she left. I stay for one week in that house but she never come back." He gave an embarrassed little laugh, as if it were his fault he was once again left alone.

Bryner spent the next ten years on the move, drifting and wandering around the countryside, working for his keep, literally working for his life. His grandfather was still in reeducation camp; his mother, who was married by now, had her new family and wanted nothing to do with him. And Bryner confessed that by this time he was so sad and angry he wanted nothing to do with her.

I asked him what he did in the countryside. "I work for two farmers. But I could not stay with the first one. His family was very mean to me. They give me rice and maybe some fish but they do not let me eat with them. I must go off alone. Always I am alone." Fortunately, he found another farmer to stay and work with. "They are very good to me. They help me."

Bryner was completely dispassionate during these talks of ours. He calmly laid out the sad facts of his young life, lining up the years and events with cool precision. I, meanwhile, was completely rattled by these revelations, alternately seething with rage and choked with emotion. How could there be such tragedy and devastation for one young child? I wondered how he could be so detached. Then I realized with regret that that was the only way he could handle all of this—all the disasters and tragedies and plain old bad luck that had engulfed him. The only way he could live was to let some little part of him wither and die, if only to ease the pain. Someday the emotion of it all might come out, but back then—and right now—he had covered himself with the only protection he could. It was his survival mechanism. And I would go home every night and weep for him. For all of us.

Finally, word had reached his grandmother in Can Tho as to his whereabouts, and in 1984 she came to get him and take him back to Can Tho. In 1985 he wandered back to Saigon again, this time staying with friends of his grandfather's "from before," a lawyer and his wife. But after the incident in front of the old American Embassy, when Bryner was arrested and beaten up after talking to the *Newsweek* reporter, even the lawyer and his wife asked him to leave. Friendship could obviously be stretched only so far. Sheltering an Amerasian was one thing—sheltering an Amerasian who gets arrested and beaten up by the police for talking to an American reporter is quite another.

So his odyssey continued. He was eighteen by this time, and while he was wandering through the countryside, his counterparts in America were graduating from high school and wondering if they had gotten into the colleges of their choice. They probably had girl friends and part-time jobs and secondhand cars they would fuss over on the weekends. They even had fathers and mothers.

But Bryner, that American teenager trapped in Communist Vietnam, was still on the move. He wandered back out near the Cambodian border and he remembers being befriended by an old South Vietnamese soldier.

"I see him on the road and at first I am afraid," Bryner recalled one day. "He is wearing old VC uniform. I think he is VC. But, teacher, I am lucky. He is not VC. He look at me and he see that I am an American, so he will help me." And once again I am amazed at the contrasts and contradictions this young man has had to live with: people who do not want him around because he is American. People willing to risk their lives and sacrifice themselves because he is American. "This old soldier, he help me very much. He give me rice. He is very kind. He gives me job." He struggles for the right words. They come out in fits and starts. He is like a lawyer building his case. A carpenter building a house. He is laying a foundation.

"You know 'tree'?" I nod. "You know 'cut'?" He makes cutting motions. "Like I cut American beefsteak," he says, continuing to demonstrate cutting motions. I nod my head. I understand. "I do this to trees." The old soldier was on his way to work in a sawmill, and for the next few months Bryner, this half-starved Amerasian teenager, worked in the forest of western Vietnam cutting trees and sawing lumber by hand. At one point in this part of his wanderings, he was even befriended by the Vietnamese Army and spent seven months as a cook for an Army encampment very close to the Cambodian border, this at a time when the Vietnamese were engaged in fierce combat with the Khmer Rouge in Cambodia. "Many times we go into Cambodia," he told me months later. "To fight?" I asked, appalled.

"Oh, no. We go to steal cows and bring back to Vietnam to eat."

Bryner had another picture in his backpack that he showed me one day. It was of a fat little American boy wearing a Batman T-shirt and clutching a stuffed toy. It was Bryner when he was about two or three years old. I asked him if he remembered that stuffed animal. He shook his head. "Did you have any other toys that you remember?" I asked. "Any toys that you played with?"

"Oh, yes," he answered quickly. "I had a yellow car. I remember it forever. It was very beautiful."

"Where did you get it?"

"My father send it to me from America. It was bright yellow. Not plastic. Not have to push it. You understand?" I understood. His father had sent him a bright yellow toy car. It was battery operated and probably made of metal.

"What happened to it?"

"My grandmother keep it. She tell me she when I gone she look at it and she remember me." He stopped. "She love me very much."

He stopped again. "But in 1984 she must sell it. She must buy rice. She have no food."

"I have a small sister," he said one day. "From my mother's other family. I meet her a few times and I love her very much. This sister is very good. Very smart. She love me, too." Then he went on to recount the remarkable story of his sister, who, as a small child, had heard she had an older brother. She had never met him, didn't even know where he was. But, as Bryner tells it, every night, for weeks after she heard about this older brother of hers, this little girl—who was maybe six or seven years old at the time—would prepare a plate of food. It was for him. Then she would put it out on a table, just in case he would come for it. " 'No! No!' she would say, if anyone came to take it. 'This for Phuong! This for my brother Phuong! Maybe he is hungry!' " And this little Vietnamese girl would sit and guard the food she had set out for the American brother she had never seen.

Today Bryner's mother and his aged grandmother both live in Can Tho, although not together. Bryner does not understand what estrangement came between the two of them much less whether he was the cause of it. His mother's Vietnamese husband, who was in the South Vietnamese Army, is a bicycle delivery man. His mother, that lovely college-educated woman who could speak three languages, sells bread in the market. What about her life? Does she wonder about the twists and turns it took? Does she ever think, What if? What might have been if Vietnam had not exploded that night in 1968 and blown her life apart? I don't know.

As for the dozens of other Amerasians I came to know, sometimes—like Bryner—I found them, usually right on the street. Or they found me, having heard about this American teacher staying at the Kim Do. I would go down and find them sitting in the lobby, surrounded by motorcycles and ticking clocks, or hovering outside on the sidewalk, waiting for me to materialize like a figment of their imaginations. But mostly it was the usual referral system, a sort of Amerasian old-boy network: every few days Bryner or Jim or Pearl would bring another Amerasian into the fold. "This boy good boy," they would matter-of-factly reassure me. "This girl my friend. No problem." It was their stamp of approval, and they were never wrong. They were my own personal Good Housekeeping Institute, determined that I would meet only the very best. Beyond that, they seemed to know just about every Amerasian who ever set foot in

Saigon. And their network was extensive, a mixed bag of young men and women of all colors and hues.

One day Bryner and Jim and Pearl arrived with Tam—he quickly became Tom—a black Amerasian who had spent the first four years of his life in an orphanage out in the countryside near the Cambodian border. Who knew the reason for his situation? Was he orphaned? Abandoned? He didn't know. And what difference did it make now, anyway? When he was four years old, however, Tom had been adopted by Buddhist monks, and was now living in a Buddhist monastery in Saigon. He had a smile that glowed, and it never left his face. And he spoke not a word of English. But he was determined. He worked hard and his proudest moment came weeks later when he was able to yell at me: "I wearing shoes!" Of course, the people near us in the restaurant were startled to hear Tom say this, especially since he was wielding a chicken leg at the time. They couldn't possibly realize it was a shout of pure discovery and delight as Tom actually heard those English words come tumbling out of his mouth.

Tom brought some photographs in one day. They had been taken when he was a child. The monks had obviously taken a lot of children into their care, for there were other youngsters in the shots. "My brothers and sisters," Tom explained, including them in his family as is the Vietnamese custom. I marveled at the philosophy of this. Even if you were alone, abandoned, cast off and cast out, if you are lucky, as Tom was surely fortunate within his own misfortune, you can still have a family. And Tom had a "family" headed by men wearing bright yellow robes. Others had families headed by women wearing long black robes or brown robes, as Catholic and Buddhist nuns likewise swept up these wartime throwaways to shelter them from the storms of life. The pictures Tom brought in were pictures of little kids on an outing—little Americans holding hands and smiling into the camera. There were temples in the background. Green trees. Flowers. Benches. I peered at the old photos. Tom looked very happy.

Tom was anxious for me to meet his "family" in Saigon, and so one day we planned it. He talked it over with the monks and it was decided: I would come to the monastery on a particular Sunday morning and meet his "fathers." I was both excited and curious. I wanted to meet these men who had been so good to Tom, who had given him a home and provided the warm center of his life. Then, toward the end of the week, Tom came in with the bad news: my visit was off.

"No can do," Jim translated. Tom's mastery of the English language, while it now included not only the wearing of shoes but the eating of chicken, was not up to this. I asked why. "They scared, teacher." I couldn't get much more than that out of Tom or Jim, but I could only guess there was some sort of unease on the part of the monks. I learned much later that around that time Radio Hanoi had announced the arrest of members of two Catholic groups in Saigon. Eleven people, including priests, had been arrested for spreading "propaganda aimed at falsely portraying Vietnam's religious policy." Prison sentences of up to ten years had been imposed. Perhaps because of this the monks were wary. Or maybe it was just a general feeling of apprehension and anxiety caused by years of religious interference on the part of the authorities. At any rate, it made me sad. I wanted to meet the men who had been so kind to Tom.

And then there was Vu, a tall, gangly teenager with just the beginnings of a beard on his chin. I met Vu late one afternoon, up near the cathedral. He was straddling a bicycle, a shy but cheerful grin on his face. When I met him, he knew only one word of English, which he used with great delight and pleasure: "Good! Good!" He relied on Jim and Bryner to translate for him. And as the days and weeks went on, his story emerged. Vu was born in 1969 in Danang up near the Demilitarized Zone, that artificial border that divided North and South Vietnam. All of South Vietnam was a hotbed of political activity during the war, but because of its precarious position hard by the DMZ, Danang was especially volatile. It was crawling with Vietcong guerrillas and infiltrators from the North. Vu's American father had been killed at the battle of Pleiku, and his mother—perhaps in a panic—had abandoned her very American-looking child shortly after that. He was about six months old and she literally put him out on the street. He was rescued only when a neighbor told his grandmother about the situation. The grandmother took him and had been taking care of him ever since, despite strong objections from an uncle. That uncle was active in the Vietcong. Today they all lived together in Saigon, Vu and his grandmother and the Vietcong uncle.

Tai simply appeared one hot Sunday afternoon when I was languishing on the roof of the Rex Hotel with Bryner and Jim and Pearl and a few others. Sweet, adorable, dreamy Tai. We were all sitting in the shade, lounging in the roof garden's wicker chairs. The caged birds were singing sweetly. The carp were splashing furiously in their hand-inlaid mosaic urns. It was refreshing up there, but still I was nearly comatose from the heat when suddenly this blond teenager appeared at the table. Again, it was a startling and disconcerting sight. And once again I forgot where I was. California? The mall? I mean, there was this blond kid, his hair punked up into a stylish do. He looked like a California surfer. He was wearing baggy jeans, a T-shirt, and deck shoes. He had a backpack slung over one shoulder, his wrist was wrapped in a cotton kerchief (a very popular fashion statement lifted right off some music video), and he was sporting aviator shades. A small gold earring pierced one ear.

Tai was eighteen years old, and spoke not one word of English. He joined the class the next day and I discovered to my sad dismay he was completely illiterate.

One day Tai brought two old black-and-white photos in for me to see. One showed a tiny little boy with pale hair staring solemnly into the camera. It was Tai when he was three years old. The other was a family group: the Vietnamese grandparents and a lovely young mother, her hands protectively resting on that little blond boy standing in front of her. That young mother, tiny and delicate, was wearing a white *ao dai*. They were all holding big cards with numbers on them. Then I realized that the photograph had probably been taken in 1975. And they were probably being registered by the Communists. I thought about what courage it must have taken for that family—that mother—to stand there with that little blond boy so much in the family embrace.

I asked Tai what he knew about his American father and he just shrugged and laughed. A few days later he held a piece of paper out to me. On it was written the complete name and military address of a U.S. soldier stationed in Vietnam in 1970. "My father," Tai said. It represented all Tai had of his American father.

A few weeks later Tai introduced me to a small woman squatting in a doorway on a stool. She had sun-baked skin and a warm smile interrupted by some missing teeth. I could hardly believe she was the delicate woman from that old photograph. Tai was lounging against the wall next to her, wearing a pair of gaudy surf jams obviously discarded by some American passing through his life. He was oblivious of the fact that he was a complete contradiction of the woman squatting on the chair. That would no doubt come later.

One day a bunch of us had all been out for lunch. Afterward we headed off for Huong's house to pick something up. Huong was seventeen years old when I met her, an absolutely lovely black

Amerasian, cheerful and loving, with a shy, crinkly smile. She was determined to speak English and worked very, very hard at it. We stopped in front of a small building and I watched Huong go into the foyer and unlock a metal grate that covered the stairwell.

"Is that where she keeps her school stuff?" I asked of no one in particular.

"No, Kelly." Raymond was with us that day so he answered my question. "That's where she lives."

"You mean she lives in this building? Upstairs?"

"No. She lives there." He pointed to the cramped area under the staircase where Huong was kneeling down, gathering up her supplies.

No matter how much time I spent in Saigon, no matter how many stories I heard or people I met or homes I visited, I continued to be shocked. I went into the building and crouched down next to Huong. "This is where you live?" I asked.

"Yes. This my house." She turned and smiled that big, wonderful smile of hers. "I live here. I live here with my mother." She gestured to her "house." It was the space under the stairs. It was about four feet wide and maybe six feet deep. It was impossible to stand up in that space. There was a straw mat on the floor and the walls were rough concrete with a few magazine pictures stuck up for color and decoration. The small American flag I had given her was up there, too. Huong saw me looking at the flag. "You give me. I like very much." Huong and her mother shared toilet and water facilities somewhere else in the neighborhood with various other people.

As I walked into that building, I had to step around another young Amerasian and her small child. I thought they were just sitting there in the entryway, getting out of the hot sun. No. This young mother—Phuong—and her child lived there, in the entryway just outside Huong's staircase cubbyhole. In the whole scheme of things Huong and her mother were the fortunate ones: they had a clearly defined space under that staircase with a grate they could pull across for security and privacy. Phuong had nothing. And she was pregnant again.

My God, I thought to myself. What have we done to these young people? First to them and their mothers? And now, in some cases, to their children? Somewhere, some American man not only had a daughter sleeping in a foyer in downtown Saigon, he also had a grandchild. A beautiful, curly-haired, big-eyed granddaughter. I

Bryner at age 3.
(Courtesy of Bryner)

Bryner at age 23.
(Katie Kelly)

Pearl and his mother, 1990.
(Katie Kelly)

Pearl and his mother, 1968.
(Courtesy of Pearl)

Trang and her mother, Luong, in 1990.
(Katie Kelly)

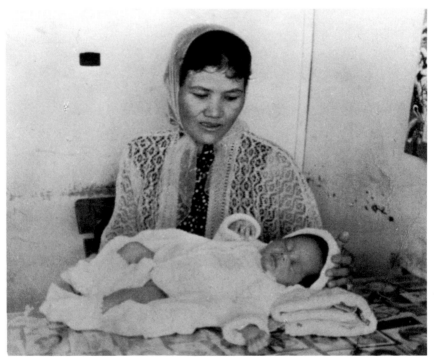

Trang and her mother, Luong, in 1967.
(Courtesy of Trang)

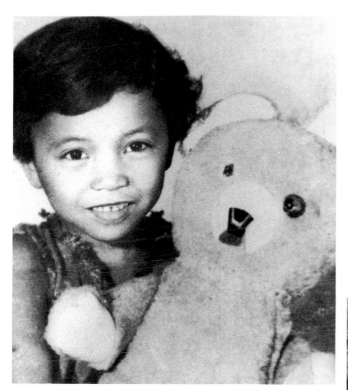

Huong in 1972.
(Courtesy of Huong)

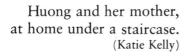

Huong and her mother,
at home under a staircase.
(Katie Kelly)

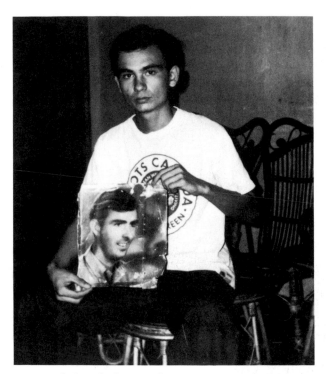

Jim with his father's photo.
(Katie Kelly)

Kim.
(Katie Kelly)

Kim and her father, Ron, in the U.S. in 1990.
(Courtesy of Ron Woolsey)

Pearl, Jim, Bryner, and Linh at Linh's house.
(Katie Kelly)

Tom.
(Katie Kelly)

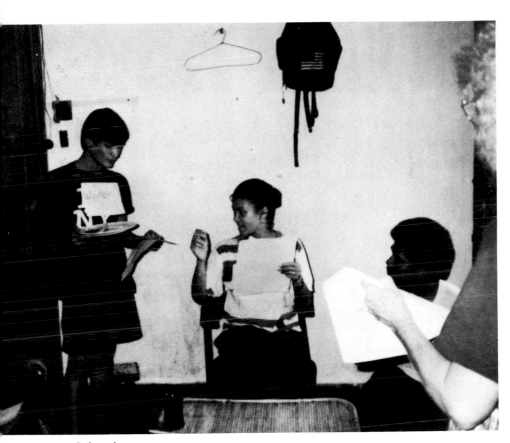

School.
(Katie Kelly)

Pearl making incense.
(Katie Kelly)

Tai and his mother
(*far right*), 1971.
(Courtesy of Tai)

Tai and his mother, 1990.
(Katie Kelly)

Phuong and her daughter.
(Katie Kelly)

Vu and his grandmother.
(Katie Kelly)

Mary and her mother.
(Katie Kelly)

Huy.
(Katie Kelly)

Cong's farewell party.
(Courtesy of Jim)

At the Givral Restaurant.
(Courtesy of Linh)

Katie outside Jim's house.
(Courtesy of Jim)

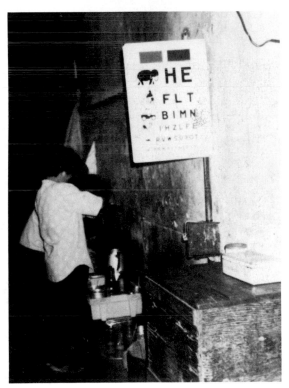

At the eye doctor's.
(Katie Kelly)

Katie with Cau's basketball team.
(Courtesy of Cau)

sat there on my haunches while Huong collected her school supplies. Good God, do men ever, ever, *ever* think of the consequences of their actions once they take their pants down? I was so angry that for a minute or two I forgot about the men who were so desperately trying to find their Amerasian children, men I knew and respected. At that moment I could only think about the abandonment. Jim's father had lived with them for five years before leaving. Pearl was a chubby little boy starting to walk when his father left. Be's father had been around long enough to father four children. Bryner's father lived in California, writing letters to his Amerasian son telling him he never wanted to see him again. These were no one-night stands.

I turned back to Huong. "How long have you lived here?" I asked her. I was hoping she would say this was a new experience, that her old house had been bigger and more generous. That for some reason she and her mother had only recently been forced under this staircase.

"Oh, teacher—I live here all the time. Whole life." She was seventeen years old. And she had spent her whole life living under a staircase in Saigon. I shut my eyes and screamed silently to myself. It echoed all the way through to my soul.

From time to time we would gather in a little refreshment stand in a park. We would meet there late in the mornings just as a change of pace from the bustle of downtown Saigon. It was cool and quiet and we would sit there for a couple of hours and "speak English" before heading off to lunch somewhere nearby. Periodically Phuong would join us there in that little park. I made sure she came to lunch with us but could never get her to come to class, although I had Jim make it clear to her that both she and her baby were more than welcome. She just smiled and shook her head. She was too embarrassed to come: she was completely illiterate. And as if her homelessness, her illiteracy, and her latest pregnancy weren't enough, she had even more problems.

Her daughter was an appealing child, and despite all the obstacles, Phuong was a tender and loving mother. The little girl didn't walk or talk so I had just assumed she was only around a year old, but one day, actually just to make conversation, I asked Phuong how old her little girl was.

"*Em bao nhu doi?*" I asked, gesturing to her little girl.

Phuong told me her child was three years old. I was astounded, then appalled, as I noticed Phuong trying to get her to stand up. Her skinny little legs had no strength. Three years old and she did not crawl or stand up or walk or talk. At that, I simply sighed and tuned out. I could not deal with Phuong and her problems. I was so frustrated I was paralyzed. There was absolutely nothing I could do, nowhere I could go to get help for this young Amerasian. There was nothing I could buy. Nothing I could pay for. All my American traveler's checks were just so much worthless paper for this young mother and her troubled child. All the money in the world could not give Phuong and her baby what they needed right then and there: a home, the ability to read and write, plus diagnosis and help for whatever was wrong with that beautiful child of hers. Vietnam— with its housing shortage and lack of medicine—had nothing to offer Phuong and her little girl. And I had no way to provide it. Staring her straight in the face, I had to turn my back on Phuong and her daughter.

This was what continued to haunt me: the living conditions of some of these Amerasians. Fortunately, as the Orderly Departure Program kicked into high gear the hundreds that once lived in and around Amerasian Park had dwindled to a handful and, finally, to almost none. They were either being processed and admitted to the Transit Center or, like so many others, had just been sopped up and absorbed by friends or the families of other Amerasians, living eight or more to half of a single room.

But there were still Amerasians out on the streets, often young families with children. Those were the heartbreakers. Long and Oanh were a young Amerasian couple. Long was a shoeshine boy who roamed Dong Khoi Street looking for customers. He was a well-known fixture around the Majestic Hotel down near the Saigon River and the Caravelle and Continental further up toward the cathedral. They had a small son, Tai, who was not quite two years old. This young Amerasian family lived across from the Caravelle Hotel, on a concrete park bench. And they carried all their possessions in two big plastic bags.

Long was born in 1970 and lived in a Catholic orphanage until he was turned out by the Communists in 1975, when they closed down all the religious orphanages. Some of the children ended up in state-run institutions, although most of the Amerasians were simply left to fend for themselves. And Long, at age five, became just another statistic in Vietnam: a homeless American child. He told me he hung around the market in Saigon, where people would at least feed him. Years later that's where he met Oanh, his wife, who had a mother and a home.

I asked him why they didn't stay with Oanh's mother.

"Oh, she let us stay. If we have money. We no have money. So—we no stay." Besides, he informed me through Linh, she already had nineteen people living with her. "No room for us," he said simply.

"Nineteen people!" I gasped at that one. I had heard of overcrowding but nineteen seemed like some sort of a record. "Your wife's mother—she has a *khach san?*" A hotel. I joked. He laughed out loud at my measly joke.

"Do you think you will ever have your own home?" I asked, thinking of his peers back in America, who, at age twenty, could certainly start thinking about a home of their own.

No. He shook his head. "That is just a dream."

His wife, Oanh, had expressed a desire to open a cigarette stand to earn more money, so some of us tourist types took up a collection for the $50 or so it would take to buy the box, stock it with cigarettes, and, presumably, pay the "fees" necessary to get permission to set up shop somewhere. I was there on opening day. I tied a piece of yarn around the box, and we had a little ceremony marking the occasion. The only scissors I had were a snub-nosed kindergarten model, but with a great deal of determination Oanh sawed her way through the red yarn. Long stood by holding the baby as Oanh shyly opened her box to display a rather meager collection of cigarettes. I could hardly hold back the tears. It had all the joy and excitement of any other ribbon-cutting ceremony. I don't even smoke but I bought two packs of cigarettes that first day.

"You first customer. I think you will bring good luck, Mama," Long said grabbing my hand. Like I said, I don't smoke but I became a regular customer buying those cheap, awful Vietnamese cigarettes every time I passed Oanh and her stand. She must have thought I was totally nuts, because I would buy a pack or two and then hand them right back to her. "Souvenir for you," I would say. "Souvenir for you." That way I contributed to her little family and kept my nonsmoking conscience clear at the same time.

Amerasians in Vietnam were different from their Vietnamese counterparts for many reasons, not the least of which was the way they looked and what they represented: war, Americans. But one of the other reasons Amerasians were so different was family. Most of them had none. The Vietnamese have a saying: "Birds have nests, men have ancestors." Imagine a child being denied the safe haven of the family nest. Of all the young people I knew and worked with, only Bieu had a real, working family unit. (And what a family: a mother, a stepfather, and twelve brothers and sisters.) All the others were either orphans or were estranged from their families or came from single-parent homes. And more often than not that parent was a grandmother. This was an added burden the Amerasians had to bear in a country that reveres family and family life. Indeed, to the Vietnamese, the family—extended and boisterous and clamorous and affectionate—is one of the most important aspects of life. It is the primary source of joy and comfort and hope, the centerpiece of life itself. The mother is the warm heart of the family but the father is the backbone, the center of strength of that Vietnamese family. And most of the Amerasians were denied this basic element of their lives. Almost from the very beginning, most of them had that central part of their lives torn away from them: a father who disappeared from the scene or was killed or otherwise denied them. Then, sometimes, the heart of their already-diminished family was torn out as the mother simply sighed and, for whatever reason war provides, gave up on her Amerasian child.

I thought about all these young people I had come to know and love. And often, it just got to be too much. I didn't have the strength to absorb all their pain. I would go back to the Kim Do and sit down in one of those yellow linoleum chairs in my room. And I would cry silently in the dark for Bryner and all the rest. Some of them—like Tom and Huy and Long and others—had been abandoned outright, given away at birth or shortly after. They had no idea who their fathers were or even who their mothers were. Huy didn't even know when he was born. Some had mothers who died or who had been killed. Still others—like Kim and Jim and Huong— had mothers who fought for them, sheltered them, protected them. Loved them. And then there was Bryner—what of this young man? On the surface, he seemed to have the best of all possible worlds: his mother was alive, he knew exactly who and where his father was. He had a grandmother, aunts, uncles. He had photographs, names, addresses. But little by little even that disappeared. The people in those photographs and letters left him or they were taken from him. Then, as if to prevent that from ever happening again, he began leaving them.

"My mother go back to Can Tho to live. I was in Can Tho in 1984 to see my grandmother but I do not go to see my mother." He told me one day. In all his life he only saw her three or four times.

A look has slipped down over his face that I cannot fathom. Sadness? Resignation? Dislike? Then I recognize the look. It is one of utter emptiness.

Again, I sat there helpless. I wanted to peel back time. I wanted to stick my foot out and trip up the course of history. Make it stumble and stall just long enough for a small Amerasian child to slip through the cracks. Change things just enough so a young GI and a young Vietnamese woman could have had the life they planned if only to give one young Amerasian the life he deserved.

"Do you love your mother, Bryner?"

He sat very quietly. Then he looked at me. "I don't know."

SCHOOL'S OUT

Among the many things I hauled into Vietnam were a lot of three-by-five file cards. I had intended to make flashcards out of them but then I discovered they were also perfect for sentence work: write a simple sentence—one word per card—then mix the cards up and let the students form them back into sentences. I had just gotten to the Transit Center one morning, armed with my latest sentences ("I am from Vietnam. I am sitting in a chair. I am walking to the door. I am opening the door." And for the more advanced among us, "The sky is blue and the tree is green"). I was headed toward the classroom, ready to spread my cards out and let the sentences begin when someone grabbed my arm and pointed toward the administration building. I took that to mean the director wanted to see me. Jim was with me so we headed over to the administration building to see what the director wanted. He was waiting for us and he and Jim exchanged a few words.

"No more classes," Jim told me.

"What?"

"No more classes."

I looked at the director. He was looking out the window.

"Why not?"

"No students."

Outside, three hundred kids thundered past to the mess hall.

"What are those—*The Night of the Living Dead*?" I mumbled to myself.

Jim started to translate, then looked at me. "Dead what?"

"Never mind, Jim. Just tell him that I see plenty of students out there."

The two of them talked back and forth and then Jim looked at me very seriously: "He say you right. Yes. Many students here. But not here long enough. Only couple days."

I looked out the window again and saw students who had been there for weeks. Tai and his friend Cong were lounging outside the snack building. They'd both been in the Transit Center at least six months. I looked back at the director. He was sitting stony-faced, staring out another window. His window didn't have any kids outside it. Maybe that was his problem: he was looking out the wrong window. Then he got up and walked stiffly out of the room.

I sat there for a moment, stunned at this latest turn of events. It was so swift. There was nothing I could do, so I packed up my flash cards and left. I didn't even get to say goodbye to my class. I had been there only three weeks.

Shortly after that encounter with the director, I was sitting in the sidewalk bar of the Majestic Hotel having a few cold beers with some of the Americans who worked with the Orderly Departure Program. I laid out to them what had happened out at the Transit Center, partly because I wanted some sympathy and partly because I wanted their thoughts on what might have happened.

"Are you kidding, Katie? You scared the hell out of those people. The very last thing they want out there is an American hanging around," one of them said.

"But he let me into the Transit Center. He let me teach. What happened to change his mind?"

Nobody had any answers nor would I ever get any. After all, this was Communist Vietnam, and not only do you not ask questions, but if you do you don't expect any answers. All bureaucracies are notoriously lax in answering direct questions. (Do you feel you have ever gotten a straight answer from the IRS? I rest my case.) But dictatorships of the right or the left don't even make a pretense of it.

After about an hour's worth of talk it was pretty generally agreed that one of two things had happened: either I had been given official permission to be at the Transit Center and it had been yanked away from me; or, worse, the director had simply let me in on his own initiative without official permission and it had just finally caught up with him and, thus, with me. Either way, I was no longer teaching English at the Amerasian Transit Center. On the other hand, nothing else had been done to me. I had not been expelled or had my visa revoked or even been hauled in for a "chat."

"You just be careful," I was warned.

By this time it was early May, and over the past few weeks a wave of unease had been sweeping through Saigon as a result of various government actions. There were newspaper accounts of an "American spy" operating out of Danang. In reality, he was an American businessman based in Hong Kong who for some reason had been arrested, held in custody, and finally expelled. Up in Hanoi, Miriam Hershberger, an American woman—a Mennonite and the first Mennonite worker allowed back into Vietnam since the war—had been invited in by the government to teach English to diplomats at the Ministry of Foreign Affairs. She had likewise been "invited" to leave, thrown out of the country on what everyone quickly agreed were trumped-up charges, which evidently caused a great deal of embarrassment among reformers in Hanoi.

Tourists reported increased difficulty in getting travel papers, visas, and permission to visit the countryside. Americans who made frequent trips to Vietnam with various medical and scientific delegations felt they were being followed. An American connected with processing Amerasians to leave Vietnam under the Orderly Departure Program reported that after work one night he had accepted a motorcycle ride to his hotel with a Vietnamese friend. After dropping the American off at the hotel, the Vietnamese man was followed for a few blocks, then stopped and questioned loudly and at length by the police.

I remembered that one afternoon back in late April, I had been at the Rex Hotel for my daily *café da* when an American man materialized. His name was John Pritchard and he was a Vietnam vet from Rochester, Minnesota. He had a bizarre story to tell: he had just been "invited" to leave Danang. Worse, his guide—an English-speaking South Vietnamese veteran—had been arrested and was still in jail. As far as this American vet could tell, they hadn't done anything wrong. He was not only curious about why he had been asked to leave but was even more puzzled by why he had simply been asked to leave Danang with no other restrictions put on him.

I wasn't in Vietnam illegally. In fact, by this time I was a fairly familiar sight around town. Face it: a curly-haired American woman being trailed through downtown Saigon by a dozen or so Amerasians would be hard to miss. But I was there simply on a tourist visa, one that had to be renewed periodically. The length of each visa varied during the year, depending on the whim of the government.

Meanwhile, confronted with all those accounts and with all the gossip and rumors, no wonder the few Americans in Saigon were paranoid. I reacted by disappearing from the streets of downtown Saigon with my Amerasian friends. We found a cultural park, where, in some long-ago burst of activity, the government had built a series of native huts representing various Asian cultures. They were lovely things, made out of native woods, thatch, and woven mats. There was a Thai hut, a Philippine hut, a Cambodian hut. Even a Vietnamese hut. The Thai hut had a gracious open porchlike affair off the back, which had been turned into a little refreshment stand. We would go there late in the morning for milk and lemonade and "English conversation." It was there my students learned prepositions: *in* the notebook, *on* the table, *under* the chair, *beside* the teacher, *in front of* Tom, *behind* Tai. Anyone walking by could have heard a chorus of voices echoing out of the Thai exhibit:

"Where is Tom?"

"Over there!"

"Where are my shoes?"

"Over here!"

"Where is Huong?"

"She is beside you!"

It became a favorite indoor sport in Saigon: trying to figure out where all this sudden antiforeign hustle and bustle—aimed primarily at Americans—was coming from. In a determined effort to figure out why the government was suddenly getting so nervous with Americans, those Americans present in Saigon—I and a smattering of tourists, backpackers, and a few Vietnam veterans—began holding a series of high-level meetings on the subject. (Note: "High level" in this case refers to the fact that most of the time these meetings were held in the rooftop bars of various hotels.) Since the rainy season was late in coming, the heat was suffocating. It was so hot that even the Vietnamese were complaining. Needless to say, given the extreme hot weather and the general laziness of the participants, it took a number of these languid and generally fairly beer-soaked sessions to come up with at least two plausible reasons for the behavior of the bureaucrats.

First, we came up with "The Russian Theory." We figured that perhaps the recent 1990 May Day demonstration in Moscow might have something to do with Vietnam's sudden skittishness toward Americans. Vietnam was no longer isolated from the international media, and thanks mostly to the Vietnamese-language broadcasts coming in over the BBC, just about everyone in Saigon knew about that enormous and angry anti-Communist demonstration in Red Square. Hundreds and thousands of angry people marching, shouting, yelling, and demonstrating against the Communist government had actually forced Mikhail Gorbachev to leave the podium in a humiliating fury. The feeling was that Hanoi had not only seen that May Day demonstration but had freaked out. Result: some overreaction resulting in the expulsion of a businessman and a Mennonite English teacher.

And second, we put forth "The Vietnamese Theory." We figured that perhaps the fifteenth anniversary of Vietnam's own "Liberation," held back on April 30, might have had something to do with all those official expulsions and unofficial "questionings." As Liberation Day had approached, rumors had come sweeping down from Danang about some Vietnamese who, to celebrate the country's "Liberation," had sneaked onto the old American air base up there and had run an American flag up the pole, the first time the Stars and Stripes had flown there since it was hauled down in 1975 when the Americans left. That also coincided with John Pritchard's invitation to leave Danang.

We held our final meeting on this subject in the terrace bar of the Rex Hotel. By and large we were pretty pleased with our findings and I felt very lucky indeed. After all, I was still here, armed and dangerous with passport and visa extensions.

(Note: The findings of our group seemed to have been right on target. By late June—just weeks after Moscow's May Day and Vietnam's Liberation Day—things were pretty much back to normal, at least on the surface. At least for the visitor. I was never allowed back to the Transit Center, but Americans were no longer being questioned, people were still inviting Americans into their homes for meals and visits, and nobody seemed unduly concerned about associating with us foreign types. And by October, even the Mennonites—albeit not Miriam Hershberger—were back with a full-fledged office in Hanoi.)

*   *   *

But in May I was still without a classroom. There were plenty of students and potential students, but without a place to hold classes we were still out of luck. It was Jim who saved the day. Jim, the dreamy teenager who wore his sunburn like a badge of honor. "Just like American boys," he would say with a smile. He was even proud of his white, hairy legs. He told me I should talk to his mother.

Jim and his mother, Lan, lived very close to downtown Saigon, so we hiked over one day. His "house" was a hulking six-story apartment building that had been home to civilian air-base workers during the war. Jim and his family—his mother and five half brothers and sisters—lived on the top floor. No elevator. Just a twisting, turning ascent through hell.

The stairs were pitch dark except for some faint light that reluctantly spilled through holes that had been chopped in the outside wall of the stairwell. I could see old electrical switches that had been pulled out of the walls and cut dead, which explained the lack of light in the halls. Along about the third floor, I caught a glimpse of someone's front door. It had been completely wrapped in barbed wire. It looked more like a piece of environmental art than an apartment door. Meanwhile, the stairs were encrusted with debris and dirt that had accumulated there over the weeks. Months? Years? Who knew.

We finally got to the top floor and then wound our way along an exterior corridor. I happened to notice a fresh dog turd steaming in the middle of the floor. I stepped over it and continued on toward Jim's apartment. For weeks I would watch the turd's progression with fascination, stepping over it each day as it slowly dried up. Months later it was still there, atrophied like that old wedding cake in *Great Expectations*. Nobody bothered to clean it up. Nobody bothered to sweep the halls or the stairs. Nobody cared.

"This my mother," Jim said, indicating a pretty woman with short permed hair and a big smile. She had obviously been waiting for us, and as we walked in she whispered some directions to a little girl, who hurried out of the room and returned with glasses of fresh lemonade for us.

"Is O.K. to drink, teacher," Jim reassured me, pointing to the lemonade. "She boil water." In addition to everything else, Saigon—indeed, all of Vietnam—had undrinkable tap water. But you could have ice in your drinks: Saigon had a water-purification plant to supply potable water to the ice-making plant. Every day, all over Saigon, you could see ice being delivered the old-fashioned way: in huge slabs, covered in burlap, that left a trail of icy water in their wake. Invariably there was someone following the iceman mopping up the water. Stores and shops that needed ice would take a delivery; then, since there was little private refrigeration, they would sell smaller chunks of ice to people in the neighborhood. I thought of the icebox in our old kitchen at home. The iceman would come to the back door with a big, square chunk of ice, which he would heave into the icebox with a huge pair of tongs, while Mom wiped up the drops of icy water that had followed him in from the backdoor. Sometimes you have to go halfway around the world just to go home.

Jim's mother greeted me, then shook her head and apologized for her English, explaining that she hadn't spoken English since 1975. "I speak good then but now—I forget. No good."

Jim had explained my problem to her the day before so she was prepared for meeting with me. And more than willing to donate her apartment for the class I had in mind.

"I live here before," she said to me. "Before" was a very specific word in present-day Vietnam, one that resonated with historic meaning. It meant "before 1975." Before the Communists came in and took over. Before the Americans left. And, what with power cuts and illiteracy and water you couldn't drink and dog turds in the hall, before everything got completely screwed up.

The apartment turned out to be one of the best I saw in my entire time in Vietnam. It had five spacious rooms, two of them opening onto a skinny terrace that was primarily used for drying clothes. The ceilings were high, the floors were Vietnamese tile, and every room had a door. Most of them even closed, although the front door was so warped it usually took two people to wrestle it into place so it could be locked. Lan even had a bed (with a mattress) and a wardrobe (with a mirror) not to mention a small television set (black-and-white) and a one-burner table-top stove (kerosene). And perhaps the best beer can pyramid I saw the entire time I was in Vietnam.

Recycling beer and soft-drink cans is something of an art form in Vietnam. Especially popular are Coca-Cola (red) and Heineken (green). The Givral Restaurant where we often ate lunch had a wall of empties behind the counter but I suppose there was a certain practical aspect to that: it showed exactly what there was available to drink in the restaurant. During the war, whole neighborhoods of shantytowns boasted shacks made entirely of flattened cans, a colorful march of Coca-Cola, 7-up, Nehi Orange, and Budweiser. Lan, however, used her empties strictly for their aesthetics: her red-and-green pyramid was perfectly centered on a low chest and rose to a point about two feet up the wall. It was the decorative centerpiece of the room.

"You can sit here," Lan explained, pointing to a set of locally made rattan furniture that occupied a corner by the front door. She gestured to the door and the window next to it. "Here you can see," she said, indicating the light that streamed through. "Cool, too." Then she shrugged and pointed to the dead fan. "No electricity." It was obviously one of the three days a week that the power was cut in Saigon. "Now we talk."

She told me she was perfectly willing to have private English classes taught in her house for Jim and his friends. She had only one condition: could she and the rest of her children attend the classes?

"Absolutely!" I assured her.

She sighed and thanked me. "Oh, I speak good English once," she said. "When Jim's father here." She sighed again. I asked about Jim's father.

"He was a good man," she assured me. "He come from Sparks, Nevada. You know that place?"

I nodded and asked her how she met him. "He not Army," she told me. "He civilian. He work at Tan Son Nhut." She puckered up her face, trying to remember the name of the company he worked for. "Not a word. Letters. RMK? Maybe. Anyway, it big American company. He fix helicopters. Sometimes I work in club near air base. I work part time. I waitress. He come every night after work. Oh, he all dirty." She wrinkled up her nose and laughed. "He good man. He work hard. This his place."

If Lan had remembered correctly, it was RMK—Raymond, Morrison & Knudson, an Oklahoma-based contractor that built air strips and base camps and repaired the war machines in Vietnam. And for those who blame only the GIs for all those lost children wandering around Vietnam after the war, they were not alone in leaving tens of thousands of American children behind. Thousands of civilian workers moved in and out of Vietnam, selling and building and maintaining that war machine. Be, a handsome young Amerasian with skin the color of burnished pecans, came from a family of four children, all of them fathered by the same civilian worker at Tan Son Nhut Air Base. Be and his equally beautiful brothers and sisters were definitely not the results of a one-night stand.

As for Lan and her American, the two of them had lived together—in this very apartment—for five years. "He come home every night. I fix food, we eat, watch TV, go to bed, get up, and go to work."

There was just one problem with this whole scenario: the guy was already married. "Yes, he have wife back home in United States. Two kids, too. Another boy named Jim!" She smiled when she said that. "The girl named Melinda." Lan explained all this with great patience and understanding. "Wife name same as yours: Katie." She shook her head and gazed out the door. "Long time ago. Long time ago." I asked her if she knew he was married when she met him—when they began their relationship.

"Oh, sure. I know." She shrugged. "But he say he divorced. I know he not marry me but I thought he good man. Good to my kids." Lan had twin daughters from a previous relationship, then they had their son Jim. While we were talking and getting acquainted, Jim had been rummaging around in a cabinet. He found what he was looking for and came over to us.

"Look, teacher." He held out a large black-and-white studio photograph of a young man. "My father." It was his father as a young man in Saigon. I was astounded. I could have been looking at Jim, the faces were so similar. The same shy eyes, the same cheekbones, the same small, hesitant smile. I was studying the portrait when Jim stuck something else in my hands. They were old, faded Polaroid pictures of a child's birthday party. I was puzzled.

"Who's this?" I asked.

"That me!" Jim said proudly. He laughed and blushed. Jim was a teenager, only eighteen when I met him, and every once in a while his voice would waver and crack, like that of every other boy stumbling out of adolescence and into maturity. I looked more closely at the pictures. It was a typical American birthday party: a fat, bald baby wearing a little romper suit and surrounded by grinning adults. I saw Jim and his aunts, Jim and a birthday cake, Jim with his presents. I recognized Lan in one, cuddling her young son proudly for the camera. Then I flipped over to the last picture. It was that young American man, this time smiling broadly. He was holding up his baby son for a birthday picture. It was Jim and his father.

I was all choked up. I didn't know what to say. "You were so fat!" I finally croaked out.

"Yes. They call me Buddha I so fat," Jim laughed again. "My mother put me in chair outside. People laugh and say I so cute. Say I baby Buddha. Give me incense like real Buddha." I thought of that fat American child sitting outside in a chair while his doting mother watched her friends and neighbors come by and admire her fat American baby. Back in 1971 when it was safe to do so.

It was all so normal and so all-American. This guy had set up an alternative family for himself in Saigon: a loving woman, a chubby son, TV at night. All that was missing was the white picket fence. Jim's father and mother were together for five years. But in the end that American man was just playing house; one day he left. They never saw him or heard from him again. Jim showed me the small cache of reminders he left behind: those photographs, some old receipts, and some blank checks with an address in Sparks, Nevada. After I got home I called the information operator in Sparks, Nevada. He was no longer there. It was like the old country-western song: no such number, no such telephone. It was all so long ago and far away.

I wondered if that father, named Jim, ever thought about this other son of his, also named Jim. A boy who was in some ways just like every other boy as he battled teenage skin, a voice that snapped and crackled as it went through its changes. Hormones that were probably raging. But a kid who was nonetheless so different. Who stood out because he sunburned so badly he practically glowed. Whose legs were not only ghostly white but, unlike his Vietnamese counterparts', were hairy as well. Like most of these young people, Jim was generally cheerful and good-natured. But every once in a while a certain kind of angry despair would grab him in a ferocious embrace.

"My mother not understand me!" he would sigh, like a quiet storm. "Not understand her American boy." One day, after what must have been a pretty bad mother-son encounter, he showed up at the Kim Do. I found him sitting on one of the hard chairs in the driveway lobby. He just looked up at me and cried with anguish: "Why she have me? Why she have Amerasian boy?" I felt such pain for this boy. Such awful pain. Adolescence is tough enough under ordinary circumstances, but to be an adolescent Amerasian must have been anguish of the most exquisite sort. I could only imagine the torment both Lan and Jim were feeling. And I was helpless. There was nothing I could do but pat Lan's hand and tell her Jim would grow out of it. Or take Jim out for a walk and reassure him that his mother really did love him. Talk is so cheap. But it was all I had and I spent as much of it as I could that day and in the sad, unhappy days that followed until that particular storm blew over.

*   *   *

One day, a few months later, when I knew her better, Lan and I were lounging around in the midday heat, talking while the students packed up their notebooks and pencils and put the room back in order. I asked her if she was in Saigon in 1975 when the Communists came crashing in from the North.

"Yes, I here. Where do I go?" She laughed. "This is my home."

"What was it like?" I asked her. "Were you downtown? Did you go out on the street?"

"Oh, I stay inside here. It was very quiet here. Some South Vietnamese soldiers were outside. I see them take off their uniforms and throw them away in the street so Communists don't know they are soldiers. But it was very quiet. Except for the helicopters. Man, they fly all day long." It was those famous military helicopters, overloaded with desperate refugees and last-minute Americans struggling to get out before the takeover was a reality. Lan and I were out on that skinny little concrete terrace of hers. There were some clothes hanging listlessly in the hot afternoon. We were squatting on two small stools, drinking lemonade and talking, like two old high school chums who finally had a breather because their kids were at football practice or band practice. "You know, Jim—he little boy in 1975. He only four years old. And all day long those helicopters keep going by." She gestured up toward the sky. "And Jim, he run out here and point up to the helicopters and say: 'Daddy! Daddy! I'm here! Come and get me!' "

BACK TO SCHOOL

Our classes started the very next day after that first meeting with Jim's mother, with the students drifting in from all over Saigon. There was a small gang waiting for me outside the Kim Do late that morning, all scrubbed and ready for our first class at Jim's house. The Breakfast Club had already met, and since I had spent the rest of the morning getting my lessons in order, now it was time for a meeting of the Lunch Bunch. Since there were only ten of them waiting for me that day we headed off to the Givral Restaurant.

This was a treat for me as well as for the kids. The Givral was a comfortable old restaurant, across the street from both the Continental and the Caravelle hotels. A survivor from "before," the Givral had been owned by a Frenchman and during the war had been a hangout for the press corps billeted in nearby hotels. CBS had rooms across the street in the Continental Hotel; NBC and the Associated Press had been just down the street in the old Eden Building across from the Rex Hotel. After Liberation the Givral had been taken over by the government, but a few of the old waiters had been allowed to continue working there. They all spoke French and English and created a clubby atmosphere for visiting Americans.

"Oh, look who's here! How many today?" The headwaiter

greeted us with open arms while a couple of other waiters started shoving tables together to accommodate us. The Givral was usually full at lunchtime. It was a haven for tourists, backpackers, and shopgirls from Dong Khoi Street. This particular day there weren't many Western tourists, just a few tables of Russians. They were easy to spot—the ones wearing all the metal teeth and acid-washed denim duds. It was only eleven-thirty in the morning but the beer bottles were already lined up in front of them.

Actually these lunches at the Givral served a dual purpose: we not only got fed very well, but they were also exercises in conversational English. And we had very strict rules: speak only English. And no smoking. Since the menu was written in both English and Vietnamese it was a terrific teaching tool, although for weeks the only words they allowed themselves to know were "American beefsteak." "Ordering from a Menu," was still one of their favorite units. This introduced them to all sorts of exotica not found on the Givral menu like fried chicken and hamburgers and hot dogs. And while they thought I was making up words like "broccoli" and "cauliflower" ("Teacher, how can you eat this? I cannot say it"), they soldiered on. The grand finale of our "Menu" unit included the likes of apple pie with ice cream and hot fudge sundaes. They hadn't a clue what those things were but I assured them they were worthy additions to their American vocabulary and well worth remembering. Nobody could say these kids weren't going to be ready for America.

Then, in a moment that can only be called absolutely inspired, I made up a unit called "The Forgetful Waiter." In this one, the customer would sit down and "Order from the Menu." But the waiter would keep forgetting things, thus forcing this exchange:

CUSTOMER: Waiter—I want a plate, please.
WAITER: Oh, yes. Here is the plate.
CUSTOMER: Waiter—I want a knife, please.
WAITER: Oh, sorry. Here is the knife.

This would continue through fork, spoon, glass, and cup until the forgetful waiter finally got the table set and the customer could then order his food. Needless to say, everyone loved playing the know-it-all customer getting more and more exasperated at the inefficient waiter. At Jim's house we would clean out Lan's meager kitchen of all its dishes and utensils as we acted out these units. The kids took turns being The Waiter and The Customer while "Ordering from a Menu" and "Paying the Bill." We did "The Forgetful Waiter" so much even Lan's dog could set the table by the time they finally tired of it. And what was I doing through all of this? Standing on the sidelines cheering them on like the coach of a Texas high school football team on a Friday night.

Slowly their vocabulary built up to include an entire place setting of eating utensils, along with a nice but imaginary selection from the four major food groups, including chicken, steak, fish, vegetables, and salad. In fact, they were so motivated that vocabulary presented the least of their problems. They ran through vocabulary drills like a marathon. It was pronunciation that became their wall. One day, shortly after their introduction to action verbs, anyone within earshot could hear Bryner motion to the chair next to him and suggest: "Teacher! Teacher! Shit here!"

That unit on "Ordering from a Menu" carried over into real life and brought this speech from Pearl to a waiter at the Givral: "Waiter!" (I think he actually snapped his fingers when he said this.) "Waiter! Please! Give me a good fuck!" he said, holding up a fork with a tine bent back at a forty-five-degree angle.

And of course they were forever telling people they were going to America, where they would, of course, live in a very nice "afartment." I suggested that, for a while at least, they opt for a small house instead of an afartment.

We sat there in the lazy comfort of the Givral, like the old friends we were becoming, exchanging gossip and observations on everything from who had gotten permission to leave the country to the latest American songs they'd heard somewhere. The Givral had a portable cassette recorder on the counter and a fairly decent collection of American tapes, which the manager would quickly drop in the slot when he spotted us coming. One day while we were sitting around after lunch, they popped in a tape. It was a medley of American tunes, and a young woman's voice began to fill the room. I couldn't quite place the voice, but it had such a familiar ring.

"Who is that?" I was actually just wondering out loud but with this gang it was like Name That Tune.

"Oh, teacher—that Miss Carpenter."

I listened a little more. My God, I think they were right. "You mean Karen Carpenter?" Could it be? Right in the middle of downtown Saigon: Karen Carpenter singing "Top of the World"?

"That right, teacher. That Miss Carpenter. The dead one."

Well, I guess it was as good a way as any to identify the tragic Karen Carpenter. "By the way, Teacher, how she die?"

I'll admit I was stumped. Karen Carpenter suffered from anorexia. How do you sit in a restaurant surrounded by a tableful of hungry Amerasians, while outside there is a sidewalk wall to wall with hungry street urchins waiting for your leftovers, and explain some Americans' ability to eat and/or starve themselves to death. How could anorexia and bulimia possibly make any sense to people whose daily lives were an almost constant search for enough food to stay alive. The idea of sticking your finger down your throat just so you could throw up a meal wouldn't make the slightest bit of sense to these kids. I did a piece once on "Celebrity Weight Loss" (Can you believe it? *Can you believe it?* "Celebrity Weight Loss"?!) And you wonder why it was so easy for me to leave TV. I learned that America is a country where people spend $50 billion a year on diet remedies to help them lose the weight that people in a country like Vietnam are literally dying to have.

Meanwhile, Karen Carpenter's brother Richard had told me during an interview that the Carpenter family believed she died after losing and then gaining too much weight too fast, thus straining her heart and causing heart failure. So I simplified and told the Amerasians she had a "bad heart." That satisfied them. They were very sympathetic to Miss Carpenter and her "bad heart."

Then, when the next song came on, something amazing happened. They gradually stopped chatting and eating and slowly, one by one, they all started to sing. Even the Russians quieted down. And there, in the comfortable silence of that old restaurant in downtown Saigon with the cyclos drifting by outside the window and the old ceiling fans brushing the air overhead, we listened to that little impromptu choir of Amerasians. James Taylor was singing and they joined him on the chorus to make one of the prettiest versions of "Handy Man" that I've ever heard. They were singing by rote, a lot of the words didn't match much less make any sense, but to me it was like hearing the sound of pure joy. And all I could do was close my eyes to hold back the tears. And think to myself: What a lucky woman you are, Katie Kelly.

Next to eating and learning English, the most important thing in the life of an Amerasian was meeting Americans. Every time there was a sighting it was a cause for great excitement. They collected these Americans like trophies, writing down their names and storing away their encounters with them in their memories. And I was shameless in using these encounters for my own purposes: the kids always found out where these Americans were from, so I would haul out my map of the U.S. and we would do a little map drill. I had a big red marker, and every time an American added a new state, we would locate it on the map and outline it in red. We already had New York identified (me), along with California (Bryner's father), Nevada (Jim's dad), and Texas (Pearl's dad). Every week they reached new geographic heights as Americans drifted through Saigon: Mr. John (Minnesota), Mr. Bob (Alabama), Miss Mimi (Illinois). But their favorite was Miss Katherine (Washington, D.C.). When they found out that was the capital of the United States of America, they were simply overcome with joy. That lasted until the day they saw a picture postcard of Mount Rushmore (South Dakota) with a rock climber hanging like a bead of sweat off the end of George Washington's nose.

Once, months ago, I had visited some Kellys who had a farm up in the Sand Hills in northwestern Nebraska. One Sunday morning after mass we packed into the camper and wandered up into South Dakota. We stopped at an old cowboy bar for lunch and I bought some picture postcards of South Dakota, which I threw into my tote bag. Somehow, they made the trip to Vietnam with me and one day I hauled them out just for a little Show and Tell. The Amerasians were mesmerized. Their goal in life—unfulfilled to this day, as far as I know—was to actually meet someone from South Dakota and trace the heavy red lines around that state. Until that time came, I (a native Nebraskan) would have to do.

By this time I knew most of the kids pretty well—Tom, Tai, Be, and all the rest—but from time to time Jim or Pearl or Bryner would add others to the mix, hauling them up those torturous five flights and squeezing them in somehow. There was Mary, who sold cigarettes with her mother out of a small stand in the park behind the cathedral; Linda, who had permed her hair, tried to teach herself English, and was training to be a tailor; Bieu, who lived nearby with her mother and stepfather and twelve brothers and sisters. Bieu was a regular, and more often than not she was joined by one of her many brothers. I was never really able to tell the boys apart because they all seemed to be the same age and look alike. It became something of a joke because after a while I just gave up and called them all Vo after the first one I had met. Although the classes were intended for Amerasians, who was I to say no when a Vietnamese mother, brother, sister, or friend came in and sat down.

There was a young man from down the hall who came with great regularity. "He Vietnamese but he good boy," Lan assured me as she shoved a stool under him. And he was indeed. His English was excellent but he wanted to work on his pronunciation and his grammar. Lan herself would sit in the back giggling over her pronunciation and swatting Jim with a piece of paper when she couldn't get a word out to her satisfaction. Lan's twin daughters also came regularly. Additionally, there was an actress from a local theatre troupe, her Amerasian half sister, and their mother. As was generally the case, the mother had spoken a little English "before" but hadn't been able to use it for the past fifteen years.

The Communists never actually outlawed English, but most people didn't want to draw attention to themselves and any association they might have had with Americans during the war, so they simply stopped speaking English. Now, however, the Communist government was desperate to have English as their new second language since they were trying to attract foreign business and foreign money into the country. Result: government-sponsored English schools were springing up all over. There seemed to be a school on every corner for every age group, with huge banners, billboards, placards, and signs announcing that "American English" was being taught inside. I spent three nights a week at one of those schools—ironically, with permission from local authorities—helping with everything from pronunciation to the latest slang. Unfortunately, these schools were somewhat off limits to the Amerasians. For one thing, they couldn't afford the tuition ($10 for a three-month course). But mostly they indicated they felt so out of place at those schools—run by the Communists and surrounded by Vietnamese people—they refused to attend. I even tried to talk one school, run by a very good friend of mine, into opening a separate class for Amerasians. Nothing doing. I asked him why, but he simply shrugged and changed the subject. I can only assume it was something he just didn't want to get involved with. And who knows? Maybe he was like a lot of Vietnamese: jealous of the Amerasians, who were now, finally, within striking distance of getting out of that miserable country. From having once been called the "Dust of Life" Amerasians were now called "Children of Gold," because if you had an Amerasian anywhere in your immediate family, he or she was your ticket out of the country.

Along with the mixed bag of Amerasians and their friends and relatives in that makeshift class at Lan's house, there was another interesting student. She slipped in very quietly one day, then came by periodically after that. She wore a lot of dramatic makeup and very high heels, but she worked diligently on her vocabulary and pronunciation. She had a notebook and a dictionary and was constantly looking up words and writing things down. Because of the illiteracy of some of the students, I didn't specifically assign homework, but I helped those who wanted to do some writing drills and dictation before and after class. This particular young woman would come in with pages of phrases and sentences, which she would insist I check over and see if they were correct.

She showed me her notebook every day and it was then I began noticing a pattern to the phrases and sentences she came in with:

"Please take your clothes off."

"Does this feel good?"

"What want me do?"

"You want stand up lay down?"

I made some suggestions, which she diligently copied down in her notebook. "I really think this should be 'What *do you* want me *to* do?' " I suggested. "And here I think you should say 'Do you want to stand up or lie down?' I think you want, um, whoever it is you are talking to to make a choice. Between, um, standing up. And, um, lying down. I think."

"Whoever, whoever, whoever." She was looking up the word. She found it and looked up. "Oh, I talk some guy, Kelly. I ask him . . ." she consulted her notes again, "Do you want stand up or lay down?" Satisfied with her progress, she smiled, closed her notebook, and stood up. "Well, must go, teacher. Have appointment. You help me a lot. Thank you very much." I could hear her high heels clicking down the tile hallway. She was a prostitute who stopped in on her way to work. She proudly told me everybody was complimenting her on her English. No wonder. She was probably the only prostitute in Saigon who had a semiprivate English tutor.

I used to think traffic in New York was bad until I got to Cairo, where traffic just stops completely, sometimes for hours on end, often to let the camels and the Mercedes sort themselves out. Saigon, it must be said, added a whole other dimension to traffic. Not that it was as crazy as New York or as congested as Cairo. It was just more lethal. There are about six working traffic lights left in Saigon, all wartime leftovers from the Eagle Traffic Signal Company in Des Moines, Iowa. Worse, there are only a few discernible traffic cops and seemingly millions of Honda motorcycles all going at warp speed. And the traffic never stops for pedestrians. You simply step into it and hope it changes its pattern and weaves around you as you work your way across the street. Most of the time it works but it is frightening. I have seen newcomers to this form of traffic madness stand for hours on a corner trying to cross a street, never getting up the courage to plunge into the midst of that motorcycle mayhem. Factor in a few hundred thousand bicycles and cyclos, women with pole baskets, and a few horse-drawn carts, and you have traffic that is not only uncontrolled but uncontrollable.

For me, it was an accident just waiting to happen. Unfortunately, I could see it coming—and was powerless to stop it. I could only sit and watch. I was on my way home from class one day. It was hot and about to rain so I decided to take a cyclo instead of walking. Minh had waited outside Lan's house for me and now we were pedaling leisurely along Ham Nghi Street, in the home stretch en route to the Kim Do. As usual, I was pondering the progress of my students. Tom had had another breakthrough: he finally was able to move his thoughts into past tense. Pearl had assumed the duties of Director of Pronunciation and spent most of his time shaking his finger at people who couldn't pronounce their *p*'s properly. "Pee! Pee! Pee!" he would yell at them. "You know—Pee! As in *Pearl!* You can say my name! *Pearl!* You can say this: Pee! Pee!"

Ahead of us, another cyclo driver was likewise pedaling slowly and methodically down the street. I saw one of his fifty-cent rubber thongs as it fell off. Later, I replayed it in my mind and I could stand aside and see myself watching languidly as that thong, in slow motion, floated to the ground. I saw that driver ahead of us give a jerk, then wheel over to go back and retrieve it. That sent my cyclo into an evasive action, which sent us directly into the path of a speeding Honda that had come barreling up behind us. It crashed smack into my cyclo and sped off down the street. We had been broad-sided by a hit-and-run Honda. There was a confusing jumble of wheels and metal and I heard a loud CR-A-A-A-A-CK! as something hard hit the pavement. It was my head. Then there were some short squishy sounds, one after the other. That was the rest of me making a melody: it was absolute 4/4 time as my shoulder, my elbow, my hip, and then my hand created some very close harmony with the street. The next thing I knew I was being helped to my feet. I could feel some hot liquid pouring out of some hole in my body and for a second I had the horrifying thought that I was wetting my pants, something I hadn't done since second grade, when Mrs. King wouldn't acknowledge my desperate hand waving. I was relieved to find it was only my blood. It was pouring out of my head, running down my face, and spilling onto the front of my dress. I could dimly hear a huge roaring sound and figured it was my brains splashing onto the street. Then I realized: The entire neighborhood had turned out. And they were all shouting and yelling to one another. After all, there was an *American!* And she was *bleeding!* All over the street! That hadn't happened since the 1970s!

The two cyclo drivers were a little bloodied. Minh had cut his toe; the other had a gash on his leg. They were also frozen with horror. They stood there paralyzed, looking at me, their mouths open. Meanwhile, the other passenger, who had not been dumped so unceremoniously out into the middle of that Saigon street, was trying to chase down the ducks that had slipped out of her grip when we all went down together. Minh finally snapped out of his daze and began menacing me with a greasy rag aimed directly at my head wound. Meanwhile, I was rummaging frantically in my tote bag for a clean tissue. I didn't want to insult the obviously distraught Minh by wrestling that filthy rag out of his hand and beating him senseless with my tote bag, but by the same token, I certainly didn't want that germ-encrusted rag anywhere near my head. By this time there was enough of my precious bodily fluid on the street to open a blood bank. Fortunately, a woman from a nearby shop came barreling through the crowd with an armload of cotton, which she held out to me. I remember wondering just what she and her family would sleep on that night, since I obviously now had their sleeping mat stuck to my head. Meanwhile, I had certainly provided just the break needed in an otherwise dull and ordinary day because by this time the crowd was enormous.

The neighbors had pretty well mopped me up and the other passenger had rounded up her ducks. And then it was decided: the American woman will go to the hospital. But first she will sit down on this small wooden stool and she will have whatever she wants to drink. So there I sat, clutching a wad of cotton the size of a mattress to my head, discussing everything from the weather in Fargo, North Dakota (Can you believe it? Some guy on that street in Saigon had relatives in Fargo, North Dakota?), to the price of a new car in America.

"Tell me," one man asked in fluent English, after they had helped me sit down, "do they still have the Ford car in America? I had a Ford car once. It was in 1965. Do you remember 1965? Oh, I loved that car very much." I assured him that yes, indeed, they still made the Ford car in America and yes, I did indeed remember 1965. In fact, it was a very good year. However, I felt obligated to point out that while they still make the Ford car, it was my unhappy duty to report that my favorite Ford car of all time (the sporty little Ford Mustang) was no longer in production. Mr. Ford, my automobile friend, was shocked and surprised and likewise unhappy so we sympathized with one another over this turn of events. I also felt obligated to tell him that despite my deep appreciation of the Ford Mustang, my favorite car in the whole world is in fact the 1957 Chevrolet Bel Air. Preferably red. Preferably a hard-top convertible. With a white top. And white sidewalls. Very wide white sidewalls.

"Is that anything like a 1957 Cadillac?" he asked.

"Well," I was forced to concede, "the Cadillac was the more expensive car and to this day it figures more prominently in popular songs about cars of that era. But real lovers of classic cars none-theless appreciate the beauty of the '57 Chevy Bel Air." Besides— that's what everyone in high school could afford to dream about. (In 1954, my dad bought the first new car he would ever own in his entire life: a two-tone Chevrolet-210 four-door sedan. He hand-carried $2,400 in cash down to Sullivan Motors and drove that beauty home, right up Fifth Street. Baby blue on the bottom, cream on the top. That was the year that automobile tail fins were just beginning to bud, like breasts on an adolescent girl. My entire se-nior year in high school is actually a photographic record of that car: me in my new Easter coat, me in my senior-prom dress, me in my cap and gown on graduation day. And in the background of every shot: that two-tone 1954 Chevrolet-210. And although it wasn't a 1957 Bel Air, I loved it nonetheless.)

Mr. Ford leaned toward me and whispered: "Now we just have Communist cars. If you ever have a chance to buy a car from East Germany—don't."

"Why not?"

"They're crap."

It was finally time to go to the hospital. I couldn't put it off any longer. I kicked and screamed and protested but my benefactors would have none of it. My self-appointed Saigon Florence Night-ingale changed the mattress on my head and we all packed off to the nearest emergency room. This included the other cyclo driver and his passenger, who, by this time, had rounded up all her ducks. She had been sitting on a stool next to me, cradling her ducks in her lap. There was nothing wrong with her but she cheerfully insisted on accompanying us, obviously not wanting to miss a minute of the fun.

We arrived at the emergency room—two cyclo drivers, a

woman with an armload of ducks, my own personal emergency medical technician, a small delegation of eyewitnesses, and oh, yes— me. The hospital staff were astounded, but they swung into action. As for the hospital itself, it was old and quiet and dim. In fact, there was not a light on in the whole place, but that only served to give it a cool and quiet atmosphere. Long exterior corridors embraced the inner workings of the hospital: the examination rooms, wards, operating rooms. The floors were tiled and mildew crept up the walls. I was ushered into an examination room, where Mr. Ford and my cyclo driver took turns giving the doctor a spirited accounting of my immediate medical history.

"Just out of curiosity," I asked Minh when they had finally finished telling the doctor what happened, "What did you tell him?"

"I tell him you fall down, go boom, much blood." That seemed to cover it.

The first thing the doctor in charge of my case did was assure me that the water he was using to clean up the dried blood and cotton stuck to my head was distilled. Then I noticed that the gloves he put on came from what appeared to be a miniature clothes rack standing on a table over in the corner, only instead of coats and hats it was festooned with rubber gloves. Then I realized, first with shock, then with dismay, and finally with sadness: the hospital's examination gloves had been washed. They were stuck on that rack to be dried and reused. Thankfully, I didn't require any stitches. It was just your basic head wound that had bled like crazy. As for medicine, I dug around in my tote bag and came up with a bottle of American Mercurochrome. There was a rush of medical personnel when they saw it. Likewise for the Tylenol, the tube of topical antiseptic, the oral antibiotics, and the Ouch-less bandages that were also floating around in there. I might travel light but I am certainly well stocked.

The other cyclo passenger had misplaced one duck but some- one cornered it in another examination room and returned it to her. As we prepared to leave the doctor whispered something to me.

"Never get sick in Vietnam." Then he paused and shook my hand. "Thank you for coming."

ENTERTAINMENT TONIGHT

It has been said that Vietnam has only two seasons: hot and hotter. The monotony of this is broken only by two weather patterns: wet and wetter. We were in hot and wet. Even that was bad news for me. I don't perspire—I sweat. I had gone beyond what others might claim as a simple perspiration breakthrough and was now in a complete meltdown. Moreover, with my Irish Afro I was now on daily hair alert. As July and August wore on I looked as if I'd stuck my finger in an electrical socket. I finally gave up altogether and tied it off with a scarf. Then I looked like a cross between Aunt Jemima and a 1940s war-bond seller. No matter. The old soldier who spent all day sitting on his motorbike across the street from the Kim Do still told me I looked like Elizabeth Taylor. And you wonder why I love this country?

Fortunately, higher mathematics is not my strong suit so I couldn't translate Celsius into Fahrenheit; thus I was spared direct knowledge of just how hot it was. Indirectly, I was dying. The heat was awful. Does the word "brutal" mean anything to you? One day some mean-spirited math grinch translated the temperature from Celcius to Fahrenheit and informed me it was close to 110 degrees. I nearly killed him. I can't tell you the number of times I ran into the air-conditioned ladies' room of the Rex Hotel, locked the door, tore off all my clothes, threw cold water all over myself, and whined.

Most days classes at Lan's were hot but tolerable, thanks mostly to an old fan she had commandeered from somewhere. She would haul it out as soon as I arrived, plug it in, and, being the selfish, sweating, sweltering American woman I was, I pretended not to notice it was aimed directly at me. That way I didn't have to share it with anyone else. But that fan was good only on those days when there wasn't a power cut. On the days the authorities cut the power I simply melted and Lan would come through with a glass of iced tea and a cold cloth so I could mop my dripping brow.

There was also a special chair for me. Everyone else sat on rattan chairs and stools and so did I for the first few days. Then Lan noticed how much I squirmed around (I kept falling through the slats) and from somewhere—down the hall, I presume—she found an old wooden chair with a padded plastic seat. When class started, that chair was always waiting for me.

Well, like the weather, we were hot into present tense one day when it happened. The power was off and there was no fan aimed at me. We were reviewing continuous present of the verbs we already knew, acting our way through "I am eating" and "I am drinking" and "I am sleeping" (my snores always brought the house down. It is important to have an appreciative audience). I had just gotten up to demonstrate the fine art of "I am standing up" and was about to proceed to "I am sitting down" when I realized there was a certain heaviness to my limbs. Well, maybe not my limbs. But certainly my rear end. Then I realized that I had sweated clear through to the plastic seat of the chair, which was now attached to me like a growth. When it fell off with a clatter I realized, for that day at least, I was at the end of my temperature-humidity tether. So when one of the students suggested we take a break and go to a movie, I was very agreeable. Seems there was an American movie playing right around the corner from the Rex Hotel. So in Saigon's sweltering heat I took the intellectual approach: is it air-conditioned? They assured me it was, and since I am game for anything, off we trooped.

I did keep mumbling things like "I am walking down the stairs," "I am riding in my cyclo," "I am buying tickets," and "I am sitting down" just to uphold our educational standards.

Sure enough, there was an American movie being shown that day. Unfortunately, the air-conditioning had broken down and the move was *A Cry in the Dark,* not one of my favorite Meryl Streep movies (all about an Australian woman accused of murdering her infant daughter all the while insisting the child had been carried off by a wild dog). And what we were watching was not a movie at all but the umpteenth copy of a bootleg video cassette. It was green and fuzzy and out of focus and so wiggly Meryl Streep appeared to have some physical disability as she jerked wildly across the screen. But the closeups were the worst: her head kept shooting up off the screen. There were no subtitles; instead there was an audio track blasting at full volume, with a woman's voice droning every single part in Vietnamese—men, women, children, good guys, bad guys. As usual, this was a full-smoking establishment, and after about five minutes the place was completely fogged in.

After an hour, there was a long intermission (while they changed the tape, I presume), which gave the audience a chance to smoke even more cigarettes out in the hallway. I repaired to the ladies room (since this theatre was also connected to the Rex Hotel the toilets were sit-down porcelain models and came complete with real toilet paper in real wall-mounted dispensers), mostly to bang my head against the wall and wonder why I had come halfway around the world only to be wreathed in cigarette smoke, washed in sweat, and assaulted by some Vietnamese woman screaming out all the words to a bad Meryl Streep movie. Since there are some questions to which there are no answers, I flushed the toilet and rejoined the kids for the remaining hour of video torture.

"Wasn't that wonderful!" the gang enthused when we hit the street afterward. I didn't have the heart to tell them it was the single most stupefying experience of my life.

I must have been a glutton for punishment, because a few weeks later, in another heat-weakened state, I let myself be talked into yet another movie. This one was the Richard Burton–Elizabeth Taylor version of *Cleopatra*. I shouldn't have been surprised when the same woman's voice began screaming out the turgid dialogue to that cinematic potboiler. On and on she droned. I wanted to throw a shoe through the screen. This theatre was down near a small neighborhood market, and since it didn't even have the pretense of air-conditioning, the doors were wide open. History may contradict me, but in this version Cleopatra seduced Mark Anthony to the accompaniment of some very large pigs squealing at the top of their lungs.

Fortunately, the projectionist had only one cassette of the movie and all the action ended abruptly in the middle of things. So everyone got up and left. Well, look at it this way: in Vietnam, at least, Cleopatra still lives.

*   *   *

Somehow these students of mine were able to keep up with the latest American songs and the latest styles, right down to some of the guys wearing little gold earrings in their lobes. Pearl even figured out how to lace his cast-off high tops the way American kids did. I couldn't imagine how they knew about these things until one day they asked me if I wanted to go "see" some music. We were near the main market in downtown Saigon and they led me off down a side street. I noticed a movie theatre on one side of the street with some badly amplified music blasting out into the neighborhood. (Did the Communists pass a law when they took over South Vietnam that decadent Western music can be played in public only if it breaks the sound barrier and is also painfully distorted? An entire generation of Vietnamese people must be suffering profound hearing loss just from these amplified sidewalk noises.) Across the street from that noise, there was what appeared to be a refreshment parlor with its own ear-splitting noise—likewise blasting forth. We went into the refreshment parlor and sat down, and it was only then that I realized that one of the noises had followed us into the place. It was not actually noise but music. We were in a video parlor.

Can you believe it? In Communist Vietnam, where economic controls are only just now being relaxed and where individual initiative is only just now being encouraged, the fastest-growing private enterprise is the video parlor, where they play nothing but bootleg videos of Western rock and roll, obviously lifted right off MTV. (The commercials are clipped out but one parlor had a tape that still had the in-house MTV promos on it. Whoever was doing the bootlegging obviously mistook those slick and clever MTV promos for part of the music videos.) Some of the videos were ancient by pop-music standards. (These kids are going to be very shocked to learn that Wham has broken up and George Michael has gone solo.) But most of them are hot off the VCRs. I saw Janet Jackson's *Rhythm Nation* in Saigon at about the same time it was debuting in New York.

We sat there all afternoon watching the likes of Bruce Springsteen, Madonna, Michael Jackson, M. C. Hammer, and George Michael. They even played a whole set of Lambada videos. I love rock and roll, and there were some overhead fans so I was quite comfortable there, drinking my fresh lemonade, surrounded by good friends. Linh dropped by for a brief period. Tai came in with some friends. It was all very relaxed and social. But still I was puzzled: why in the world would the Communist authorities allow this? It appeared to be the quickest way to promote and promulgate American decadence and corruption, because these are A-1 propaganda films: slick music videos showing happy American kids wearing snazzy American clothes dancing to American rock music. This is where Tai learned about guys wearing earrings. This is how Pearl learned to lace his high tops. This is where they all learned to dance. Why didn't the Communist government control this? After all, that's what they do best: control. Why show people these American music videos? Why not show them stuff like *America's Most Wanted* or *A Current Affair*. Stuff that shows us murdering and maiming one another. For the Communists *Rescue 911* would be politically more appropriate than music videos: murderous highway accidents, violence in the streets, deadly high-rise fires. C-SPAN would be better than this. (Note: The government did step in shortly after that and impose some tight controls on one form of imported song and dance: no more Lambada videos on the grounds that it would cause too much "thinking" about "the sex." Maybe. Personally, I'd keep an eye on George Michael and his buns.)

Cong was a big, handsome young man I had met out at the Amerasian Transit Center. He was a black Amerasian, tall and ebony-colored with a thousand-watt smile. And when we met he simply went into a tailspin: he loved everything about America, and to see a real, live American standing in front of him was almost more than he could bear. If smiling could kill, he was practically terminal. I gave him an American flag and he nearly exploded. Then he ran off. He came back a few minutes later, adjusting a GI fatigue jacket. He was wearing an American Army-issue hat and carrying that American flag. The only jarring note was his Vietnamese thongs. He wanted his picture taken with me.

"He an actor," the kids told me.

"Get outta here," I scoffed, giving them my best "You're Kidding" look.

"No, no, teacher. Cong—he an actor. Very famous. Very rich."

They were right. Cong was indeed an actor. And he was indeed quite famous among Vietnamese moviegoers. And he was probably rich, at least by Vietnamese standards, since he actually got paid to act in movies. Seems that whenever the Communist regime set out to make yet another anti-American movie about the war they would hire Cong to play the evil GI. After all, he was big, he was American, and he was black. Translation: to the Communists he embodied American evil. Cong loved it, and all the rest of the Amerasians thought it was a big joke. After all, Cong made money on the deal. As for the movies? "They all bullshit, teacher," I was told firmly by Jim. The others agreed. "All bullshit. Nobody believe that stuff anymore."

Like so many of the black Amerasians, Cong had been abandoned. He drifted around for a while, shuttled from one orphanage to another, before being taken in by a Chinese woman and her family. And now he was about to leave Vietnam. His paperwork had been processed and he was just waiting out at the Transit Center to be issued his ticket out of the country. Weeks later came the news: he had his ticket. Cong was leaving Vietnam, headed first for that mandatory six-month stay in a refugee camp in the Philippines and then on to his very own personal promised land: America.

"Big party, teacher. Cong want you to come." By this time my students had met a young American named Eric (Connecticut got outlined on the map) and he, too, was invited to join everyone at Cong's farewell party. At the appointed hour a huge army of Amerasians was waiting outside the Kim Do to walk me up to the party. They were dressed to the nines in clean T-shirts and blue jeans. Others had been dispatched to the youth hostel to pick up Eric and make sure he made it to the party. It was set for 7 P.M., and there was excited talk about going to a disco afterward.

I didn't quite know what to expect but I was amazed at the extent of the party: it was held in a restaurant that I had eaten in many times before, a rather elegant outdoor restaurant a couple of blocks behind the cathedral. And Cong had taken over one entire end of the place. All told, there must have been thirty or forty people at the party, and the food and beer and Coca-Colas kept coming. Soup, fish, rice, meat dishes. I was dazed at the proliferation of food and drink.

"This must be very expensive," I whispered to Bryner.

"Expensive? What that mean?" he whispered back.

"Cost much money."

"Oh, no problem. Teacher, we tell you Cong very rich. Remember, teacher: he movie star."

I then pointed out that in reality that meant the Communists were actually paying for this party. They looked at each other and then everyone got hysterical. They thought it was a huge joke that Cong—an outcast black Amerasian who had made his money acting in Communist propaganda films—had therefore been paid by the Communist authorities and was thus able to afford such a send-off for himself. A send-off celebrating the fact that he was finally escaping from Vietnam and headed for the very country he had been paid to portray as wicked and evil and decadent. The irony was not lost on these Amerasians.

All in all, it was a swell party. Everybody ate tons of food, had a few beers, took loads of pictures. There were little vases of fresh flowers at each table, and since I never travel without my stash of American flags, pretty soon every flower arrangement also had a small American flag stuck in it.

They all wanted to have their pictures taken with the Americans, especially Eric, that handsome all-American boy from Connecticut. So when a gang of them crowded around him, I obliged. Then it struck me: most of these young men were Eric's age, in their early twenties. He had done and would do things they could never dream of doing, all of them very basic: get an education, make some choices. And his after-college choice: bum around for a while. During the time Eric spent in Saigon, I would spot him around town, writing in his journal, taking photographs. He was friendly, gregarious, curious. And he was on the move. Then I looked around at the other American kids sitting at that table with us: Bryner, Jim, Pearl, Cong, Tom, Tai, Bieu, Huong, and all the rest. Even if they got to America, these young Americans—most of them near Eric's age—could never even hope to catch up with the likes of Eric. It wasn't their fault. And it certainly wasn't Eric's fault. It was just the awful reality of their awful situation. It made me very sad.

Then I noticed someone was missing. "Where's Jim?" We all looked around. Tom looked under the table. That was a big joke and everybody laughed. But still Jim wasn't anywhere in sight. A little buzz went up and someone went back to the toilet to see if he was there. Nope. We forgot about him for a while—all that food, all those photographs to be taken. Then I felt someone shaking my shoulder. Jim had been located. A few of us trooped outside to the sidewalk. It had rained while we were eating, but since we were sitting under an overhang it hadn't mattered. But outside, the streets and sidewalks were slick with rain. The restaurant was on a quiet side street behind the cathedral. If your eyesight was good, down at the far end of the block you could see a corner of the Foreign Ministry.

The sidewalk outside the restaurant was lined with makeshift shelters for some of Saigon's homeless. We found Jim in one of these shacks. He was sprawled out on his back, lying on a straw mat, his arm thrown over his eyes. I got worried and bent over him. Behind me, some of the kids were giggling at the whole scene.

"It's O.K., teacher. Jim all right. No problem." Bryner was trying to reassure me that there was nothing to worry about.

"What do you mean, no problem? He's passed out on the sidewalk. What's the matter with him?"

"Jim no drink good."

I pointed out that to my knowledge he hadn't even finished the one beer he had. They shrugged. Turns out Jim was indeed one of those people who doesn't drink very well: one drink and he's under the table. Only in this case, one drink and he was out in a shack on a straw mat on a sidewalk in Saigon. Then I looked around me. There was a family of smiling, unconcerned Vietnamese sitting under the tarp with Jim, looking at us looking at Jim. There were six of them. And this is where they lived. Their possessions were stacked neatly in one corner in various heavy plastic tote bags. There were a charcoal stove and that sleeping mat. That's all. I learned that down the street was a public toilet and a spigot for bathing, cooking, and washing clothes. During the day, Saigon's trees and walls and fences were festooned with the drying clothes of its homeless people.

Against my wishes, we left Jim there, sleeping off his glass of beer. They assured me he'd be O.K., although I simply couldn't imagine doing likewise in the American counterpart, New York City. Jim was obviously well looked after because he showed up for lunch the next day as if nothing had happened. A few days later I happened to walk down that same street. Those insubstantial shacks had disappeared, as had all the people, swept away like dust by the police in one of their periodic forays against the homeless of Saigon.

Cong's party wound up at a disco back downtown, just off Dong Khoi Street. We started to walk, and since it was Sunday night, we were quickly caught in a unique display of local culture. I hadn't seen this since Albion, Nebraska, on a Saturday night back in the fifties. We called it "cruising." In Vietnam it's called *Chay vong vong*—"run around and around." Back in Nebraska we'd just load into somebody's car and drive around downtown for a few hours. Since downtown was only about two blocks square, we had to be careful to drive very slowly or we would have ended up in Petersburg. Or maybe even Iowa. Downtown Saigon, 1990, wasn't much different from Albion, Nebraska, in 1954. It was *American Graffiti,* Saigon style. It seemed as if every motorbike and motorcycle and bicycle in all of Saigon had been pressed into service. The whole exercise is mostly for young people—cruising, flirting, gig-

gling—but I saw whole families jammed onto motorbikes or bicycles for nothing more than hours of riding round and round and
round. Down Dong Khoi Street, across Ton Duc Thang, up Nguyen
Hue Street, across Le Loi, back down Dong Khoi Street. Repeat
until approximately 11 P.M. and then go home. If it's Friday night,
come back and do it all over again on Saturday night. If it's Saturday night, come back on Sunday night. If it's Sunday night, come
back next Friday.

The first time I got caught in this mess, the traffic cops outside
the Caravelle Hotel laughed themselves silly at the sight of me trying
to cross the street. Tonight was different, though: I had an Army of
Amerasians doing recon work for me. Cong barreled through the
crowd, clearing a path for us. Pearl grabbed one arm, Be the other,
while Bryner guarded the flank and Tom brought up the rear as
traffic closed around us. Somehow, we all made it across the street
and continued on our way to the disco.

It wasn't one of the fancy ones at any of the hotels frequented
by tourists or visiting businessmen. This one was on a side street
and was obviously frequented by Young Saigon. And no wonder: it
had a huge video screen. Bon Jovi was the *group de jour* when we
arrived.

Pearl moved off immediately and began trolling the tables.
Within seconds he had the prettiest girls in the place trailing him
around while we all sat around smiling and shaking our heads and
saying, "Oh, that Pearl!" He had obviously pulled his old "I'm an
American visiting Vietnam" routine, because pretty soon he came
bouncing up to the table with a couple of beauties in tow and
introduced them to me.

"This my mother!" he yelled, pointing at me.

And the place was packed with young couples dressed in the
latest styles and doing the latest dances. Except for the fact that
everybody had dark hair and was short, it could have been Queens
or Nebraska. Indeed, the most amazing thing about going to a
Vietnamese disco is seeing how Western it all is. Everybody dolls up
in his or her latest duds and hairdos (lots of mousse and hair gel)
and cuts loose. And everybody seemed to be right on top of the
latest moves, including maneuvers worthy of Janet Jackson or Va-
nilla Ice. But every half hour or so, the strangest thing happens:
everybody starts to cha-cha. I couldn't believe it the first time it
happened. I thought maybe my Vietnamese beer had gone bad on
me when Bon Jovi flickered off the video screen, the lights came on

over the dance floor, and everybody began to cha-cha. It was like being marooned in the Catskills on Memorial Day weekend.

Bryner and Pearl and Huy picked me up early the next morning at the Kim Do. Huy was a handsome young Amerasian, a good friend of everybody's, and I would see him around town periodically. He had no idea who his mother was, where he was born, or even when he was born. He wasn't a regular but periodically he would join us for class. One day while we were having a conversation session in that little Thai hut in the cultural park, Huy took out something he had brought to show me: some old Polaroid pictures. They were pictures of him as a baby and one was a picture of his mother. Those fading Polaroids were his only link to his unknown past. Huy was by far the hardest-working Amerasian I met in Saigon: he drove a cyclo. And I was appalled that morning, but he insisted on loading all three of us into his cyclo and pedaling us out to Tan Son Nhut Airport some ten miles away. We were off to say goodbye to Cong.

One of the most social events in Vietnam is what I like to call "The Going to the Airport" ritual. You have to see it to believe it. Many of these flights can only be described as refugee flights: Amerasians and their families *getting out*. Old soldiers released from reeducation camps *getting out*. Family members *getting out*, off to be reunited with husbands or wives or children who escaped years and years ago. Entire neighborhoods must empty out whenever someone catches a flight. Friends and family flock to the airport, sometimes taking up entire buses. And no wonder: they may never see that voyager again. So everybody dresses up, stocks up on gifts to load the departing passenger down with, and then they all trek out to the airport. Often they end up spending the day out there. Vietnam is very whimsical about departure times for these flights. I think they do it on purpose. It is their last chance to harass Amerasians or old soldiers or anyone else lucky enough to be processed out of that poor, sad country. And they do it in the most petty way possible: delaying the flight for hours. Busloads of Amerasians and their families with tickets out of the country arrive on flight day from the Transit Center, and to see them off, everyone else comes too. In the middle of it all is a stray tourist or businessman or a load of Russians hauling back thousands of illegal cartons of cigarettes to be sold on the black market back in Moscow. It is an absolute zoo out there as hundreds and thousands of people mill around. To keep things from breaking down completely, no one is allowed inside the terminal except the lucky passengers waving their tickets over their heads like flags.

We found Cong, and to his credit, his flair for the theatrical was still very evident. He called himself the "Last American Soldier to Leave Vietnam" and had outfitted himself accordingly. He was all decked out in his U.S. Army fatigue jacket and a web belt, and he was carrying an old Army-issue backpack. I noticed he had sewn the American flag I had given him onto it. I looked a little more closely and saw that on one of the white stripes he had written: "In God We Trust: Amerasian Coming Home." And on his luggage, a metal footlocker that he had painted Army green, he had painted an American flag and two hands clasping. He saw me looking at the flag on his backpack and the inscription on it.

"Love America," he said, touching that forty-nine-cent American flag. This was the only English he had picked up in the weeks since we met. My God. What would happen to him? What was waiting for him in the country of his dreams? Cong had no such fears that morning, however. His smile was bigger than ever. We hung out with Cong and his growing entourage for a couple of hours. He and the other lucky refugees would go first to Manila, then on to that refugee camp on the Bataan Peninsula. But the Vietnamese authorities kept delaying the flight, and finally when it was announced that his 10 A.M. flight to Manila wouldn't leave until 5:30, we called it quits and left.

"You're sure you don't mind?" I asked the guys.

"No, problem, teacher. We see him in Philippines. Then we all see you in America. No problem." They were happy for Cong, happy for themselves.

Jim's mother had been insisting that we go out some time. I met her at her house one night, had some tea, and then she announced: "O.K., Kelly—now we go to my job."

"Your job? What is your job? Where are we going?" She was a part-time waitress during the war so I thought maybe we were off to a restaurant.

"We go my theatre!" There was the usual assortment of Amerasians with us—including Jim and Bryner and Pearl and Tai—and it took three cyclos to accommodate us. Off we went, to Lan's theatre. It seems Lan was an actress.

"So—how'd you get into the theatre?" I asked. It was déjà vu. I felt like an entertainment reporter again, only instead of being backstage with some Broadway Tony nominee, I was sitting in a cyclo being pedaled through the darkening streets of Saigon.

"Oh, I born there!" she said, laughing. "My parents in the theatre. Actors. I born, I become an actress. From time I am little girl, I act on stage."

"In America we would say you were 'born in a trunk,' " I told her.

"That about right, Kelly."

"Are you an actress now? Will we see you in a play?" I asked, intrigued by all this.

"Oh, no, Kelly. I no actress now. Had to quit," she said firmly. "Couldn't go on the road anymore. All those kids." She had a point. It was the lament of actresses the world over: family ties, family pressures. Lan, by then, was the single mother of six, having had three more children in another relationship after Jim's father left her. So she gave up her acting career but remained with the theatre troupe, becoming its general manager. Every night the troupe performed in Saigon she went to the theatre to check up on the cast and crew. Tonight she was off to pay them.

The place looked more like a warehouse than a theatre. It was huge and nondescript, although there was a wild-colored billboard outside, which I supposed concerned the evening's theatrical offering, although it looked more like an oversized, full-color police sketch of the week's most wanted. Lan headed for a metal door grate, and we all slipped through what was obviously the stage door and into an outdoor alley that led to the backstage area.

Now, all New York theatres have stage-door entrances. Some even have those similar side alleys leading to the rear of the theatres. And as an entertainment reporter I had been through many of those doors, down many of those alleys, but never in my life had I been in a place like this. New York's theatrical alleys are there simply to move massive sets and props and costumes, to facilitate the delivery of expensive floral arrangements in and out of the theatre, and to let actors and stray reporters backstage. Once that's done, those alleys are relatively empty and very quiet. Not this one. Like every other bare spot in Saigon, this alley was teeming. It was carpeted with people, food stalls, dogs, cats, bicycles, Hondas. Food was being prepared: women were hacking dead chickens, smacking fish around, stirring rice, ladling soup. People were eating. Dishes were being washed and then filled up again. Coffee was brewing, tea was steaming, beer was cooling. Smoke from the cooking fires and steam from the food rose in billows and hung in the air like a curtain. And everywhere people were roaming back and forth as if it were one huge party.

"Come on, Kelly. Don't get lost." Lan grabbed my hand and pulled me through the crowd and the steam and the smoke and up a rickety flight of wooden stairs. I stumbled over a doorsill and landed in someone's lap. He? she? looked very startled. So did I. They do a very different kind of stage makeup in Saigon, very dramatic and emphatic. Mostly it consists of lots of blue eye shadow. It was Bingo makeup gone crazy.

The curtain went up late that night. After all, there was an American backstage and she had to be examined. I could have been USDA approved, the inspection was so precise. When they were through with me, they stuck a chair in the wings, pushed me into it, and presented me with an ice-cold lemonade. Then I poked my head around the curtain and looked out into the theatre. It would have sent a New York City fire inspector to combustion heaven. It was an all-wooden theatre: wooden seats, wooden floors, and two wooden balconies on either side of the stage for the lighting crew. Those crew members sat directly beneath the theatre's huge illuminated NO SMOKING signs. They were chain-smoking.

Then I looked at the audience. Let me tell you, this was real theatre for real people: it was a sea of cone hats. Remember that famous picture from *Life* magazine of the movie audience in which everyone is sitting bolt upright wearing 3-D glasses? This was the Vietnamese version of that old photograph, only instead of 3-D glasses this audience was wearing cone hats. The place was packed to overflowing and everyone seemed to be eating and smoking and spitting betel juice, that mildly narcotic and completely ubiquitous substance chewed by almost every adult in Asia. First it turns your teeth red, then it rots them out completely. And all a chewer does is dribble and spit. I tried it once in New Guinea. I dribbled. I tried to spit. I threw up.

Whole families had turned out for an evening of cultural uplift at the theatre—mom, dad, the kids, grandpa, grandma—eating, spitting, and watching the proceedings with gusto. People obviously felt free to wander; after a while the whole theatre seemed to be a rolling sea of movement, with people drifting up and down the aisles, stopping here and there to chat or exchange babies. From time to time someone—usually the male lead—would go and knock a patron of the arts off the apron of the stage. He did this periodically throughout the evening.

The sets were right out of the senior class play: painted cardboard and plywood. They shook ominously every time anyone went near them. This bothered me a lot when three people had to climb one piece of scenery for a second-story window scene. The actors were real pros, however. They just hung on for dear life and kept going.

I never did figure out exactly what was going on there on that stage. As best I could tell, it was a domestic farce involving mistaken identities, mother-in-law jokes, and lots of naughty references to sex. There were two couples and a running argument about whether one wife should or should not work. The action was also loaded with sight gags involving two staples of life in Saigon: beggars and cyclo drivers. In fact, the cyclo jokes constantly brought the house down. The first time the cyclo was driven on stage the audience went nuts. It caused the kind of furor I had only witnessed at the Metropolitan Opera in New York during a production of *Aïda* when live elephants were paraded onto that cavernous stage during the "Triumphal March."

As for the action on this stage, it proceeded broadly to the big Act One production number, which was just an excuse for the handsome male lead to come out with two tarty backup singers for a prolonged disco scene. The lights dimmed, a mirrored ball dropped down, highlighted by a pin spot, and the audience went berserk. The male singer was a handsome guy wearing tight pants, who began phonetically singing every song from *Saturday Night Fever* while the two backup singers shimmied and boogied behind him. Both wore strapless tops, miniskirts up to their crotches, fishnet stockings, and heels so high you would have needed a degree in civil engineering to walk in them. Meanwhile, I was sitting in my chair wearing an old I ♥ NEW YORK T-shirt, a sun dress, a pair of shower thongs, and a coat of sweat. It was so humid in that theatre I could feel my hair start to bubble. Suddenly the chair was pulled out from under me, I was hauled to my feet, and a firm hand was placed on my back.

"Your turn, Kelly!" Lan gave a shove. I could hear her laugh as I slid onstage. It was like Tom Cruise making his underpants entrance in *Risky Business*. Unlike Tom Cruise, however, I stood there completely frozen. Likewise the audience. Now, this was the disco scene and I wasn't alone up there. Indeed, by this time there were a couple of dozen people dancing up a storm, including Bryner and Jim and Pearl and Tai. But all the audience was able to zero in on was this strange American woman, who suddenly appeared out of nowhere, sliding in on her rubber shower thongs and wearing an expression of sheer horror on her face. The audience became totally immobile. Not a single person spit on the floor for a good sixty seconds. Small children were brought to bay by my presence. Then there was bedlam. People began shouting, kids were wailing, and betel juice began flying everywhere. And a woman's voice could be heard above the din: *"She American!"*

And I was standing there like a dope. If I moved my head one way, I could see my students. They were dancing like mad but they were also looking at me. And they had that universal teenage look on their faces that indicates that some adult is dangerously close to making a fool of herself and thus bringing everlasting shame down upon them. If I moved my head another way I could see Lan off in the wings. She was smiling broadly and flapping her hands, encouraging me to do something.

Then I felt something rising within me, taking over my being and my body. I couldn't contain it. I was about to go out of control. I couldn't help it, your honor. *Something was going to happen!*

Now, I must confess: I am a frustrated tap dancer. It is a long story going back to Saturday matinees at the Rex Theatre in Albion, Nebraska, where I sat dazed and dazzled for years, entertained by the world's best tap dancers, who came every Saturday afternoon to dance up there on the silver screen just for me. Then, every fall at the Boone County Fair, a road show would come to town and perform on a portable stage set up on the racetrack right in front of the grandstand. It was a wonderland for me. The people in that show were actually alive and right in front of me. Broadway couldn't have been more exciting, even if I had known what Broadway was. The highlight of those performances always came at the end when they turned off the racetrack lights and turned on the black light. All the shoelaces on the tap shoes turned fluorescent orange and glowed in the dark. I may have wept with sheer joy sitting there in the darkness of those prairie nights watching those orange shoelaces dancing in front of me.

Then—wonder of wonders!—Mary Jane James moved to town. She was the wife of the new florist, but that wasn't the half of it: she was also a *tap-dance teacher!* I watched my friends flock to her class. I tried to do likewise, until harsh reality caught up with me: the lessons were fifty cents apiece. No go. Every Saturday morning I would sit outside the door—on the pathetic pretense I was waiting for my friend Mary Ellen Curran—listening to my friends hop-shuffle-step-flap-ball change. Believe me, you cannot learn to tap dance simply by listening to a class of Midwestern fourth graders.

Fate, and that journalism degree of mine, obviously guided me to New York, because it was there I had my first big break. At Carnegie Hall. I was thirty years old when I took my first formal tap lesson in a tiny studio at Carnegie Hall. And I found it in the yellow pages. So what if everyone else was six years old and came with mommy? At the end of the lesson and in front of the whole class, the teacher—a black woman who was dancing on Broadway at the time—came over and said to me: "Miss Kelly, did anyone ever tell you you have natural rhythm?" That did it. I immediately became the World's Oldest Living Bad Tap Dancer, a title I feel has gone unchallenged to this very day. I went on to tap dance on the *Today* show (off camera and to the horror of the executive producer) and with Dick Cavett (another Nebraskan and not a bad tapper, by the way) on the *Morning Show* in New York. I even auditioned for the road company of *42nd Street*. (Don't worry: it was a gag. I took a camera crew and did a feature piece on the experience. The crew were so disgusted they wanted to put in for hazardous-duty pay. I kept losing my balance and slamming into them during the turns.)

So here I was, frozen to the floor in the middle of a stage in Saigon. Offstage, Lan was still smiling and waving her hands at me. What to do? Are you kidding? This was my chance. My big break. I'm not stupid. Besides, I know a captive audience when I see it. I slid my feet deeper into my thongs. The disco number was grinding away, and believe me, that audience in Saigon witnessed the most stirring dance recital the world has ever known. It was a little eclectic, ending up to be part tap (face it: a person can tap dance only so long in thongs), part Lindy, and part Twist. I even tried to moonwalk, grateful that not a single person I knew from New York was anywhere near that theatre that night. Thailand would have been too close. (I once interviewed the choreographer for Michael Jackson's *Beat It* video. Sometimes I am absolutely shameless: I actually talked him into trying to teach me to moonwalk. I think I am safe in saying it didn't work. Every time I tried, it looked as if I were cleaning dog poop off my shoes.)

But I can say in all modesty, in Saigon that night they loved me. Dozens of cone hats went straight up into the air. Graduation day at Annapolis could not have seen more hats in the air than my incendiary performance in that Saigon fire trap. And when that disco scene was over—finally!—I received thunderous applause, with the audience giving me the universal stamp of approval: "America! Number one! America! Number one!"

I felt like Sally Field at the Academy Awards. They liked me. They actually liked me. I noticed my students had looks of relief on their faces. I hadn't disgraced them.

"How you feel, Teacher?" Pearl asked me later.

I quoted my favorite philosopher, James Brown: "I feel good!"

10

GOING NORTH

Mr. Thieu had been put in charge of me. And he was very insistent that I see the Temple of Little Richard.

"Little Richard?"

"Oh, yes. Little Richard." We were standing in a small stone courtyard. "Do you like?" He gestured around, indicating a graceful little temple. I agreed that it was quite lovely, but I was puzzled nonetheless.

"Tell me, Mr. Thieu, just exactly when was this temple built?" Now, I'm no math whiz but I used to listen to Little Richard back in the fifties, and this building looked a whole lot older than cars with tail fins and girls with ponytails.

"Oh, Kelly, it is very old. It was built in the eleventh century."

"Now, Mr. Thieu, I can understand why some people would build a temple to Little Richard. But—in Vietnam? In the eleventh century?"

"That is very simple," he explained solemnly. "We have always been great scholars in Vietnam. Why—we read all the time."

Yes. Of course. This was not the Temple of Little Richard. This was the Temple of *Literature!*

* * *

I had thought it was time for a little serious sightseeing. And so, with the applause of the assembled multitudes (well, at least the ones who happened to be caught in that local theatre the night of my Saigon stage debut) still ringing in my ears, I decided to get out of town. Besides, I figured my students needed a little break from both me and English grammar. So one day in September I headed north to Hanoi. And in Hanoi Mr. Thieu, a serious young man from the Department of Tourism, had been assigned to me. And here we were, at the Temple of Little Richard.

"Well," he asked me. "You would like to see the Hall of Mammaries?" Now admit it: you'd be intrigued, too—right? As Mr. Thieu so meticulously explained it, this complex was once a university of the old royal court. And when the students were through with their exams (in the Temple of Little Richard) they would repair to the Hall of Mammaries, where they would Organize Their Clothing.

Now, I remember chewing a few pencils during a geology final at the University of Missouri, but I don't think I ever mussed up my clothing so much I had to go to a separate building to pull up my zippers. So I thought about this. I knew I could figure it out if only I put my mind to it. Finally it came to me: after their exams, those eleventh-century students would go to the Hall of *Memories*. To clear their minds. And while there they would straighten their robes so they could go give thanks to Buddha for his guidance in their exams. Or something like that.

I am particularly fond of the way Communist countries name their hotels: the Democracy Hotel, the Freedom Hotel, the Liberty Hotel. I guess the whimsy or the fantasy appeals to me, since old-time, hard-line Communist regimes wouldn't know democracy or freedom much less liberty if it came up and bit them on the ankle. I was staying in the Democracy Hotel. It was an old French hotel, a shadowy relic of its Colonial past. My room had towering French doors that opened onto an exterior hallway. Inside, the room was sparsely furnished but cavernous. The bathtub was like a car up on blocks. I discovered why when I entered the room and slid all the way to the other side, crashing into the wall and freeing up some loose plaster that came tumbling down like face powder. The floor was so uneven that in order to balance the tub a block had been put under first one leg, then the other, and so on around the tub. This had been done two or three times, which meant the tub had been hoisted ever higher and become ever more precarious. To get into that tub was a feat of engineering that eventually involved borrowing a chair from the hotel dining room just to make my first Great Leap Forward and into the tub.

Large cockroaches waddled across the floors like potentates exploring their realm. I was the interloper. And no one had even made a pretense of sweeping out the corners of the room. Dust and debris had collected there through the ages. Archeological digs could have been organized in the corners of the Hotel Democracy. Electrical wires came and went around the room, coming from who knows where and leading absolutely nowhere else. And blooming like a rose on a wobbly table next to the bed: a bright red television set. It had obviously never been plugged in. Perhaps it had never been used. Not only was there no plug to receive it, it didn't even have a cord. (Thinking perhaps it was a cleverly disguised refrigerator—oh, these fun-loving cadres up North!—I tried opening it and retrieving a Coke. No such luck.)

But despite that towering bathtub and fake TV set, the Democracy Hotel was obviously the place to be. The Hanoi Hot Spot, so to speak. Compared to my pre-*glasnost* visit to Russia in 1982, I was struck with how open the place was. The bar–dining room opened right onto the street, and there wasn't a guard or doorman in sight. People just wandered in off the street. *Vietnamese* people. In Russia, hotel guests were hardly allowed into their own hotels. In Saigon, although the restaurants and shops and stores are open to anyone and everyone, the hotels are a different story. There the doormen kept fairly tight control of things, obviously to prevent a general wandering in and out and socializing.

Meanwhile, the dining room–bar of the Democracy was decorated with a fair mix of people, tourists and natives alike. There was a long table of dour Russians downing vodka and watching each other's noses turn red. I fell in with an Irish film crew at the bar, then struck up a conversation with a Vietnamese math teacher who had dropped by for a beer and a smoke. A particularly loud blast of noise from the Russian sector caught our attention.

"So—what do you think of those Russians?" I asked him, gesturing to their table. They were pretending to bite the heads off their vodka bottles by this time.

"Oh, I hate them," he said jovially.

"But they're Communists," I said reasonably.

"That's why I hate them. I hate Communists."

"But they are your comrades, living in another workers' paradise." I was smiling, he was smiling, so we both knew we were kidding. A little bit.

I swear he said "Bullshit." Or at least the Hanoi equivalent of "Bullshit." "My wife is a teacher," he explained patiently, to this American woman with the brains of bread dough. "She teaches engineering in college. She earns six dollars a month. Six dollars a month!" He went on to tell me that he and his wife had a one-room apartment and shared the kitchen and the toilet with everyone else in the building. They had only one child and planned to have no more, a decision that had absolutely nothing to do with the government's new push for family planning (headed up, interestingly enough, by General Vo Nguyen Giap, considered by most American military men to be one of the most brilliant military men not only of the Vietnam War but of any war of this century. He certainly had his work cut out for him in the population battle: Vietnam's population had doubled since 1960, now hitting a record 68.4 million in a country roughly the size of California with its population of 29 million). But to the math teacher and his wife it was more basic: "We can't afford it. There is no social welfare here. There is nothing here. This country is dying."

He had a point there: with a per capita income of only $180 per year, Vietnam is one of the poorest countries in the world. And in addition to Communism, an economic system that couldn't operate a profitable lemonade stand let alone an entire country of hard-working people, one of the many reasons for Vietnam's economic decay and decline is America. More precisely, an American attitude that is both vengeful and punitive. Or, as one of my intellectual heroes—Pogo—put it: "We has met the enemy, and it is us."

Fifteen years after losing the war, not only has the United States government refused to resume diplomatic relations with Vietnam, it has also strictly enforced the Trading with the Enemy Act. Under the provisions of this act, American businesses are prohibited from doing business there and thus giving any employment opportunities to the Vietnamese people. Moreover, the American government has gone out of its way to isolate Vietnam economically by strongarming its allies—particularly Japan—from doing much major business there. These American restrictions are not only a punishment to the Communist government and its economy but they are a punishing reality to the Vietnamese people. This trade embargo has kept Vietnam's already badly managed economy on its knees, thus encouraging a hemorrhage of refugees out of Vietnam.

I asked the math teacher why Vietnam's economy was such a mess. I guess I wanted to see just how deep the resentment was and how open people were willing to be about it—and how much America would be blamed for those problems.

"Well, that's easy," he said. "Vietnam is so isolated. America won't trade with us and won't let anyone else trade with us so we can only deal with other Communist countries." He looked at me and gave a wry grimace. "Can you imagine. Doing business with Romania? That is a joke. But mostly it is because this country is run by the generals."

I was a little shocked by this kind of openness. I was, after all, in the North. In Hanoi, for heaven's sake, the birthplace of Vietnam's Communism. "But those generals won the war. They defeated the imperialist Americans. Drove the bullies out and united the North and the South." He looked at me as if my brains had just fallen out on the floor.

"That doesn't mean they can run a country!"

He had a point. And it was a point I heard from one end of Vietnam to the other.

It was time for The Big Moment: my visit to Ho Chi Minh's tomb. We parked on an empty street. Ahead of me stretched a wide, totally deserted boulevard. I was turned over to a young Vietnamese soldier, who began to march me straight down the middle of that wide boulevard. Mr. Thieu had already relieved me of my purse and then reminded me to keep quiet, not to look around, and not to scratch my nose. I was a nervous wreck. My sneakers kept sticking to the pavement and squeaking, giving me a drunken, lurching quality. I felt isolated out there on the boulevard, squeaking and lurching down a long aisle to nowhere. Suddenly, the soldier began gesturing insistently to me. What did he want? What have I done? The tomb, a huge marble edifice, was looming closer and closer and the guard was still picking at me. I was close to panic. Then, through my pounding adrenaline, I figured it out: obviously doing my best Prince Philip imitation, I was marching *with my hands behind my back!* when in fact I was supposed to be walking *with my hands down at my sides!* I dropped my hands so fast I had khaki burns on my thighs.

And just in time, too, because we had hit the red carpet. It was plastic. My sneakers made even more noise. I was turned over to a pair of guards, who silently pointed me inside the mausoleum. A blast of icy-cold air hit me. I climbed a flight of marble stairs and there he was, out of reach, perched high atop a catafalque and suspended in a bright halo of light. It was Uncle Ho. He was tiny, pink, and glowing. If he had been Irish my relatives would have been standing around complimenting the mortician for his terrific work ("Doesn't he look natural?" "Why, he looks like he could just sit up and talk to you!"). I learned later that Ho had only recently returned from Moscow, where he had been totally refurbished.

Now the gossip in Hanoi was that up in Beijing, their traditional enemies the Chinese had decided that Mao likewise needed a little fixing up. So the Chinese, who were feuding with their fellow Communists in the Kremlin at the time, tried to spruce up the Great Helmsman themselves. They made such a mess of it that Mao, who is sort of on everybody's Ten Most Wanted List these days anyway, was really out of circulation, until somebody had the bright idea of shipping him off to Hungary (or was it Romania? Bulgaria?) for a complete overhaul. The reviews were not in on that production, but the Vietnamese had obviously heard of that fiasco, so when it came time to fix up Uncle Ho they sent him straight to Moscow for his renovation.

I wound up my morning by visiting Ho's little house, a charming two-story wooden structure that looks like an understated beach house, open and airy and restful. It is built in a small grove of trees directly behind the more ornate French Colonial building that once served as residence for their colonial administrators. There is a small lake alongside the house, where, I was told, Uncle Ho used to feed the carp. I spent a few minutes doing likewise. I smelled like fish chow the rest of the day.

They weren't pushing the war down my throat in Hanoi. In fact, I was the one badgering everybody about it. Mr. Thieu, my minder, finally agreed to show me the infamous Hanoi Hilton, the prison where the American pilots shot down over Hanoi were kept. It is smack in the middle of Hanoi, outlined by a high concrete wall painted the same soft ocher color seen on many of the French Colonial buildings in Hanoi. I stood at the entrance while Mr. Thieu watched in dismay as some soldiers rushed forward. They just wanted some American cigarettes. I told them I didn't smoke.

I stood there for a while looking at that despicable place where so many hundreds of American POWs had been held, tortured, and brutalized. I wondered where the men were who had endured that place. I knew what happened to the Americans: some had died there, tortured to death. The rest had been released on that glorious

April day in 1973. But what about their captors? What happened to them? Did they ever think about the agonies they inflicted?

"What was this before it was a prison for the Americans?" I asked Mr. Thieu as we left.

"A prison," he told me.

"What is it now?"

"A prison."

Well, that was keeping the circle unbroken. "So what kind of crooks are in there?" I asked Mr. Thieu.

"People who lie and cheat and steal from the people."

"Oh, you mean bureaucrats?" I joked.

"Right." He also added that everybody figured there were a fair number of political prisoners in there, too—people who just plain disagreed with the government.

"In a democracy we would call those people the losing party," I joked.

"You mean like Michael Dukakis?" Mr. Thieu said, grinning, then fell over laughing. "I read *Time* magazine," he said, by way of explanation.

Mr. Thieu also agreed to take me to Kham Thien (Heavenly) Street, which had been blasted to rubble during Nixon's Christmas bombing of 1972. According to Hanoi Tourism, more than six hundred people were killed outright and twenty-five hundred were wounded. In one house alone, eight out of nine people were killed.

"What happened to the ninth?" I asked Mr. Thieu.

"Oh, he was away fighting the war," he replied.

Today, everything seems back to normal. The only reminder of that bombing run is a small courtyard with a crude monument. It is set well back off the street. Meanwhile, out on the street life goes on, uneventfully. The most exciting thing that day, next to an old lady with a load of squawking chickens for sale, was the unexpected appearance of an American in the neighborhood. And after I reassured them that I wasn't Russian (*"Nyet lien xo! Nyet lien xo!"*), they really got excited.

"We hate the Russians!" one old lady with betel-stained teeth reassured me in French.

"Americans! Number one!"

"Why do you hate the Russians?" I asked them.

"They're so cheap!"

"No money!" one man shouted.

"Money no good!" another added.

"They no talk to us!"

"They not nice!"

"Americans: friendly!" The old lady tried to give me a chicken from her basket. I looked at her as if she were daft. We dropped more bombs on Vietnam than were dropped during all of World War II on all of Europe, Africa, and Asia combined.

"But we bombed you!" I cried, gesturing to the little courtyard with the crude monument. The crowd laughed and dismissed that argument as totally idiotic.

"Long time ago. War. Bad. Forget it."

At my request, Mr. Thieu did take me to the War Museum. He poked along behind me while I strolled past antiaircraft guns and an assemblage of downed planes with American insignia on them. Little yellow flowers were peeping through the wreckage, a delicate contrast to the twisted metal. Inside the small, dark museum there were exhibits from the war: photos, uniforms, some weapons. It was so dark you could hardly see them, though. Out in the middle of the room, I noticed a small display. It was a collection of photographs, along with a row of large leather boots and some helmets. I walked closer through the gloom, then caught my breath. They were all from downed American pilots. And rising up from the middle of this collection: a collage of smiling American faces. Pilots. It was in the shape of a cross.

Outside, hundreds of small Vietnamese children ran in childish confusion as their teachers tried to move them into orderly lines. Their laughter came softly into the room.

Hanoi was a complete change of pace from Saigon. Saigon is all energy and drive and business and the roar of motorcycles and cars and trucks and buses. Hanoi is the whoosh of cyclos and bicycles with only the occasional car or motorbike to break the silence. Economically, Saigon is the wide-awake sound of money changing hands. In contrast, Hanoi is drowsy and half-asleep. Although I must admit, in the year or so since my last visit Hanoi seemed to be stirring, waking up. Capitalism was creeping in, with more shops, more stores, more stalls. More people trying to sell more things to more customers. I was stunned at the array of clothing, cosmetics, video stores, electronic goods, even photocopy shops, usually a big no-no in such controlled societies. Whether anybody could afford to buy the VCRs and TV sets—much less have the electricity to use them—I didn't know. But they were there. I wandered into a big state-run department store. There was a measly array of rather chintzy goods, mostly cheap plastic toys and household goods. There were no lights on so it was dark and rather gloomy. But it was cheerful: Roy Orbison's "Pretty Woman" was going full blast on the loudspeakers.

Outside again, I passed a small shop—a sliver of a store tucked between two doorways—selling audio cassettes. On the wall: posters of American rock groups. Heavy metal. AC/DC and Twisted Sister and Def Leppard.

Hanoi itself was once a lovely and graceful city, filled with authentic Vietnamese architecture and old French Colonial buildings, including a treasure trove of French Art Deco design from the twenties. One extraordinary example of Art Deco whimsy caught my eye. It stood on a corner, almost obliterated by the old-fashioned electric poles and cables that were likewise there jockeying for position. It was a good-sized stucco house and it was painted a light, frothy blue. But it was the little porch that caught my eye. Its support poles were shaped like champagne bubbles that got larger and larger as they fizzed up to the top of the porch.

Today in Hanoi, however, everything is worn and tired and shabby and literally crumbling away, not from American bombs but from neglect. Splotches of black mildew crawl over everything. Vines pull at already crumbling balconies and fretwork. And everywhere a maze of heavy electrical wires crudely attached to the exteriors of the buildings tear at their fragile faces.

I wandered out one night, into the still, quiet Hanoi darkness, past those silent old buildings with the mildew creeping across them. The whoosh of the cyclos had died down and it was almost pitch dark, both electricity and light bulbs being in short supply. I ended up in a Hanoi disco where everyone was dancing discreet fox-trots and two-steps. I even saw one sophisticated couple doing the Peabody. It reminded me of college. I dated a guy at the University of Missouri who could do the Peabody. He had red hair and freckles. He dumped me when I quit school one year to bum around Europe. I was too weird, he said. I think "independent" was the word he wanted. I danced with two children, a matched set, their parents and grandparents staring at us in smiling, open-mouthed amazement. Round and round we went, those parents and grandparents spinning around us as we danced to the music. It was Glenn Miller playing "In the Mood."

In Danang, I was turned over to Mr. Do and installed in a brand-new Volga. We left Danang immediately in a torrential rainstorm, headed north for Hue. I wanted to see the Citadel, the most sacred spot in Vietnam, which was, during the Tet Offensive of 1968, the scene of twenty-five days of some of the fiercest fighting of the war. Today, there is hardly anything left of the Citadel, and what still stands is coated with that mildew that crawls like a cancer over most of the buildings in Vietnam. Inside, the former Forbidden City is completely gone. In its place is a vegetable garden. The Imperial Reception Hall still has two big chunks gone from the roof. The government claims they were blown off by American bombs during the Tet Offensive. Others argue the French did it years before. No matter. The roof is still caved in and the rain, soft and warm, was coming down in silken threads. Nobody assigned to me mentioned the mass graves they found after that 1968 offensive: the graves of more than three thousand civilians, some buried alive, all massacred by the Vietcong. It all made me very sad.

Later that day, we took a small boat down the Perfume River to the Thien Mu Pagoda, a small Buddhist monastery. We were strolling through the damp, quiet grounds when I glanced over and caught sight of something vaguely familiar: an old car, up on blocks.

"Mr. Do—what in the world is that?"

"Oh, that is a very important old car."

"Well, Mr. Do, where I come from, we put a lot of old cars up on blocks but I would never call them important. Lemons, maybe. Heaps and junkers, perhaps. But—important? Never."

"But this car very special, Kelly." He proceeded to tell me that on June 11, 1963, two monks—from this very monastery—got in that old Austin and headed south to Saigon. And when they arrived, they stopped the car and one of the old monks got out and set himself on fire. It was the first immolation of the war. And there, in the background of an old photograph showing a monk burning to death on a street in downtown Saigon, was this old Austin.

"I was there, Kelly. I saw this happen."

"Tell me about it."

"Well, the monk—he stop the car. The other monk, the old one, he get out and walk off a little ways, sit down right in the middle of the street. Oh, cars and trucks and everything stop. Then some other monks and nuns come and pour gasoline over him. Then they set him on fire. I think they use a cigarette lighter. It burned very hot and very bright. There was a terrible smell, and then the body just give a little sigh and fall over."

Madame Nhu, the sister-in-law of South Vietnamese President Ngo Dinh Diem, later referred to this incident as "a barbecue." As more monks went up in flames, she told an interviewer: "Let them burn and we shall clap our hands."

Sign in a room of the Pacific Hotel in Danang: "Pets, firearms, explosives, inflammables, and other STINKING THINGS! are not allowed in the hotel."

A few months before, I had visited Danang with some friends from the East Meets West Foundation, an American humanitarian group established by Le Ly Hayslip, a Vietnamese woman who chronicled her incredible story in her best-selling book, *When Heaven and Earth Changed Places*. Le Ly had left Vietnam in 1970 and had been coming back since 1986, first to visit her family and then to also bring in much-needed medical supplies to the Danang area. In 1990 she brought a delegation of doctors and volunteers along with more medical supplies to deliver to various hospitals and clinics in the city and to the small clinic she had built the previous year in her family's village a few miles outside Danang. I joined up with Le Ly and about ten other people and went with them to deliver some of those medical supplies to Danang General Hospital, the biggest hospital in the area. It was one of my first behind-the-scenes visits to a Vietnamese hospital, and I could hardly believe it.

The by-now-ubiquitous rubber glove tree was there, festooned with surgical gloves that had been washed and were waiting to be reused. Plastic Coke bottles were being used for IV drips. In the Intensive Care Unit patients were lying in beds lined up under the open windows. Outside, a display of faces decorated the wrought-iron window grates, scant inches from the critically ill patients. They were breathing and coughing and blowing cigarette smoke all over the patients. One face even dropped its cigarette down on a patient and the owner had to reach in to retrieve it before it set the bed on fire. And over it all: the smell of stopped-up squat toilets.

The conditions in this hospital were not so much a result of what the doctors and the staff were doing as of what they just simply could not do because of what they did not have: the basics, including soap. And the well-educated, dedicated, and frustrated doctors here earn $8 a month from the government. This, of course, compares to the Hanoi University professor who earns $6. Or the worker in the Saigon fish factory, who can now earn the princely sum of $20 a month.

The hospital staff celebrated our presence and expressed their gratitude for the supplies Le Ly and the rest had brought in (including a $25,000 colonoscope donated by a California doctor) by hosting a lunch for us at a local restaurant. When we sat down and the incredible food began to arrive, one of the doctors leaned over and whispered to me: "This is so wonderful. We are glad you came and brought us all that equipment. Now we can eat."

Unfortunately, one of the things that we were eating was little French-fried songbirds. Three platters of them arrived, their little fried wings folded neatly against their little fried bodies, their little eyes fried shut forever. The Americans were stunned. Then a hand reached over and grabbed a bird, popped it into his mouth, and a soft crunching sound shattered the silence. Then the diner stopped, his mouth full of little fried bird, and looked at us—looking at him. The platters were quickly whisked away. And in the silence that followed we could hear the sounds of the kitchen help cleaning up after us: little soft crunching sounds. At that moment, I had a very serious Big Mac attack.

In addition to the clinic Le Ly had already built in her home village just outside Danang, the local officials in Danang had turned over a large chunk of property to her. Her plan: to build a rehabilitation village to serve people from the area—soldiers from both sides, old people, young people, children—anybody who needed physical rehabilitation. Joined by representatives from the Danang Red Cross, some children from a nearby school, and some local officials, we all trooped to the site one morning for a dedication ceremony. Ironically, in 1965, almost exactly twenty-five years before the day that Le Ly turned the first shovel of earth for her clinic on China Beach, the U.S. Marines had landed, coming ashore by the thousands. It marked the start of the most massive buildup of the war. A buildup that would put some 540,000 American troops into Vietnam by the end of the decade. Before it was over, some three million Americans would serve in Vietnam.

I don't know what I expected but I was shocked when I saw the property. It was vast and catch-your-breath beautiful. And it was also prime: it ran along a wide stretch of China Beach, its soft, blinding white sand stretching down into the crystal blue of the South China Sea. It was very quiet the day our particular group of Americans stood on that beach. I felt wrapped in peace and serenity. At that moment I wanted to stay there forever. And forget about everything. Forget about those Marines from twenty-five years ago. They were young men then. Where were they now? Were they allowed to grow older? Or did they die? Did they suffer? Were they ever whole again? I wanted to forget about clinics being planned to patch up wounds a quarter of a century old. Wars go on. We will always be building clinics. Suddenly a jet screamed overhead, tearing apart my silence. It was a Russian jet based at what was left of the old American air base just down the road. My moment was gone, shattered by the ironic roar of that Russian jet.

One morning I took a stroll along China Beach. I had been warned not to stray too far inland because of all the unexploded mines and bombs that still pepper the area. People are still being killed and maimed by the war's leftovers. Within seconds of leaving sight of the hotel I was completely alone on the beach. I walked for a few minutes then sat down on the soft, white sand. I sat there, quietly contemplating the blue sea washing up onto the blue horizon miles and miles off in the distance. A large glob of wet sand hit me right between the shoulder blades. It was followed quickly by another one, which landed right on top of my head. I rolled over to get out of the line of fire, then looked back and watched another load of sand land right where I had been sitting. Is this really happening? Twenty-five years after the Marines landed, am I sitting on China Beach being shelled by incoming rounds of wet sand? I walked over to where the sand was coming from and found myself peering down into a deep hole. There, at the bottom of the hole, was a woman armed with a shovel. She was digging slowly and methodically, tossing the sand up and out of the pit she was creating. Twenty-five years after that massive seaborne assault by the Marines and fifteen years after the Communist takeover of South Vietnam, people can still find that war's valuable leftovers. This woman was digging for metal—shell casings, tin cans, barbed wire, oil drums—anything she could sell for scrap.

A small boy came up behind me and watched me watching the woman, who smiled widely up at me but never stopped her methodical digging. The little boy motioned me to follow him, making it clear I was to walk exactly where he walked. As he led me away from the beach, I could see he was following a faint path that wound through some scrubby beach grass. From time to time he would point out some items of interest: an old U.S. Army boot lying in the sand, a neat pile of rusted barbed wire, a U.S. helmet.

Then he bent over and picked something up, brushing the sand off it. "Souvenir for you," he said, holding something out to me. It was hot to the touch, having been heated by the warm sun that washed over the beach. I looked down at it. It was a heavy fork with a hole in its handle. I turned it over. It was an old fork from an

American Army mess kit. How long had it been here? Who did it belong to? Where was he now? Home again, happy, safe, and secure? Maybe. Maybe not. I slipped the fork into my skirt pocket, holding it lightly in my hand. My guide had turned around and was leading me back to the beach. Then he slowed down and waited for me. I still had my hand around that old Army-issue fork, still warm to the touch as if someone had dropped it only moments before. As we walked along the soft sand the little boy slipped his tiny hand into mine. It was warm, too.

As Mr. Do and I drove south out of Danang, a heavy gray mist pressed down on us. But within about an hour the mist lifted, the sun broke through, and Vietnam in all her glory blazed forth. We were hugging the coast, and periodically on that drive we would dip down and meet the South China Sea head on. There were bays and inlets and white, white sand beaches washed by gentle waves. We stopped at one beachside restaurant. Do and Vu, the driver, preferred to sit inside and eat and smoke. I bought some baked chicken and rice and green beans, put on my souvenir cone hat, and went down and picnicked alone on the deserted beach. I sat there, my toes dug in the warm sand, watching the waves roll in.

There were almost no other cars on the narrow road that day. Instead it was clotted with bicycles, oxcarts, shuddering old buses, hundreds of children on their way to and from school, men and women staggering under the weight of shoulder poles and baskets. The history of American involvement in Vietnam drifted by on small road signs: Chu Lai, My Lai, Pleiku, An Khe, Cam Ranh Bay. We were aiming for Nha Trang, a coastal city, and we reached it about ten hours after leaving Danang. The surf roared and crashed on a sparkling beach that stretched down to the sea from a wide boulevard that ran the length of the city. I stayed in a hotel on that boulevard overlooking the sea. The stately old French Colonial mansions that line the boulevard have been turned into government offices and bureaus and agencies.

Nha Trang was once an American command and R & R outpost, but today there is absolutely no evidence that the Americans were ever there. Indeed, except for a dwindling population of Amerasians, there is little obvious physical evidence anywhere in Vietnam that America spent nearly two decades there. Since we left so unceremoniously on that April day in 1975, the rubble has been cleared, the landscape is recovering from the chemical blitz it endured. Vietnam, like its people, is a forgiving country.

And the millions of tons of military equipment we abandoned all over Vietnam—everything from airplanes to aluminum cans—have been recycled and absorbed back into the Vietnamese society. Old three-quarter-ton Marine trucks are now local buses, chugging between villages. Even trucks that didn't make it are put to use: I saw one abandoned troop carrier being used as a bus stop. The tires had long since gone. Even a couple of rims had disappeared along with every item of its innards, both under the hood and in the cab. It had settled at a precarious angle along the side of the road, and people would climb in to relax while waiting for the bus, which in all probability would be an old U.S. Marine vehicle.

Earthmovers and caterpillars and airplanes have been cannibalized, broken down, re-formed, and made into everything from fences to roofs to who knows what. At a coffee shop on the perimeter of the old Marine base at Khe Sahn, scene of the most brutal siege of the war, spent howitzer shell casings are used like patio stones to make a verandah. In a small amusement park outside My Tho in the Mekong Delta, I saw old war scrap that had been fashioned into a children's carousel. From time to time, however, the war looms up like a phantom: a ghostly American tank mired in the dust outside the infamous tunnels of Cu Chi near Saigon. And back in Hanoi, the remains of a B-52 shot down during a bombing run over Hanoi are still stuck in the mud of a small lake.

"You're beautiful. Don't ever change."

Mr. Do was practicing his English as we barreled down the road toward Dalat. As usual, the narrow road was filled with people, animals, bicycles, children going to school, grain drying on the side of the road. Children and dogs skittered back and forth onto the road, then scattered as we came through. Periodically a dull thump would echo back through the car. Vu, the driver, never stopped. Never paused. Never looked back. I kept whipping my head around to see if any children had been toppled by our rampaging vehicle as it tore through the countryside. I never saw a crowd of concerned people. Never saw any heartbroken parents or devastated neighbors. Then I realized in horror: he was wiping out half the dog population of Vietnam.

This was terrible. My ASPCA card burned a hole in my wallet. My conscience was on fire. Another thud shook my principles. I could feel them rattling, taunting me. I was about to speak out (although what good would that do? The driver didn't speak a word of English) when another thud shook the car and he turned and with a big smile addressed me and my conscience: "Dinner!"

Well, O.K. So he knew one word. And we continued zooming down the road.

"Bull-sit," Mr. Do continued.

"I believe you mean 'bullshit,' " I replied.

"Yes. Bull-sit," he repeated. "Am I pronouncing it right?"

"Absolutely not," I assured him. So we spent the afternoon working on his pronunciation, concentrating on "shit" in all various aspects. He was particularly impressed with the use of "You are a big bag of shit" as a quick but effective insult. His fallback phrase quickly became: "You have shit for brains," although no matter how much pronunciation work I did with Mr. Do, it still came out: "You have sit for brains." No matter.

We were in Dalat, high in the cool mountains in the interior of Vietnam. Dalat was that old French Colonial resort town used by the Vietnamese upper classes as a retreat during the hot months, a refreshing break from the heat and humidity of the lowlands. As we drove through its winding streets, still lorded over by towering and sweet-smelling pine trees, I wondered if any of those once-elegant villas had belonged to Bryner's grandfather and his family. Today bedding was flung over once-elegant balcony railings. Laundry decorated the old porches and verandahs. Periodically I would see pigs snorting through the overgrown gardens, still ablaze with brilliant flowering bushes.

I was assigned to the old Palace Hotel, once a mountain retreat for the French and, later, for the Americans. It was shabby and a bit grim these days, but in its heyday the Palace must have been spectacular. It is an overgrown chalet with dark wood, towering French doors, shutters, fireplaces—the works. The lobby was two stories and cavernous. Two massive French doors opened onto a stone terrace and a view of a sweeping lawn that led to an enormous lake.

I took a walk around the grounds, now scuffed and scrubby. There was an old tennis court off to one side. Had it once been grass? Clay? Who knows? It was covered with broken concrete now. Some barefoot kids were batting a dead tennis ball back and forth. They were using chunks of wood.

Some other children, wandering home from school, spotted me as an American (I think they heard me speaking English to the horse that was tied to a tree on the front lawn). I was immediately pressed into service for an impromptu English class under a huge tree on the

Palace's front lawn. By the time we finished, an hour later, the class included the caretakers and the man who came to retrieve his horse. And there is just no escaping Vietnamese kindness: Nguyet, a sparkling child of about ten, returned the next morning and presented me with two old postcards (including one from the newer hotel down at the bottom of the hill) wrapped in lined notebook paper and tied with a piece of embroidery thread. She had pressed her teacher into writing me a note in very formal English thanking me for my generosity in speaking English with them.

Palace Hotel Rule #8: "Guests are not allowed to move out the room furniture without the manager's acceptance."

Mr. Tu had arrived at the Palace Hotel in 1942, an eighteen-year-old straight from Hanoi. He has been a waiter in the Palace dining room ever since. I was the only person in the entire dining room, a cavernous space with a wall of elegant French doors that open onto an enormous stone terrace. He has seen them come and he has seen them go. He has met all the high-ranking visitors who have strayed through Vietnam in the past forty-six years. Presidents Diem, Thieu, Ky. General Westmoreland. Defense Secretary McNamara. Senator Robert Kennedy. And, yes, Emperor Bao Dai.
   "Emperor Bao Dai! You really met Emperor Bao Dai?" I cried. This was exciting. Bao Dai had abdicated in 1945, skipped out of Vietnam, and gone immediately to Paris, where he became a playboy, drinking whiskey and soda and cavorting with the International Set. "What was he like, Mr. Tu?" I prepared myself for some firsthand, hidden insights into this playboy prince. Mr. Tu thought for a long time and finally gave me his studied opinion of the last Emperor of Vietnam:
   "He was very tall and . . ."
   "Yes? Yes?"
   "And he had very long arms."

We left Dalat early the next morning on the final stretch of the trip back to Saigon. The air was cool and crisp and overhead the sky was a brilliant, crackling blue. I had gone to bed in all my clothes and slept under a blanket and still I was cold. It felt great. All along the road the countryside blazed forth at us. Everyone who has ever been to Vietnam—soldier and civilian alike—is awestruck at the beauty of that country. In the highlands, the countryside rolls gently, periodically lifting itself like arms to the crisp blue sky. The rice fields are a carpet of emerald green. Palm trees sweep the sky. Red and yellow hibiscus blaze like flames along the road. Thatched houses sit like little live-in haystacks along the sides of the road and up in those green hills. The first time I saw those exquisite greens flung out over the landscape—paddies, palm trees, jungle hillsides thick with vegetation—I nearly wept. The countryside is a palette of greens that wash as far as the eye can see, changing colors until it reaches the horizon. Later, I could only describe Vietnam as a tropical Ireland. My Asian homeland.

The approach to Saigon, like the approach to any city, was a jolt as the softspoken gentleness of the rural landscape gradually gave way to the rude reality of urban sprawl. Shacks, dirt, noise. Suddenly, the very real world of Saigon crowded in on us, outspoken and insistent.

HOME VISITS

Lionel Richie would have been pleased: Bryner was walking on the ceiling. Meanwhile, Tom was pointing up to the floor. We had all gone happily back to school after my two-week sabbatical in the North and were now confronting "The Room." And everybody was in a state of confusion, trying to tell the difference between the floor and the ceiling. They had done a great job of figuring out that you sit in a chair and eat at a table and write at a desk, even though most of them had never seen a desk in their lives. For some reason, even "wall" flowed into their vocabulary with ease. "Floor" and "ceiling" had become their latest trial.

Lan, who could obviously tell the difference between her floor and her ceiling, had wandered out to the kitchen during this part of the lesson. I could hear her chopping and rattling away out there. At one point a little girl came running through the class and sped out the door. I heard her footsteps rushing down the hall and then disappearing down the stairs. A few minutes later she came rushing back up the stairs, through the room, and into the kitchen. This went on for the rest of the class as Lan occupied herself out there, until we heard a loud crash and the sound of glass breaking. Without hesitating, both Jim and Bryner jumped up and went out to help clean up whatever Lan had broken and spilled all over the floor.

When class was over, Lan came to the doorway and stood there wiping her hands on a towel. I could tell she cooked the way I did. Her face was red and shiny and she was covered with flour. But at least she was smiling.

"O.K.," she said. "You eat now." I nearly choked. She was holding out a heaping platter of deep-fried okra. "Here your plate. Here your fork. You eat." Then she sat down, obviously pleased with herself. I ate the whole platter while approximately twelve people sat around watching me eat and taking as much pleasure in it as I did. Food is an important social ritual in Vietnam. I, at least, was very social that day.

When I first visited Vietnam in late 1988 as a tourist, having foreign visitors in your home was strictly forbidden. Few if any people would risk any sort of casual contact. It was just not worth the hassle with the police. Reporters after a story had to make furtive visits under cover of darkness, posting lookouts at the ends of streets and hoping no one would turn them in or, worse, that the people being interviewed would not be grabbed later and hauled off by the police. Even returning Vietnamese, home to visit their families, were subjected to rigid regulations governing a simple visit to an old mother or brothers and sisters or even their own children whom they hadn't seen for years. For the gracious, generous, gregarious Vietnamese—particularly those in Saigon—this must have been one of the worst aspects of Communism: the shutdown of their own innate sociability. But by 1990 all of that had changed and Saigon was reveling in an orgy of home entertaining.

As an American, I was in great demand. The invitations came pouring in. I became the Jackie Kennedy of downtown Saigon. The social sweetheart of orphans, Amerasians, shoeshine boys, and cigarette ladies. The first person who scored what was probably the coup of the 1990 social season, thus solidifying his social position in the community for years to come, was Hung, my cyclo driver from the old days at the Que Huong Hotel. I had gone there one day after I had moved to the Kim Do simply to sit and schmooze with the gang outside the hotel, when Hung just up and loaded me into his cyclo and pedaled me out to his house to meet his new wife, his three kids, and his mother-in-law. They all lived together in one excrutiatingly tiny room. During the day, they stacked their sole wooden bed up against the wall so they would have enough space not only to enter the room but to actually turn around in it and live

in it. (Let me point out: when I say wooden bed, I mean wooden.
Everything is wooden including the part you sleep on. Even in
hospitals the beds are wooden. Sometimes, if you are lucky, a
woven straw mat is slipped between your haunches and the wood.
And if you are really lucky, you can buy cotton-stuffed sleeping
pads.) Hung pulled the bed down and we all sat for an hour drinking fizzy orange soda and smiling at one another. I looked at more
of their wedding pictures, then took some photographs of my own,
and Hung pedaled me back to the hotel. Score one hospitality point
for the home team.

Linh was also insistent that I come visit his house. I had loaned
him $6 to pay his rent one month so he wanted to show me what
he had gotten for my money. Bryner, who had no home at the time,
was temporarily living with Linh and his aged landlady. So one day,
with Pearl and Jim along, we headed off to visit Linh.

His home was half of one room on a quiet alley. There was a
wooden bed in the front, which Linh and Bryner shared, while the
landlady took the wooden bed in the back. The bathroom was a
hole in the ground behind the house. Out back there was also a
water spigot shared by the neighbors. It was hot and we were dusty
and sweaty, so while the guys went out and took their shirts off and
splashed water all over themselves to clean off and cool down, the
landlady brought out a basin of cold water, a clean rag, and a tiny
sliver of soap for me, her guest. Then she dragged up a stool and sat
smiling at me while I washed up.

That hot afternoon in Saigon washed me with memories as
well. Back home in Nebraska, my sister and her husband had a farm
just outside town. For years there was no running water, just an old
pump out in the yard. I remembered all those hot, dusty Nebraska
afternoons when we all cleaned up out there in my sister's yard,
using a tin basin, a thin towel, and a bar of strong soap. There was
also a metal cup hooked onto the pump, and we would drink gallons of that sweet, cold Nebraska water drawn up from the depths
of the prairie. All the kids would hang around out there because
there was always some goofy man in the family who would bend
over and stick his head in the basin and make loud, bellowing noises
and shake water all over everybody. We would all laugh until we fell
over in the dust. It was the 1940s and entertainment like that was
cheap and easily available. Then we would all go inside and eat
roast beef and mashed potatoes and gravy and a piece of somebody's rich homemade pie. Afterward, the men would go into the

parlor and smoke and talk and then, one by one, fall asleep where they were sitting. The kids would crawl under the table or behind the big black cookstove in the kitchen and likewise fall asleep to the quiet murmurings of the women clearing the table, doing the dishes, talking softly through the heat of midday.

I stood there, in the equally enervating midday heat of Saigon, splashing cold water on my face. I could hear Linh and Bryner and the rest of them splashing around in the back, talking and laughing quietly among themselves. It wasn't Nebraska, but for a minute or two it could have been. Months later I found a photographic record of that day: Linh and Bryner and Pearl and Jim are sitting in a row on the hard, wooden bed in the front of that room in Saigon. Their faces are freshly scrubbed, their hair is wet and slicked back. Bryner is wearing an old cowboy-style shirt a passing tourist gave him. It was faded blue cotton and had little lariats embroidered across the front. They could have been Nebraska farm kids, all scrubbed and clean from a session at the backyard pump, sitting in a row waiting for some stray dad to get goofy and splash cold water on them. Only none of these kids had dads. Half them didn't even have mothers.

At the adult English school where I helped out three nights a week, I met a fascinating young woman in one of the classes. Tho was married, had three children and an Amerasian half brother. And because of that half brother, they were all preparing to be processed out of Vietnam. While they waited, everyone in the family was studying English at that government-sponsored school. Somehow, Tho and her husband had enough money to afford private English schools for the whole family, even their small children. Her oldest daughter—an appealing seven-year-old—attended English class from 7 A.M. to noon every Saturday.

Tho had me over one Saturday morning for "breakfast," an incredible array of food, including a centerpiece of boiled chicken feet. The food, as usual, was delicious, so I ate furiously. (I kept my eye on those chicken feet. I wanted to make damned sure there were as many chicken feet in my bowl when I finished as when I started.) She and her husband became so concerned about me that those Saturday-morning "breakfasts" became a ritual. They were worried that I didn't eat enough, that perhaps I was lonely, that I needed a family around me. There was no explaining to them that I was (1) eating like a pig in Saigon and (2) also had a better social life in

Saigon than I ever had in my hard-working, career-driven, crime-ridden life in New York.

One day, after yet another early-morning feast at their house, Tho and her husband and I were sitting around talking. Their three children were all home and were watching English-language tapes on their VCR. Then Tho's husband put a cassette into the VCR to show me some stuff he had just videotaped around Saigon. "For souvenir," he explained. "So we can remember our old life when we get to our new life in America." There were shots of their neighborhood, of the family going to church, of a family outing at the zoo, scenes of downtown Saigon. I then realized I was sitting—albeit on the floor—in the midst of some pretty heady stuff: a mountain of material possessions.

Ky, the husband, sighed. "Oh, I borrow the video camera. But we used to have our own," he assured me, again sighing deeply. "We used to have a color TV." He sighed again. "We used to have a red motorcycle." Then they both sighed. "We used to have lots of money."

"What happened?" I asked.

"We put it in the bank." Then they peered closely at me. "Do you have banks in America?" I allowed as how, yes—we did. This was long before the S & L crisis, so when they asked me about the viability and security of American banks I wasn't just throwing out a load of sheep dip when I told them how safe and secure banks in America were. They sighed again. "We put our money in the bank. And we lost it all."

Indeed, one of the biggest scandals rocking the Communist government in 1990 was the banking scandal. After 1975, the Communists wrecked the banking system and had just recently started to allow banks to operate again. Trouble is, they forgot how to do it. Especially how to regulate them. As a result, these new banks had become the roach motels of finance: people put their money in, it didn't come out. And suddenly bankers were living in big houses, driving big cars, wearing fancy clothes and, well—you get the picture.

"How much money did you put in?" I asked my friends.

"Ten thousand dollars."

"Ten thousand dollars!" I was aghast.

They nodded sadly. Tho seemed ready to cry.

"How much did you get out?"

"Two thousand dollars."

No wonder they were in a state of distress. Sitting there, surrounded by boiled chicken feet, I had one more question: "Where did you get all that money?"

They both smiled broadly. "Oh, we smuggled."

Hmm-m-m. "What did you smuggle?"

"Drugs."

Oh, my God. Here I am—dangerously close to the infamous Golden Triangle, where the world's most lethal drugs are grown and harvested and from where they eventually make their way to the street corners of the world. And I am obviously sitting in the midst of some of their major distributors. I was horrified. "What . . . what . . . what did you smuggle?" I asked. Heroin! Industrial-strength marijuana! Morphine! I was ready for it all.

"Oh, you know. Tylenol, Bayer, Maalox."

Yes, there I sat, surrounded by the world's major Maalox smugglers. It was a sobering experience indeed. In Saigon in 1990 there was obviously as big a market for American pharmaceuticals as there was for heroin and marijuana.

"Oh, we have that other stuff here in Vietnam," Tho assured me, obviously not wanting to be left out of the international dope loop. "But, Kelly—you can make more money with a bottle of Tylenol. Everybody have headaches in Vietnam. Everybody." she nodded her head knowingly. "Yes—Vietnam is a headache."

There were six chicken feet when I went in. There were six chicken feet when I went out.

Crime did not start or stop with those Tylenol smugglers or bank schemers, however. Smuggling was a major problem. In August even the Army newspaper, *Quan Doi Nhan Dan,* was compelled to comment on the massive amount of smuggling going on, particularly on the boarder between Vietnam and Cambodia. They called it a "smuggling epidemic," with "tens of thousands of people smuggling goods across the border day and night." A whopping 65 percent of the goods for sale in Saigon were said to be contraband. "Representatives of public organs, mass organizations, factories, and enterprises find their way to the border to buy tax-free goods." Everything from electronic equipment to, well—Tylenol.

A major crime wave involving American cigarettes even swept Saigon over that summer. American cigarettes—particularly Marlboros, either smuggled in from Thailand by way of Cambodia or brought in legally through their Asian distributors—were openly available all over Saigon at a cost of $1 a pack. (Remember: this is a country that earns an average of 50 cents a day.) And those American cigarettes had become the biggest status symbol of all in Saigon, so young men began mugging people to get the money to buy these cigarettes. Or so the authorities claimed when they moved in and cracked down. On October 1 the authorities banned the sale of foreign cigarettes. Overnight, not a single pack of American butts could be found for sale.

Blue jeans were also a hot commodity for petty thieves preoccupied with status but unwilling or unable to pay the steep price ($10 to $15) for them. One of my students had washed his blue jeans—a gift from a departing tourist—and hung them on the inside of his window grille to dry overnight. The next morning they were gone. And he lived on the second floor rear of a building. Someone had seen his blue jeans drying in the window and had somehow shinnied up two stories and stolen them. But the worst case of stolen blue jeans was reported in the newspaper: someone had actually gone to the city morgue and stolen a pair of blue jeans. Off a body.

Immediately after we met, Nguyet, Kim's mother, proceeded with her plans for a dinner in my honor. It would be the first of many as Nguyet quickly absorbed me into her household. Nguyet was lonely and distraught after Kim left Vietnam, frantic with worry until the first letter arrived from the refugee camp in the Philippines. Thanks to inefficiencies on both ends, it took long and painful weeks for that initial letter—written the first week Kim was in the camp—to arrive. They must have been the longest weeks of Nguyet's life. She would often arrive at my hotel and just sit in the lobby holding my hand and weeping quietly over Kim. I think, among other things, she saw me as a link to her daughter so we would sit and reminisce about Kim and dream together about their new life to come in America. Fortunately, as the weeks wore on Nguyet managed to become somewhat resigned to what was now turning into a long wait to get Roan-na's case reviewed so they could both proceed to the Philippines to join Kim. "Roan-na not retarded," Nguyet would insist. "She just slow. She shy, too."

Generally on those nights she cooked dinner for me, I would be taken out and brought back by Minh in his cyclo, and he too would be fed. Then one night she arranged with Bui, a friend of hers, to pick me up and bring me out to her house. Nguyet and Bui were business acquaintances: Nguyet had sold cigarettes outside the Rex Hotel while Bui, who owned an old motorcycle, had staked out the Palace Hotel two blocks away. There he would sit, day after day, offering to guide tourists around Saigon on his motorcycle. He spoke excellent English and was a generous, accommodating man. She thought I would like to meet him.

"Besides, he good friend Kim father," Nguyet explained. Bui and Kim's father had become friends during one of his many trips to Vietnam, first to find Kim and then to visit her while her paperwork slogged through the two warring bureaucracies.

"Bui O.K., Kelly," Nguyet had assured me. "He good man. Good man. He pick you up, bring you my house. We eat. No problem, Kelly. He stay. He know I very good cook."

So Bui, a former chief petty officer in the old South Vietnamese Navy, picked me up one night on his aging Vespa and we started out to Nguyet's house. I had armed myself with what I knew by then were the appropriate Saigon hostess gifts—a freshly plucked chicken, five loaves of bread, and some big bottles of Saigon beer—and off we went.

It was rush hour in Saigon, which just means that along toward late afternoon traffic gets denser than usual. And with almost no working street lights and not a single traffic cop in evidence, traffic is a dicey endeavor, a lethal mixture of cyclos, overloaded bicycles and motorbikes, with a few cars, trucks, and buses just to add an edge of mortal danger to the scene. Safety devices like seat belts or baby seats in cars or helmets for bikers and motorcyclists are unheard of. My own recent encounter with Saigon pavement was still very fresh in my mind. Likewise the Australian neurosurgeon I had met recently at the Givral. We had begun to talk and I discovered he had been asked to come to Saigon to deliver some lectures to the doctors at various hospitals.

"Why is that?" I asked him.

"Head injuries," he replied, succinctly summing up the problem. All over Vietnam, people are hurtling off their bicycles and motorbikes and landing on their heads, suffering severe head and spinal-cord injuries. And in the general poverty of Vietnam—where surgical gloves are washed and reused, where burn victims lie like open sores in their beds, where there is even a black market in American aspirin—there are few if any surgical or rehabilitation programs to help these accident victims.

"They still use hand drills over here," he said, discussing neurosurgery techniques.

So there I was, balanced on the back of Bui's aged Vespa, hanging on for dear life, traffic whizzing past my unprotected head.

Nguyet lived in a distant quarter of Saigon, down a series of side streets that kept getting smaller and smaller. Finally, even those gave up and turned into pathways cutting between some rickety one-story shacks. The final approach to Nguyet's house was over a broken sewer line that had filled a ditch with an ugly black goo. Someone had thrown a board across it for people to walk on.

The houses back here were little more than a series of thin wooden partitions thrown up to create long rooms to separate one family from another. Nguyet's was almost at the end of the path. The fronts were made of heavy mesh screening with ragged wooden doors. That mesh screening in the front of the house made it seem more like a cage than a room where people lived. I wondered what Kim's American father thought the first time he visited his daughter there. Corrugated tin had been thrown on top of the flimsy partitions to make a ramshackle roof.

Typically, Nguyet shared a big room with other people, in this case two elderly people who lived in the front half of the room. In addition to Kim and Roan-na, Nguyet had four other children including a daughter who was married. So at one time, shortly before Kim left, all eight people had lived together in the back half of that room. These days, only Nguyet and Roan-na were living there. The only furniture was an iron bed with an actual mattress, a chest for kitchen items, and another chest for everything else. Most of their possessions were kept in an assortment of tote bags and old suitcases stacked against the wall. A curtain separated the two halves of the room. There was no running water, but a big concrete cistern took up one corner. The bathroom was a hole in the floor off to one side. Nguyet had put up some sort of wall to give at least a semblance of privacy. Cooking was done on the floor with a single small charcoal cooker made out of clay.

And Nguyet was in full swing when I got there. At first I couldn't find her. She was squatting on the floor, surrounded and half-buried by food, family, and neighbors. There was a confusion of food and people down there on the floor—salad greens, vegetables, rice—with everybody involved in the chopping, hacking, peeling, mixing, and stirring that went on to put a meal on the table. All this in a country where there was basically no refrigeration, no running water, and no fuel other than charcoal for stoves that looked more like pottery ashtrays than kitchen equipment that could actually turn out a full-scale meal.

"Oh, hi, Kelly! You come! Good see you! Come in! Come in!"

She jumped up, wiping her hands. Then I noticed a shy black girl, still squatting on the floor, smiling behind her hand.

"This Roan-na," Nguyet said proudly, indicating that shy young girl. "This Kim's sister. She American, too!" she said proudly. Roan-na stood up and, with Nguyet urging her on, put out her hand for an American handshake. Roan-na was a lovely eighteen-year-old with Nguyet's big smile very much a part of her personality.

I learned later that this dinner had been an all-neighborhood affair. In fact, buried in all that food being prepared down on the floor were two neighborhood women who had rushed to Nguyet's aid. Neighbors had also come up with a table to eat on, some chairs, a fan, and a cassette player complete with an American tape (Michael Jackson, what else?). They plugged the fan in, opened the beer, whacked off a big chunk of ice with a huge knife, and served me the first glass of iced beer.

It was an orgy of food that night. Nguyet and her neighbors had prepared fresh curried soup, beef with peanuts, a chicken dish, wispy Vietnamese noodles, and handmade *cha gio,* those delicate and delicious Vietnamese spring rolls. The meal ended with an array of fresh fruits that seemed always to be in season in Vietnam: mangoes, papayas, bananas, grapes, and other fruits that I couldn't identify but had come to love. I was popping grapes into my mouth with gusto when Bui began explaining American grapes to the dinner set.

"These grapes are nothing," he said to the dinner guests. "Do you know that in America the grapes have no seeds?" A gasp of disbelief went up from the crowd, by now sitting wide-eyed around the table. "And one American grape is the size of two of these measly things." He shook two delicate grapes under the noses of his audience, then put the two grapes into his mouth. I could hear the seeds cracking under his teeth. "These Communists. They don't know how to do anything."

"You ever been to Philadelphia, Kelly?" Bui asked me on our second after-dinner bottle of Saigon beer. Nguyet was bustling around cleaning up after the meal, and Bui and I were sitting around talking. I allowed as how I had been there once, and since Bui was so enthusiastically pro-American I felt it prudent to reassure him that I liked it very much. "Me, too. Oh, I like Philadelphia. Very beautiful. Very beautiful."

"Bui! You have been to Philadelphia?"

"Oh, of course. I lived there six months." Turns out Bui had been in the Vietnamese Navy from 1958 until 1975. And because of this, he had been sent to America twice for training. "You know Great Lakes?" he asked. I nodded at his reference to the Great Lakes Naval Training Station, just outside Chicago. "I have been there, too. Kelly, I have been to America many times." He began counting on his fingers. "I was in America in 1964. I was in Philadelphia and Norfolk, Virginia. Then in 1968 my ship sailed to Guam. I consider that part of America." Far be it from me to argue that point with him. "And in 1971 I spend seven months at Great Lakes studying electrical maintenance. Great Lakes is in Illinois, where it gets very cold in the winter. It gets so cold there is ice on the sidewalks." To the after-dinner crowd, this was close to unbelievable. "Yes, I tell you this. Ice. Oh, I fall down many times. What do you know about doughnuts, Kelly?"

What do I know about doughnuts? Oh, Bui. You silly man. What *didn't* I know about doughnuts. I mean, didn't my mom and dad once own a doughnut shop in Albion, Nebraska? I proceeded to dazzle him with my knowledge of frosted, glazed, and jelly doughnuts. He hadn't heard of frosted jellies or doughnuts with sprinkles, but he was happy to hear of them and was quite impressed. He translated the wonders of American doughnut making to the crowd sitting at the table. They were duly impressed.

"Oh, that sounds wonderful, Kelly. I like American doughnuts very much. There was a kiosk right outside the front gate at Great Lakes. There they have the best doughnuts. I think maybe they were the best doughnuts in the world." He paused, a dreamy and faraway look came over his face. "Do you know if that doughnut kiosk is still there? I would certainly like to go there and eat another American doughnut."

He paused. "They have much better doughnuts in Chicago than in Salt Lake City." I think I was gaping at him by this time.

"How do you know Salt Lake City, Bui?"

"Why, I traveled there by Greyhound bus." Bui was unbelievable. Seems he had once had a fifteen-day pass from his naval training duties at Great Lakes, so rather than waste any precious time on that particular trip to America he hopped a Greyhound bus for a fifteen-day round trip to California. And to him everything about that Greyhound bus trip was wonderful. The bus stations, the food, the vision of America slipping past his window. Bui was bowled over by the Great Plains, the Rocky Mountains, the Great

Salt Lake (although he apologized for saying he didn't much care for the doughnuts in Utah), and the Pacific Ocean. I noted that he had really seen the sights, but I was curious.

"After all that, Bui—the mountains, the prairies, the ocean undoubtedly white with foam—what impressed you the most?"

Without a moment's hesitation, Bui replied: "Sacramento."

Sacramento? Sacramento, California? Why in the world would a man who had taken a picture-postcard trip halfway across the United States, seen the towering peaks of snow-capped mountains and great salty lakes and the vast rolling expanse of the Pacific Ocean—why would he then pronounce Sacramento to be the most impressive sight?

"It was so clean, Kelly." He shook his head. "Never have I seen such a clean city."

"Bui, you spent months in America. You traveled halfway across the country. You met people. You visited Americans in their homes. What did you like best about our country?"

"The weekend," he replied without missing a beat.

"Which weekend?" Had I missed something?

"Any weekend. Never have I learned of such a thing: two days off." In addition to his military training, Bui also worked part time. He told me he worked as a gardener, he cleaned up in restaurants, he got a job as a dishwasher. He kept himself busy. "I wanted to earn some money and I wanted to learn about America," he explained. Then he leaned forward and explained the concept of a weekend for the dinner crowd. They were hanging on to his every word by this time. "Imagine: every Saturday and Sunday you don't work. And still they pay you. I find this very wonderful indeed." There was a great babble from the table that Bui translated back to me.

"They find the idea of the weekend to be very wonderful, also," he said. "But what they find most wonderful of all is having the job so you can have two days off from it. Now *that* is wonderful."

Things had quieted down. The neighbors had gone home. Bui and Nguyet and I were sitting around the borrowed table on our borrowed chairs while the borrowed fan continued to stir the quiet air. Bui and I were sipping beer. Nguyet had made tea for herself, while Roan-na was sitting on the bed playing with one of Nguyet's two cats. Bui had already confessed that before Liberation, while his beloved Americans were still in Vietnam, he used to watch American television. His particular favorites were *Mission: Impos-*

sible and the old *Batman* series, starring Adam West. He sighed. But that was very long ago and awfully far away.

"What happened after 1975?" I asked. "Were you in reeducation camp?"

He shook his head. "No. I was only a chief petty officer. I wasn't important enough. But you know, Kelly, I think the whole country is a reeducation camp." He told me how he had gone down to his ship, at anchor in the Saigon River, the day the Communists moved in on Saigon. "Our commanding officers told us to take off our uniforms and go home. So I did. Imagine. Just like that, it was over. After all those years, it was over."

As the months went on and both the political and the economic situation became more and more unsettled and desperate in Saigon, indeed in the entire southern part of Vietnam, Bui decided he had to make a move. Just as there wasn't a family in Vietnam during the war that wasn't affected by that war, there now wasn't a family in South Vietnam that hadn't been affected by the end to that war, especially by escapes and escape attempts. Indeed, over the past fifteen years escapes and escape attempts became the norm in Vietnam, with people from the South eventually being joined by those from the North in streaming out of Vietnam. So in 1978, with two of his sons—aged eight and fifteen—Bui made his own escape attempt. It failed.

"We were all so scared, but, Kelly, my kids were great. They didn't cry. I trained them well. We could see the soldiers. They had guns. I told my kids before 'Keep mum!' " He made a shushing gesture at his mouth. "And when the soldiers closed in on us I tell them again: 'Keep mum!' We were far from Saigon, over by the Cambodian border, trying to get a boat out of the country. Finally the soldiers went away and we could escape."

"What did you do?" I asked.

"Took the bus back to Saigon." He said this in a matter-of-fact way, as if making such a life-changing decision and then facing down that life-threatening challenge was a normal, everyday occurrence.

"What was the worst thing about that escape attempt, Bui?"

He looked at me with disdain and I felt somewhat guilty for asking such an insensitive question. Then he took a deep breath and answered: "The bus ride." I couldn't tell if he was serious or if he was joking. "Kelly—you have been on Vietnamese buses. They're awful. Nothing like buses in America." Bui was off again, dreaming into reality the time he spent in America. "Why, that bus I took to

California—oh, it was wonderful. It was like I imagine an airplane would be. The seat was very comfortable. There were even windows. And they were very clean. Do you know—there was even a bathroom?"

Bui and his sons tried again, two years later in 1980. Again, they made their way to the Cambodian border and once again tried to leave Vietnam by boat. This time they actually made it down the part of the Mekong River that flows across the border between Vietnam and Cambodia. "There were twenty of us. We were in a rowboat. My two sons were with me again. Oh, I hoped we were going to make it. But, no. Suddenly we were surrounded by soldiers again. They fired on us. Over and over again they shot at this rowboat. People were scared to death. What could we do? We all jumped out. Many people were killed. There were bodies all over. And much blood. We were not even in the sea. Not even close to freedom. And all those people died."

Bui and his sons were not so lucky this time. They were captured and arrested and taken to a work camp near the border. His ten-year-old son was kept for two weeks, his seventeen-year-old for six months. Bui himself was kept for three years.

"They put me in leg cuffs after I was arrested," he told me. He demonstrated how they did it: an iron rod was driven into the ground and he was put into leg irons and then chained to the rod. He was kept in leg irons, chained to that rod, for two weeks. "We had only one bowl of rice a day to eat. No newspapers. Sometimes the guards would forget and wrap our rice in old pieces of newspaper. That is how we could read a newspaper. The Vietcong ran this camp." I asked him if he was ever mistreated. "Of course. All the time. Mostly they beat me for talking. Just for talking to other people." He shook his head. "We even had to stay away from the guards. We had to stay five meters away from them. If we got too close, they would beat us. They were afraid we might try to assassinate them. It was stupid of them to think that: they had the guns."

Outside, the bustle of late afternoon had quieted into dusk. I could hear people scuffing through the dirt. Now and then a door would creak open, a dog would bark. These were the quiet, familiar universal sounds of a day ending and an evening beginning. The comforting sounds of ordinary life.

Bui leaned forward. His eyes had filled with tears but they were blazing. "Kelly, I am a gentle man. I believe in God. I believe our Lord loves us. And I love my Lord very much. But I tell you this,

Kelly: I want to kill them. If I had a gun I would kill them tonight. I hate them so much. I would assassinate them. Right now." He wiped his hands across his face. "I would assassinate them all."

Through all this, Nguyet and Roan-na had been sitting quietly. In addition to the dead chicken, the beer, and the loaves of French bread I had brought to Nguyet, I had also stuck some picture books into my tote bag for Roan-na. They were from some "Learn to Read" series I had picked up in the main bookstore near the Kim Do. They were in basic Vietnamese and English and I figured they might be of some use to her before she hit the classrooms that were waiting in the refugee camp in the Philippines when—if—they were allowed to leave. She flipped through the pages and then closed the book and smiled at me. Suddenly, an awful realization hit me.

"Can Roan-na read?" I asked Nguyet. She shook her head. "She didn't go to school at all?" I asked. Again, she shook her head. I was surprised. "But Kim went to school." I knew that Nguyet had kept Kim in school as long as she could, taught her from what little storehouse of English she herself could remember, then encouraged her to learn English anywhere she could: from Bui, from tourists out on the streets, from English-speaking neighbors.

"Yes, but Kim white American child. That bad enough. Roan-na black American child." She took Roan-na's face and gently touched her cheek. "Oh, I send Roan-na to school, Kelly. She go. She like school. She slow. Not smart like Kim smart. But she want to go. She want to learn. But the teachers and the other children—they . . ." Nguyet looked to Bui for help in finding the word she wanted.

"They taunt her," he said.

"They call her names. They call her 'American.' They call her 'My den.' Black American. 'My lai.' Half-breed. They call her 'bad girl.' She not a bad girl! She American girl. They mean to her." She grabbed Roan-na's arm and thrust it under my nose. "Look. Look what they do to her." I looked down and saw thick scars decorating her arms. "Look what they do to Roan-na. They cut her. They hit her and call her names and they cut her." Judging by those thick scars on her arms, Roan-na had endured as much as she could before refusing to go back to school. From then on, she stayed close to Nguyet, her fiercely protective mother.

But that was only a part of Nguyet's struggle to keep her family together. By the end of the war Nguyet had six children—including her two Amerasian daughters. In all the confusion when the Communists were sweeping through the country, she and her little family had left Vung Tau and joined the stream of refugees pouring into Saigon. Nguyet and her children ended up living on the streets for nearly six months before being rounded up and sent off to a work camp in the countryside for another six months. Then they were shuffled back to Saigon and life on the streets.

"Oh, it very hard, Miss Katie. I have many children. I have my American babies. They little babies. Everybody say—get rid of those Americans! I say no! They my babies. I love them very much!" Against all odds, this single mother of six kept her fragile little family together. Nguyet—and countless other mothers—opened up stalls and sold anything they could. She eventually set up her cigarette stand in downtown Saigon, staking out the Rex Hotel. When Kim was old enough, she was sent out on the streets to peddle postcards and peanuts. Even that was difficult.

"The police don't like American children," Kim once told me. "So they hit me." She was so matter-of-fact about this it nearly broke my heart. And once again I was overwhelmed by the reality of the situation: These were American children. And to be an American—an American child—trapped in that country after the war was to be a prisoner of your heritage. A prisoner of freckles and pale skin and black skin and curly hair and green eyes.

And now, because of those experiences, Roan-na could neither read nor write. Worse, she had been judged mentally retarded when perhaps it was just a case of illiteracy. And it was now jeopardizing their final approval to go to America and thus be reunited with Kim.

Nguyet got up and unlocked the wooden chest that acted as a partial divider between her family's space and the landlady's space. I could see her riffling through papers, pulling some out and laying them carefully on top of the chest right next to the tape player, which I now noticed had been switched to an Easy Listening tape of some sort.

She finally found what she wanted and came over and sat down by me. She unfolded one paper—written entirely in Vietnamese—and pushed it over to me. "I go hospital tomorrow morning. Seven o'clock. You come with me?" I looked at the paper and did indeed see the name of a hospital—Cho Ray—and tomorrow's date. I didn't see anything about 7 A.M. though.

"You have an appointment? For seven o'clock?"

"No. But we go there. We wait." This was part of the medical procedure she and Roan-na still had to endure to work their way through the bureaucracy. You were given a date, you showed up, you waited. Sooner or later, if you were lucky, the bureaucracy would catch up with you. "I pick you up six-thirty." She smiled, patted my hand, poured some more beer in my glass.

Sure enough, Nguyet and Roan-na showed up outside the hotel promptly at six-thirty the next morning. By the time we reached Cho Ray Hospital the place was already jammed with people who were there to take their physicals. Women were running around in pale blue examination gowns, trying to keep both the gowns and their paperwork together. Everybody was giggling like mad at the indignity of it all. To me, it was absolute chaos, but Nguyet kept a tight hold on things and moved slowly through the procedures.

"You come with me now," she whispered, grabbing my hand and pulling me into a room. Then she and Roan-na disappeared behind a curtain. I sat there for about ten minutes, then suddenly Nguyet broke through the curtains. I knew immediately something was wrong. Her face was like chiseled stone.

"What's the matter?"

"No good. No good." Her eyes were glistening with tears and her jaw was set so firmly I thought it would crack into pieces. She started talking but she was so agitated I couldn't understand a word she said. "No good!" She shook a piece of paper under my nose. She finally calmed down enough to make me understand that there had been what could only be described as a monumental screwup by the bureaucracy. And she and her daughter were paying the price. As best I could understand, all of Nguyet's crucial medical examinations, including this one, were scheduled by the Vietnamese authorities. She had been given one year to complete all of the medical procedures. Through no fault of her own, today's examination—which should have been just a formality, the last one before finally being given permission to leave—was now a few days beyond the one-year cutoff point. And now, according to the officials at the hospital, all the previous examinations and appointments and judgments were worthless. Roan-na had to start all over again with a new examination and new evaluation by the Vietnamese mental-health authorities.

"Please. You help me," Nguyet's voice cracked and broke.

Oh, my God. This was awful. I felt as if someone had punched me in the stomach. I was speechless with shock and dismay. I sat there for a moment, staring at Nguyet, utterly paralyzed by this turn of events. Pretty soon that shock and dismay turned to something more positive and certainly more productive. I got mad.

"Where's the doctor?" I demanded of Nguyet. "Who told you this? Go get him. I want to see him."

She pointed to the curtain.

"Does he speak English? Find someone who speaks English." This was incredible. I was actually behaving as if I knew what I was doing. Actually, I was just marking time. What could I tell this woman? What could I do for her?

Fortunately, we found a young doctor who not only could speak English but who was sympathetic to Nguyet's case. The mental-health clinic she had to go back to—to start Roan-na's examinations all over again—was in a completely different part of Saigon, and since it was impossible to telephone the clinic (no telephones) and make an appointment, I asked the doctor if he would write a note detailing the problem on the back of her health form and request an immediate appointment for a new evaluation. He agreed, and while Nguyet and Roan-na ditched their blue robes, he wrote the note. We flew out of the hospital, jumped into two cyclos, and sped off to the mental-health clinic. Appropriately enough, considering what the Vietnamese authorities think of any emotional, psychological, or mental problems, it was located right next to a garbage dump.

Now, my old Irish mother went to her grave firmly believing in guardian angels. I, however, became quite cynical very early in my life and tossed guardian angels onto the dust heap along with the tooth fairy and the Easter bunny. The luck of the Irish? Get real. But something was working in our favor that day. Would you believe: at that Vietnamese mental-health clinic there just happened to be an American psychiatrist in from the State Department's processing center in Bangkok? Further, he was evaluating patients. And, best yet, he agreed to hand-carry his recommendations back to Bangkok with him, which would greatly speed their processing. Without knowing any of that, however, at the clinic I scratched out a request for an interview, which I tucked into my passport and gave to someone to take somewhere and give to someone. I still didn't know what the hell I was doing, but Nguyet was so distraught by this time I figured I had to do something. Giving my passport to a total stranger whose only connection with the clinic was that she was wearing a white coat seemed appropriate at the time. She could have been a cook for all I knew. Or a patient. Or a very lucky

Vietnamese woman who would soon leave the country under the unlikely moniker of Kathyrn Ann Kelly, born in Omaha, Nebraska, in 1936.

Well, within seconds a large American psychiatrist came into the room and was immediately set upon by two women babbling furiously and waving bits of paper under his nose. He didn't know what hit him. His only out was to schedule an immediate appointment with Roan-na. Which he did. Nobody was more surprised than I was.

Roan-na, usually cheerful and placid, seemed reluctant to go upstairs for her reexamination. When we got into the evaluation room, I could see why: Vietnamese psychiatrists wear Army uniforms. I could imagine Roan-na's reaction when she had that initial interview of hers, over a year ago. We were ushered into a cramped room and seated at a large table that took up most of the space. We sat down and were immediately confronted by this glowering mass of khaki uniforms. It was beginning to look like an inquisition. Or a pre-Miranda grilling. Fortunately, the American psychiatrist conducted the interview. And he was, as Nguyet later put it: "Good man. He good man." He very quietly questioned Roan-na. Checked to see if she could count to ten (she got a little confused), knew the difference between a chicken and a pig (she did), and could carry on a conversation (she could). Then he asked her what she did all day.

"I go to movies," Roan-na replied immediately. The Communists all got I-told-you-so looks on their faces and began whispering to each other.

"Who did you go to the movies with?" the psychiatrist asked.

"Oh, I go alone." Roan-na was beaming by this time. The uniformed psychiatrists buzzed again, then glared at Nguyet. The implication was clear: to them she was a bad mother. I could see the iron in Nguyet's spine stiffen and then kick into action. You simply do not cast aspersions on mothers like this. In a move worthy of an international diplomat, she pointedly ignored the Vietnamese authorities and nailed the American doctor with a look that could pierce steel. Eyes glistening, she quietly told him her story in Vietnamese, which was translated into English for him: that after the war, she was a single mother with six children to raise. That she sold cigarettes on the street corner outside the Rex Hotel to earn enough money to keep her family together. That she put her kids in school and kept them there as long as she could. But because Roan-na had been hounded from school because she was not only an American but a black child as well, she would take her along with her to her cigarette stand in front of the Rex Hotel. There was a cinema right next to the hotel, and Nguyet knew everybody who worked there. And they let Roan-na in to go to the movies to pass the time.

"Roan-na good girl," Nguyet reassured the panel firmly. "She good girl. She want go school. She no can. She like movies, so I let her go movies."

Upshot: the American psychiatrist not only treated Roan-na and Nguyet with respect and kindness, but he upgraded Roan-na's original diagnosis of "severely retarded" to "mildly retarded."

"Oh, Kelly—I so happy!" Nguyet said. "Now, Roan-na has mental health. That good." We all celebrated by going across the road and having fried-egg sandwiches and fizzy orange soda pop. It had been another good day. Now we all had mental health.

Nguyet had become one of my best friends in Saigon. Although we were almost exactly the same age, if Vietnam has Jewish mothers and Irish women can qualify to have them, she was mine. She was my bowl of chicken soup. She worried and fussed over me constantly. And periodically she had good reason to.

One day, my friend Tien invited me to his home for lunch. Tien was the director of the English school where I went three nights a week. The lunch was a joyous family affair celebrating the return of Tien's eldest son from America. Seven years before, Tien had put two of his sons—then aged ten and sixteen—onto a boat and sent them sailing off into the void that was the South China Sea. He hoped the voyage would eventually take them to America. They spent two years in a Malaysian refugee camp but finally they got to America. They had done well, were both in college, and now the eldest was coming home to visit for the first time. The family graciously invited me to attend a party in his honor.

It was a sumptuous, joyful affair. Everybody was there: Tien, his other children, aunts, uncles, cousins. There were toasts and tears and great food that the women had spent hours preparing in honor of this son's return from America. And when that delicious home-cooked food was proudly put on the table, I smiled and got up and walked to the doorway, stuck my head out into the courtyard, and threw up all over the family dog.

Something had obviously gotten to me, but fortunately nobody paid the slightest bit of attention to me and my behavior. Nobody was going to embarrass me much less interrupt the proceedings of this joyous, overstuffed family meal and make a big deal out of the fact that I had just barfed all over the dog. One of the women did slip me a vial of that magic elixir that everybody in Vietnam delicately dabs on every ailment from cuts to cancer. To me it smells suspiciously like Vicks Vapo-rub. Then, when the meal was over, they loaded me in the back of an old panel truck they had scrounged up from someone in the neighborhood and took me back to my hotel so I wouldn't have to bounce home in a cyclo.

I staggered into the Kim Do, hauled my body up to the top floor, and with my stomach as lumpy as the mattress, I sighed and stretched myself out on the bed. I was looking forward to simply passing out for the night. I was also feeling dreadfully sorry for myself. Then they started showing up. Concerned friends from all over Saigon who had heard about my plight began arriving at my door. And of course Nguyet and Roan-na were the first. Somehow Saigon's Rumor Central, the most efficient operation in Saigon, had activated itself and put the word out: She's sick. She threw up all over somebody's dog. The two of them arrived with pained expressions on their faces and bags of fresh fruit in their hands. Then they both kicked their shoes off and crawled onto the bed with me.

"How you feel, Miss Katie?" Nguyet asked, holding my hand. Mine looked like a bear paw next to hers. I mumbled something incoherent. Then Linh arrived with some bananas. He was followed by Bui, who was quickly followed by a couple of Amerasians. They all crowded into my room and took up their positions. My bed was fairly full by this time. Indeed, I had to struggle a little to maintain my position on it, but with a gentle nudge and a prod, I was pretty much able to carve out a little territory for myself, although Linh's foot did get a little heavy on my ankle there for a while.

"How do you say 'I threw up!' in Vietnamese?" I demanded weakly. Would that be the hint that finally bopped them over the head? The one that would encourage them to leave? I was feeling very sorry for myself.

"*Toi oi!*" they chorused back.

"Well—*toi oi!*" I mumbled. "*Toi* very much *oi.*"

Fortunately, they all kept each other pretty well entertained. In fact, they would forget about me for long stretches of time. Periodically, I would get up and stagger to the bathroom and throw up, then wobble back, push through the crowd, and get back into bed. I felt like my Grandma Doyle: an Irish woman laid out at her own wake. This went on for the better part of an hour, and while I hated to break up such a swell party, finally, in a weak voice, I took matters into my own hands. I simply asked them to leave.

"Oh, O.K., Miss Katie. We go now," Nguyet said with a smile, pushing people toward the door. "You rest, be quiet, tomorrow you be Number One again." Then she turned and looked at me. "You know, Miss Katie—not good you have so many people here when you sick. Goodbye for now." And then they all left. And I went back to bed surrounded by banana peels, orange rinds, and fruit pits. I found the mess oddly comforting.

New York might have seven million people but it invites a kind of solitude. We all learn to put a little distance between ourselves and the next guy, who could be anyone from a serial killer to someone plotting a leveraged buyout. Here it was different. Very different. Families are not only extended, but so is society. And it is very inclusive. There is no such thing as a table for one in Vietnam. Indeed, the very concept of privacy as we know it does not exist in Vietnam. And for somebody like me—an only child, a divorced woman—who grew up with privacy as her birthright to be jealously guarded over the expanse of a lifetime, this openness was new. We might bang on each other's screen doors in Albion, Nebraska, but in New York City those doors had triple locks, even socially. Let's do lunch sounds simple enough but it would produce all sorts of consultations and intricate schedule jugglings just to have a simple lunch or dinner or movie. But this—this was different. And I liked it. Most of the time.

Some of the time it quite honestly drove me nuts. Since there were no telephones—and no answering machines to screen your calls—the direct approach was always taken: someone would just appear in the lobby and sit and wait, sometimes for hours. I would come back to the Kim Do all hot and sweaty and want nothing more than to stagger up those three long flights of stairs, hurl some obscenities at a few bats, and take a shower. But there would be Hung or Linh or Nguyet or someone. And they would smile and grab my hand and say, "Hi. We wait for you. So good to see you. How are you?" Now I ask you: who could resist that? I tell you: not I.

The Great Kim Do Upgrade (Cont'd): I staggered down to breakfast the day after my *toi oi*. I was still a little woozy but I made it down the three flights of stairs to the lobby. Hey. Wait a minute. What's wrong with this picture? Something was missing. It was the lobby. Who took the lobby? Where is it? I blinked. Once. Twice. I looked around like a crazy woman. I looked to the right of me. It was gone. I looked to the left of me. It was still gone. Oh, you wild and crazy Vietnamese. You wacky, fun-loving Communists. What did you do with the lobby, you silly things? I wasn't alone in my confusion. There were about a half-dozen other hotel guests milling around down there, peering this way and that.

"Hey! You come in here! Now!"

We looked over and saw a door that had not been there yesterday. Miss Congeniality was standing there, her *ao dai* fluttering delicately around her legs. In my still-woozy state she seemed almost—well, I don't want to overstate the case—but she seemed almost human. She was holding the door open, motioning at us. And what was that on her face? Could it really be—a smile?

We walked through the door. It was like Dorothy going from black-and-white to Technicolor. It was like a wonderland, Auntie Em. It was definitely not Kansas. Overnight, a new lobby had materialized where before only . . . who knows what had been there. All I know is that it ran adjacent to the parking lot–clock shop that had been the lobby only hours before. What was now the new Kim Do lobby had been completely blocked off and closed up before. I guess I had seen it but figured it was just a place to store rubble.

But now—now this! A real lobby. O.K., so it was a sea of yellow linoleum-covered furniture. Look over there! There were proper display cases for souvenir items that would soon be sold. And there! There was a bar in the corner. (We knew this because of the intricate arrangement of empty Heineken cans rising nearly to the ceiling.) There was even a swinging glass door. And a real air-conditioner! Can you believe it!

As time went on it became painfully apparent that this was really the Potemkin Village of hotel lobbies: the display cases remained empty, the only things to be seen in them a growing collection of dead and decaying insect life. The bar—presided over twenty-four hours a day by that towering pyramid of empty beer cans and later a bust of Ho Chi Minh—appeared to be open only between the hours of 6:30 A.M. and 7 A.M. That was when the person who obviously lived behind it got up and began getting ready for the day: stretching, smoking, hawking, and spitting up a nighttime accumulation of whatever it is Asian men accumulate in their bodies that has to be hauled up like toxic sludge and then spit out on the nearest available floor. The swinging glass door had nothing to do with the door frame it was stuck into, and kept screeching on the tile floor every time it was shoved open or shut. Hotel guests, who would adhere to the yellow plastic as soon as they sat down in the chairs, could be seen by everyone outside on

Nguyen Hue Street clapping their hands over their ears whenever anyone opened the door. To the passers-by outside we appeared to be screaming silently, like people trapped in an Edvard Munch drawing.

The air-conditioner was very efficient though. It kept things at or below freezing, although periodically it would spit up all over everyone, sending slivers of icy water splashing down on unsuspecting guests.

Miss Congeniality seemed to be enjoying all of this.

"You comfortable?" she would cry gleefully.

Teeth chattering, ears ringing, we would all nod ferociously.

ON THE BEACH

Now, generally I don't like going to the beach. Any beach. For one thing, I don't tan, I burn. In Tibet I burned right through No. 36 skinblock and weeks later was still leaving large portions of my face on the towels in Katmandu. Moreover, the idea of lying on a beach oiled like a Perdue fryer, only to be threatened with a sunburn today and skin cancer tomorrow, always seemed pretty boring to me. But it was hot and humid in Saigon. And so it was decided that a refreshing trip to the sea was in order. And Vung Tau, a hugely popular resort town on the South China Sea about two hours northeast of Saigon, was the beach of choice.

The town of Vung Tau itself was built primarily as a playground for the rich during the French period. They called it Cap St. Jacques. During the Vietnam War Vung Tau was both a popular R & R spot for American troops and an enormous American supply base as well. I had been to Vung Tau on my first visit, and in my mind's eye it was less a place to work on my sunburn than the perfect place to relax.

The day I had spent there on my first trip, in December of 1988, was wonderful. The beach was almost completely deserted. Rows of empty chairs and umbrellas stood in a silent line in the soft sand that edged the incredible blue of the water. Vendors carrying pole baskets full of steamed crabs and cold beer patrolled the beach. My own solitary stroll was interrupted by an invitation to join a family party in progress. We were among a few people there that day and I spent a thoroughly pleasant couple of hours eating fresh steamed crabs and drinking cold beer with total strangers all under the sheltering protection of a big beach umbrella.

Yes, a quiet excursion to a nearly deserted beach sounded like a good idea. I could sit under an umbrella under a palm tree under my industrial-strength sunblock while communing with nature (translation: I could take long naps undisturbed by motorbikes, loud noises, or flying bats). Additionally, I could intellectually refresh myself (translation: an American leaving Saigon had given me an entire paperback library of Louis L'Amour westerns). So, obviously overwhelmed and finally overcome with visions of palm trees and white sand and warm crab and cold beer, I decided to make an excursion of it and take some of the kids along. Some days I am dumber than on other days. This was one of them.

Now in addition to those rattletrap Czechoslovakian buses that belch and snort their way around Saigon, there was also a small fleet of brand-new eight-passenger minivans that made the trip to Vung Tau each day for about a dollar each way. I figured I could pack eight of us into a van and we'd go down for an overnight stay with me as the chaperone. So I broached the idea one morning during a meeting of the Breakfast Club.

"Oh, wow!" they all yelled. I took that as a yes. So we got down to the intricate business of making plans for our invasion of Vung Tau. I took a typically American attitude, invoking the fairness doctrine and incorporating all our odd notions about the equality of the sexes, figuring we could divide things up evenly: four boys and four girls. Then, if the initial trip was successful, we could repeat it over and over until everyone had a chance to take to the waters. They took a typically Asian attitude: the girls got all silly and giggled and blushed and held back and finally refused to have anything to do with the plan whatsoever. The guys could care less about quotas or equality of the sexes or even-handedness or anything else. So it was settled: they were going to the beach.

The chosen few ended up being Bryner, Jim, Pearl, Vu, and Linh. And the plan was this: Vu would meet me at the hotel at 5:30 in the morning and then take me to the rendezvous point, where we would meet the others. Then we would all catch the 6 A.M. bus, which would put us into Vung Tau about 8 A.M. After finding a hotel and checking in, we would be on the beach by 8:30. What a terrific plan. Whose great idea was this anyway?

First of all, I forgot about Saigon Time. Saigon Time is a lot like Moroccan Time or Greek Time or Mexican Time or Egyptian Time. All of which are a lot like Scarlett O'Hara Time: tomorrow. And tomorrow is not only another day, but eight o'clock is a lot like nine o'clock, which is very much like ten o'clock when you stop to think about it. Sit down. Relax. Have some tea? One moment please. Come back later. Americans, Canadians, a few Japanese, and a handful of misguided countries in the European Common Market are the only people in the world who have actually been known to go out and meet time head-on. Very confrontational. Vietnam is simply like the rest of the world, to whom time is simply something that you sidle up to as if you didn't want to startle it. Which explains why I was sitting on my haunches in front of the Kim Do Hotel at five-thirty in the morning.

All of which meant, of course, that first I had to get out of the hotel, which turned into more of a production than I had thought it would be. As I staggered through the darkened lobby I could feel vague stirring noises all around me. Imagine my surprise when I discovered they were people. They were the hotel workers, sleeping all over the place. Imagine my next surprise, when I discovered we were all locked in. They actually locked us all into the hotel at a certain hour. I guess I'd never gotten in late enough or up early enough to have found this out before. I woke somebody up and he had to laboriously push aside the solid metal grate that covered the doorway, which went up with a series of shudders and screeches. As I watched the Kim Do tomb being unsealed, I tried not to think about raging fires sweeping through that wooden tinderbox, roaring up that old wooden staircase, and frying hundreds of bats on its way straight to my room on the top floor.

Saigon at five-thirty in the morning is breathless and still as if it is just catching its breath, recovering from the day before and anticipating the one that is about to arrive. The silence is remarkable and beautiful. I squatted down on the sidewalk, waiting for Vu to arrive. The handsome older woman who sold candy and peanuts in front of the Kim Do was sleeping on her old plastic chaise longue, a large towel thrown over her head for privacy. During the day when she napped she tossed a washcloth over her face. I guess she didn't need as much privacy during those daytime naps as she did at night when she was down for the longer snooze. She had obviously spent the night. Did she live there? I could only guess she did.

Without the horrors of daytime traffic in downtown Saigon, the streets were nearly deserted, and there was a spirited soccer match underway at the intersection in front of the hotel. Up and down Nguyen Hue Street, joggers sped by in the early coolness. They were all barefoot.

I squatted there watching an old lady start a fire in her small pottery stove, then put a blackened, battered aluminum kettle on to boil. The stove was crudely made out of local clay and had a Coca-Cola can cut up and secured around the bottom to keep it from breaking and cracking. You could also get those little stoves with Heineken bottoms or Fanta bottoms, but I was assured that Coke was the can of choice. I looked at the big clock that topped the ornate face of Communist party headquarters at the top of Nguyen Hue Street. I noticed with American precision that five-thirty had come and gone and six o'clock—our departure time—was fast approaching. And I'll admit: I was getting a bit antsy.

I know it's bad form, but I'm always on time. In fact, I'm a real Midwesterner when it comes to being on time. No matter what time I'm told to be at a dinner party, that's when I arrive. Over the years, because of my prompt arrival, I have read thousands of magazines and listened to hundreds of people take showers. My dad would always get us all up at five-thirty on Sunday morning so we could leave the house at six o'clock so we wouldn't be late for seven o'clock mass and communion down at St. Michael's Church. St. Michael's was all of five blocks from our house. Five short blocks.

I glanced back up at the clock on Party Headquarters. It was now precisely 6 A.M. Departure time. And then I did an amazing thing. I shrugged. And continued watching the woman at her charcoal stove. The water was beginning to boil and she offered me a cup of tea. I accepted. And as I squatted there on the sidewalk watching our departure time come—and then go—it occurred to me that, despite being a bit antsy and anxious, I was being surprisingly calm about all this. Then it slowly dawned on me that before or after class I could often be found placidly sitting around for hours on end just like this, talking and schmoozing and gossiping and just generally wasting time. I would spontaneously drop down on my haunches right on the sidewalk to chat if I ran into someone I knew. I could often be caught strolling up and down these by-now-familiar streets, stopping here and there to talk with shopkeepers and stall owners and old guys just hanging around on their motorcycles. How odd. Was that really me, sitting patiently for manicures I not only didn't need but didn't really want simply because someone wanted to "souvenir" me with yet another coat of pink glitter polish and I didn't want to be rude and say no?

I had to admit that even my step was slowing down. I didn't walk as fast as usual. For one thing, I couldn't. It was so hot and humid I would have melted down to a minuscule glob of sweat within minutes. So these days I strolled. I sauntered. I meandered. I even kept my mouth shut. This may have been forced on me simply because of the language barrier, but for someone who earned her living by shooting off her big mouth, this was a welcome change indeed. I no longer had to listen to myself talk. And neither did anyone else, for that matter.

There was also something totally relaxing about no telephones. No TV. No mail. And for a while anyway, no news really was good news. In my Vietnam-induced time warp, it took weeks for Saddam Hussein to invade Kuwait. To the American public, that invasion might have occurred almost instantaneously on the evening news, but for me it didn't start until a couple of weeks later when *Time* magazine finally got to the newstand. And by that time there wasn't a damn thing I could do about it. Or anything else, for that matter. For a whole year I couldn't do anything about the hole in the ozone or the world's population problems or the disappearing wetlands. For a whole year, I couldn't even do anything about myself. Imagine—a whole year without pantyhose. Now there's real relaxation. I may have found the true meaning of Women's Liberation.

Ah, but enough's enough. And after forty-five minutes even the New Me had tired of this waiting-around thing. Our rendezvous time of five-thirty was history. Six o'clock had come and gone, and still no sign of Vu. I was kissing six-fifteen goodbye and pacing the sidewalk in front of the Kim Do, frantic about our excursion to Vung Tau, when Vu suddenly appeared in a cyclo.

"Hi! We go!" he said with a grin on his face.

"Vu! The bus leaves at six o'clock!" I frantically pointed at his watch. "Bus! Six o'clock!" It was now six-twenty, and by my calculations, the bus was already minus us plus twenty minutes down the road by this time.

"Yes! Six o'clock!" he agreed, still smiling. "Good! Good!"

Yeah, right. Good. Good. At least he was improving. He could tell time in English now. Not that it did any good, mind you. I was having a serious attitude attack. I was also ready to belt Vu. I squeezed into the cyclo and we took off down the street with me mumbling to myself. After about five minutes the cyclo slowed down and Vu jumped down. "O.K., Teacher. Get out now." We were unloaded on a deserted sidewalk with not a minivan or a collection of Amerasians in sight.

"Here?" I asked. Yes, sometimes I can be as dumb as gravel. Today you could hear the loose chunks rattling through my head.

"Yes. Here. We wait."

"Wait for what?" I asked. The end of the world? The great flood? I think I was pouting by this time. Because by this time it was well after 6:30 A.M. I had visions of an excursion bus full of happy campers barreling down the highway to Vung Tau. Without us.

"O.K., Teacher. Now we go." Vu was smiling happily and gathering up our belongings, including a tote bag I had filled with French bread, a jar of peanut butter hauled over from New York City, and a few packages of La Vache Qui Rie (The Laughing Cow), which is not only the world's worst processed cheese but its sturdiest. It is the only cheese in the world that can exist for centuries in direct sunlight with temperatures hitting 100 degrees Fahrenheit or more. Those little round cardboard wheels of Laughing Cows can be found baking and simmering in the hot sun on just about every street-corner cigarette and chewing-gum stand in Saigon.

Then I looked up and through my pout I saw a brand-new white minivan pulling to a stop in front of us. The doors flew back and four very familiar young men tumbled out. Bryner, Jim, Pearl, and Linh were all dressed up in their best beach gear: clean T-shirts and clean shorts. Jim was wearing someone's cast-off Izod shirt with a pair of khaki walking shorts. He looked like something out of a Gap advertisement. Unfortunately, he had pulled his tube socks all the way to his knees, which made him resemble a suburban mailman. Linh was wearing a new blue T-shirt brought in by a tourist from Canada. And it was very special to Linh: it was not only new to him—it was *new* period. No one else had ever worn it. Pearl fell out looking like the chairman of a fraternity hospitality committee. He was smiling broadly and holding a battered guitar.

Seems they had all gotten to the rendezvous point on time. Vu had been dispatched to pick me up, and the driver had been told to wait. When we didn't show up at the appointed hour of 6 A.M. they just told the driver to go to the hotel and get me. Our paths had obviously crossed somewhere so the van came back to wait for us. No problem. No problem. They all piled into the back of the van, along with a few patient Vietnamese passengers, who seemed to take this kind of scheduling folderol in stride. I was ushered into the front and given the seat of honor (a/k/a The Death Seat). A woman holding a big, fat baby sat in the middle seat. Given the way most people drive in Vietnam and considering the road hazards (potholes the size of small villages, water buffaloes big enough to stop a Scud missile, and armies of small children and dogs wandering haphazardly into the roads), I had visions of that child being launched like a ballistic missile through the windshield. Then I noticed that there didn't seem to be any seat belts for any of us. I pointed this out to the driver, but he was very reassuring.

"No problem," he said with a shake of his head and a big smile. "No problem." Then he threw the van into gear and we shot off, the four of us sliding around dangerously on the front seat. I was horrified. Then I turned and made a final head count: there were fifteen people in that eight-passenger van. They all smiled and waved cheerfully at me.

It was a fairly uneventful trip up to Vung Tau. The baby, who resembled a drooling Happy Buddha wearing a T-shirt, was incredibly well behaved. Although just as I was wondering if these non-diaper-wearing babies ever have any accidents he peed all over my leg and then sprayed the front windshield.

"No problem!" the driver reassured us all with a big smile. "No problem!"

After about an hour I remembered that none of my crowd had had anything to eat, so I called back to remind the kids there was food in one of my tote bags. I also wanted to order up a peanut butter sandwich.

"No problem, teacher," Pearl reassured me happily. "We love Sloan's Crunchy Peanut Butter." They had cleaned out the entire jar of peanut butter.

As we got closer more and more palm trees came into view. Sand began appearing along the roadside. Then the sharp tang of salt air bit into the air. It seemed a bit warm but I figured what the heck. With fifteen people jammed into an eight-passenger van, it was bound to feel a bit toasty. I just chalked it up to overcrowding. Meanwhile, I couldn't wait to feel more of those refreshingly tangy ocean breezes. To relax under the shade of a palm tree and observe the endless expanse of sea and shore and sky. I wanted to loaf around under a load of sunblock and watch the world pass by.

Oh, now, this looks good, I said to myself as we pulled into a courtyard. We seemed to be in a brand-new resort complex. It was small and quiet and tidy. There were palm trees waving in the breeze and flowers growing in profusion. And across the road you could actually see the beach and the ocean. Already I could see myself lolling in a beach chair. Already I could feel the sand between my toes.

As we all piled out, the driver reassured us he would be back to pick us up the next afternoon for the return trip to Saigon. Everyone in the van waved goodbye and I went in to register, telling the hotel clerk we would need three rooms: two for the guys and one for me. This was a government hotel and, as usual, it was on a two-tier price system: foreigners (anyone with hard currency) paid twice what Vietnamese or Russians or anyone else from the socialist world paid with their internationally worthless and otherwise unwanted dongs and rubles and zlotys.

"You want AC?" the clerk asked. I ducked. I couldn't help it. It was pure reflex. It sounded like she was clearing her throat, about ready to spit. I thought for a moment Miss Congeniality might have a relative here in Vung Tau.

"I don't understand," I said.

"You want AC? Air conditioning?"

I told her it wasn't necessary. A nice ceiling fan would do.

"O.K., great. I give you AC." I couldn't help it. I ducked again. As for the AC, I didn't pursue it any further.

A cleaning woman put down her broom, rounded up our keys, and shuffled slowly across the road with the six of us trailing behind, lugging our backpacks, one of which now contained an empty peanut-butter jar. It was only eight-thirty in the morning but I noticed that the sun was already blinding. I didn't remember the sun being so bright the last time I was here. Of course the last time I was here it was December. The hot season. This was June. The hotter season. As we walked through that overwhelming light I had a world-class perspiration breakthrough. Funny, I thought to myself. I don't remember being this, er, damp before. It eventually came back to me: December was the wet season. This was still June, the wetter season. It didn't take major surgery on the by-now half-baked and nonfunctioning portions of my brain to tell me that hot and wet equal humid and that does not spell relief no matter how much you fiddle with it. Boy. I couldn't wait to get to my room and turn on the AC. Or just sit under the fan, whichever came first.

We walked past a swimming pool, empty except for those three dead animals huddled at one end. What could they be? Big rats? Small dogs? Lunch? We staggered up some torturously white steps and across a rooftop terrace, also freshly painted an eye-searing white. If I squinted hard enough I could see that the terrace offered a panoramic view of the beach and the South China Sea. Other vacationing fun seekers, who had obviously come up to the terrace for that breathtaking ocean view and the photo opportunity it presented, were also lurching across that white expanse, clutching their eyes in a desperate attempt to protect them from the pain of the reflected light. One of them slammed directly into me. We both went reeling. She was so disoriented I had to help her up. All around me I could hear people spinning and smacking into one another as the bright sun took its toll. Nobody said a word. There was just dead silence punctuated by a series of dull thuds and thumps as the bodies collided with one another. By the time we all made it across the terrace, the body count was alarming. I was glad to be swallowed up by the darkness of the hallway.

The cleaning woman held out the fistful of keys she was armed with, gestured to a series of rooms, and left. None of the keys were marked or numbered in any way, but then again—what difference would that have made? None of the doors were numbered either. As the morning wore on and the heat mounted, we all engaged in an act of sheer desperation: trying to match the right key with the right door. After about fifteen minutes we realized that what we had actually been doing was locking all the doors, so we had to go back to the beginning and start all over again. Finally, after a half hour or so we matched keys to doors and began sorting ourselves out.

The Russian air-conditioners in the rooms had ceased to function years before. Unfortunately, with the installation of those socialist monuments to inefficiency the authorities had ripped out all the ceiling fans. Mine now dangled like a taunt, a threat, over my bed. Not a breath of air stirred the humid heat that was likewise hanging in the rooms. Oddly enough, in a touch of first-class sophistication, each room did have a small courtesy fridge stocked with ice cubes, two Cokes, and a bottle of water. And everything was actually cold. Meanwhile, out in the hall the communal toilet had stopped up, probably about the same time the air-conditioners had broken down. As the day wore on, the smell rose in direct proportion to the temperature-humidity index. It was only the thought of that air-cooled beach that kept me going.

I had forgotten to pack my bathing suit but who cared. Not me. I was just going to sit under an umbrella in the shade of a palm tree, remember? We all held on to each other and made it safely across that white terrace, down those white stairs, then ran down to the beach through the sand. Actually, we had to run because the sand was so hot it burned right through the soles of our shoes. A few

minutes in the hot ocean water, though, and our feet cooled down
enough so we could continue our assault on the beach.

Linh rounded up the chairs and beach umbrellas, Bryner found
a few small tables, while Jim located some inner tubes that could be
rented for a very small fee. Vu just stood around sighing and pro-
claiming everything to be "Good! Good!" Pearl had disappeared
immediately but would return periodically with some bikini-clad
beauty in tow. He worked that beach like a Hollywood agent working a room. While everyone disappeared into the water, I made
myself comfortable, waiting for cool breezes to waft my way. Funny
—the more I sat there, the more uncomfortable I became. I wiped
my face. I wiped my arms. I wiped my legs. I was sitting under the
shade of an umbrella, on a beach hotter than any place I had ever
been in my life. Slowly the horrible realization began to dawn on
me: there was not a breath of air stirring. And what air there was
in Vung Tau was heavy and oppressive and stultifying. The place
was boiling hot. About as refreshing as a lobster pot.

Periodically, I would totter down to the water and soak down
my legs in a vain and desperate attempt to cool off. It didn't work.
All I did was get my underpants wet. Meanwhile, the humidity was
so awful nothing dried, and as a result I sat around the rest of the
day in wet, salty underwear. I was quite sure I had never been so
uncomfortable and so miserable in my life. It got worse. I hadn't
brought a complete change of clothing with me—just a lot of
T-shirts. So the khaki jump suit I waded into the water with was the
same one I had to wear that night to the disco. And it was there I
discovered to my dismay that the salt water had dried in just such
a way as to leave a damp-looking ring on my seat.

Meanwhile the empty, deserted beach of my first visit was
nothing like this overcrowded, claustrophobic mess. Buses would
snort up and heave hundreds of people out onto the sand. One
section of the beach had been taken over by dozens of huge Russians, who had hunkered down, displaying what had to be the
world's supply of blinding white flesh. It rolled off into the distance
as far as the eye could see. Compared to the Vietnamese, they were
gigantic. Monstrous. It was like dropping a rock in a full glass of
water: if just one Russian hit the beach, an entire multigenerational
Vietnamese family would be displaced by the plop.

Periodically, one of the Gang of Five would rush up to explain
enthusiastically all the good times they were having. I restrained
myself from belting them. I was too weak. The only thing I was

looking forward to was lunch. I began daydreaming of cold Coca-Colas, cold coffee, cold food, cold COLD!

About this time Bryner ran up and plopped down beside me. He was all wet and covered with sand. I asked him if he was having fun and he smiled and nodded. We talked back and forth about nothing in particular. The weather. The beach. Vu's sunburn. Pearl's skinny white legs. Jim's white, hairy legs. Out of the corner of my eye I could see Pearl laughing and glad-handing his way up and down the beach, while next to me, Bryner was sitting quietly.

Then it hit me with a jolt: these two kids were me. Both sides of my own personal coin. Pearl was my goofy, bright side, letting a smile carry him through his rough spots. Bryner, on the other hand, was my shady side. Not dark or grim or gloomy—just out of the sunlight. Over the months we had known each other, I noticed how he would sit in the midst of things and withdraw from his surroundings. Gather in his own self and tuck it away so others wouldn't notice it or bother it. He was friendly but basically shy, outgoing when he wanted to be or when he felt he knew someone well enough to relax his grip and let go of some little part of himself. He could also be moody, going into sulks and pouts and silent, interior storms that no one could pull him out of. At those times I could almost feel him fighting those interior battles with himself. I did it with myself. I could feel him talking, arguing, reasoning, wrestling with himself, and—finally—breaking loose from whatever had grabbed onto him and held him so tightly, so he could emerge and join the rest of us again. Sometimes it was scary. It was like watching myself. We were so alike we could have been the same person. He could be me. Or my kid brother. Part of my family.

There are those who believe we each have a psychic double somewhere in the world. Could whole families have one as well? Could this be ours? A Kelly, disguised as an Amerasian sitting on a beach in South Vietnam? Could we have overlooked him at some point? Misplaced him somewhere along the line? My family was so big that at family gatherings we were always taking inventory to make sure the right kid went home with the right family. Sometimes we slipped up. When I was a kid, Sunday afternoons meant Kelly family visits with kids and moms and dads stacked in happy confusion all over the place. And every once in a while, when it was time to go home, someone slipped out of the family grip and got left behind. But things would sort themselves out the next Sunday and Pat or Mike or Sharon would end up with the right family again. Is that what happened here? Was this one ours, a Kelly kid we had somehow misplaced who ended up in Vietnam?

As I sat there on the sand pondering all this, I looked over at Bryner and noticed something I hadn't seen before. He had a thick scar up near his eye. I asked him how he got it.

"Remember? I tell you at Jim's house, about when I was a little boy?" he said. I nodded while he collected his thoughts, gathered his English words together. "In 1975, when I was a little boy, and my mother does not want me? I go to the countryside and work for the farmers? Remember?" I nodded my head again. "I go near Tay Ninh." Tay Ninh was truly in the countryside, out near the Cambodian border, in fact.

"How did you get there?" I asked. In 1975 Bryner was only eight years old.

"I take a cow."

"You took a cow?" I was thinking in terms of transportation so this didn't make much sense to me.

He nodded. "Sure. I take a cow for a farmer. Someone tell me I can take a cow, get some money. You know—a job."

"Oh. O.K. So you deliver a cow to a farm in the countryside. And the farmer gives you a job." He nodded back at me. "What did you do there? What was your job?"

He thought for a while, then he reached over and grabbed a stick. He smoothed out the hot sand in front of him, and I watched him draw a portion of his life in the sand in front of me. It was a little boy, wearing a cone hat, sitting on top of a water buffalo. The buffalo was huge, its horns flaring out from the side of its head. The little boy, perched like a small bird on top of that massive beast, was Bryner.

"That my job," he said pointing to the water buffalo. "I work." He fumbled for the right words. "Rice. Rice." I looked down at the drawing. As a small eight-year-old American boy he wore a cone hat and sat on top of a water buffalo and worked in the rice fields. He did it to save his life. "First, I just take care of these big cows. Later, when I am bigger, I work very hard. I cut grass to feed them." He demonstrated making bundles and bales of grass. "I carry them, here." He pointed to his shoulders. "Everything in Vietnam, done by hand."

I sat there, looking out over the South China Sea, wondering what eight-year-old boys in America were doing in 1975? Playing Little League baseball and riding their bicycles, I supposed.

* * *

I guess I nodded off a bit, but when I surfaced and wiped the veil of sweat from my eyes, I saw that most of the kids were sitting in front of me on the sand. A vendor with pole baskets full of eggs and cooking equipment had joined them there, likewise squatting in the shade of our umbrella. I figured the eggs were hard-boiled and offered to buy a round for us. Great. Jim immediately lopped the top off of his egg just as I was about to reach out and get one for myself. But wait. I noticed there was something gray floating and bobbing around in there. I was about to caution him against eating it when he jabbed a small spoon into the egg and put that wet, gray mass into his mouth and began chewing. Omigod. Is that a *feather* stuck to his teeth! I looked at all the other eggs and suddenly realized—those things aren't hard-boiled eggs. Those wet, gray things in there are *baby birds*! Little bird embryos. Bird fetuses. Feathers. Eyes. Beaks. These kids are eating little baby birds, their wet feathers stuck uselessly to their little wet boiled bodies.

To this day I'm not quite sure they understood why I suddenly shot up out of that beach chair and tore pell-mell down the sand. I cam back with an ice-cold Coca-Cola but it was less the pause that refreshes than the only excuse I could find for leaving quickly enough not to throw up all over everybody. I had stopped eating veal because I couldn't stand the idea of some cute little baby calf with its cold, wet nose and big eyes looking up at me from my dinner plate, thinly disguised as veal piccata. Same with Mary's Little Lamb. And deer. (What! Eat Bambi's mother? You must be kidding.) The idea of a live lobster thrashing around in a pot of hot water made me add that to my list. Even to this day, at odd moments, I wonder about those little deep-fried birds I met in Danang: were they dead before they hit the fat? And what about those little beach birds? Did they suffer much when they hit the water? If I had any courage at all I'd become a vegetarian. I came back from my unscheduled jaunt down the beach and sat there, sweating bullets, questioning my moral fiber, and trying to calm the rolling thunder in my stomach.

Then reality intruded. Real reality. Tragedy had struck: someone had stolen Linh's brand-new blue T-shirt right off his beach chair.

"It's not here, Mama," he said, turning all our beach gear out onto the sand. "It's not here." His face was absolutely stricken. Out of a string of hand-me-downs and secondhand clothes cast his way by departing tourists, he had lost his most prized possession: something brand new. I was heartbroken with him and for him. Fortunately, it knocked some sense into me and I stopped whining out loud about how hot and miserable I was. And for a moment I stopped worrying about baby calves and Bambi and unborn birds. Reality was often worse, even if it simply came in the form of a stolen T-shirt.

We never found Linh's T-shirt but we were lucky nonetheless: we found a beachside restaurant that had a huge pedestal fan. I wanted to spend the rest of my life there. The restaurant was big and airy and, with that fan flowing directly on me, I was actually quite comfortable. There were some enormous windows shaded by a large overhang. They were thrown open to a magnificent view of the water and the beach, and periodically a bit of a sea breeze would actually blow up and amble through. The guys gave lunch about fifteen minutes, then shot back down to the beach. Since there were no other customers in the restaurant, I stretched my part of lunch out for hours, just so I could sit in front of that fan. This didn't seem to bother the restaurant help at all. In fact, when lunch was over they all came out and joined me in the main part of the restaurant, falling asleep on the floor space under the windows. It wasn't quite what I had fantasized—spending my day at the beach sleeping it off with the kitchen help—but it was better than vaporizing down on the sand.

We had dinner in yet another deserted part of that resort complex. All those who had crowded onto the beach that day had obviously been day-trippers who had been shipped back to their places of origin as night fell. Dinner was a fairly comfortable affair. We had confiscated every portable fan in the place and were all lounging around just waiting for the evening's fun to begin: I'd promised them that trip to the disco. Suddenly Pearl turned his back on us and began doing—what's this? Mime routines? Yes. Turns out Pearl was a fabulous mime. His first one: man and woman kissing passionately. (For those of you who never made it to San Francisco during the late sixties and early seventies when it was the mime capital of the world, this is when the mime turns his back, puts his arms around himself, and runs his fingers up and down his own back so it looks like two people are locked in a passionate embrace and smooching like crazy.) We all fell on the floor.

He turned around with a big, self-satisfied grin on his beet-red face. "That Pearl," Jim said admiringly. "His face gets very red." He was blushing like crazy. Pearl then went on to do some classic mime routines: walking, running, flying a kite, tripping over invisible objects, death, sadness. He was wonderful. He was a one-man Shields & Yarnell. Even the kitchen help came out to watch and applauded like crazy every time he wound up a routine.

"Pearl! You are terrific!" I said.

"Yes! Yes!" he agreed, nodding his head.

"Where did you learn how to do that?"

"Oh, I learn my home."

Bryner leaned in to amplify that explanation. "When Pearl little boy, he live next to . . ." They all went into conference on the missing word. Fortunately, someone in this gang was always packing a dictionary, so the word was quickly found. "He live next to theatre. He go in."

Seems that at one point in his childhood Pearl had indeed lived next to a theatre. And that theatre had a mime troupe in residence. And Pearl, that little American boy, would sneak in and watch the mimes rehearsing. Pretty soon, he knew all their routines. He was also blessed with a natural theatrical flair. A few months later, when some of us were relaxing at the Rex Hotel, Pearl launched into his routine in front of a group of Australian businessmen. They were ready to pitch money at him. I thought how badly these kids had been used and what wasted talents some of them obviously had. Pearl was a mime. Bryner liked to draw. Linh was nearly fluent in English. Vu played the guitar. What else was there within them— and all the others—that was being wasted? How could a government—no matter how hateful and vindictive and vengeful—waste brains and creativity and initiative like this? Allow these qualities to die just because these young people were Americans?

Pearl proudly took me out to meet his mother one day. They lived miles from downtown Saigon. And they lived on the kindness of strangers: Pearl and his mother shared their corrugated tin lean-to attached to the house of a family friend. The household—the usual extended Vietnamese family—had absorbed the two of them completely. Pearl considered the boys in the family his "brothers" and the matriarch was likewise his "grandmother."

Pearl's mother was a lovely woman, fiercely proud of her son. The day I visited she hauled out one of his old grade school report cards.

"Look, look," she said proudly, pointing to his grades.

I took that old report card in my hands and thought of my own mother likewise showing off my first report cards with the universal pride of mothers everywhere. "Was he a good student?" I asked.

"Oh, yes," she said firmly. "He good student. He very smart boy." She had been able to give him five years of education before the Americans left and the Communists came in and ruined everything.

"What did you do then?" I asked, referring to that awful day in 1975 when the Communist North Vietnamese troops stormed into Saigon.

"I ran away," she said, a hint of anger washed with sadness still in her voice. "I go to the country with my American baby. I so afraid. All womans with American babies go long way and hide. So afraid. It very hard to live. We have no food. Always afraid. But I tell them—you must kill me before you kill my baby."

Pearl's father had been in the Army, stationed in Vietnam in the late sixties and Pearl was born in 1968. "Did his father know Pearl? Did he see Pearl?"

"Oh, yes. He love Pearl very much. He hold him. Then Pearl walk and his daddy help him. Walk with him. Have big picture of him holding Pearl."

"Do you have that picture?" I asked.

She shook her head. "Oh, no. Pearl daddy go back America. Take picture with him. To Texas." Pearl's father, who held him and talked to him and helped him learn to walk, left for Texas, taking with him that big picture of himself and his son. And the mother and son never heard from him again. Pearl's mother never married. Never had another relationship. Never had another child. She devoted her entire life, her whole being, to her American son.

Looking at this handsome, cheerful, talented young man sitting in front of me, I mourned the loss of it all: the woman who lost the love of her life. The son who lost his father. The father who knew his son. Who held him and loved him. A father who not only gave him life but named that life and then lost him. No letters. No cards. Nothing. Pearl and his mother suffered that loss every day. I wondered about that American father. Did he realize that he, too, was suffering a very profound loss, the loss of this terrific kid? This wonderful young man?

The disco of choice was at the Palace Hotel, a long cyclo ride from our beachfront digs. There was a live band and—what luck! We strolled in just as things got going. Their first tune: "Beer Barrel Polka." Oh, good fortune was smiling on us tonight. For a brief moment I thought I hadn't left Nebraska. The last time I'd heard "Beer Barrel Polka" played by a live band was at my nephew Gary's wedding when he married a Polish girl from Columbus, Nebraska.

As for the disco in the Palace Hotel in Vung Tau, well, compared to that disco off Dong Khoi Street this one was positively sedate. There was no oversized video screen playing bootleg MTV videos, no sparkling mirror ball, no young bloods dressed to the nines. The customers here were mostly hotel guests, and I guess a live band playing tunes like "Beer Barrel Polka" didn't inspire much boogying. The arrival of an American woman and some extremely good-looking "American boys" was a cause for minor celebration, however.

I did notice some attractive young women in the place. I figured they were teachers or office workers or something. One of them—wearing a white blouse and black skirt and wire-rimmed glasses—looked like a Wall Street secretary taking a break. They immediately got up and table-hopped our way. As usual Pearl took charge and within minutes was introducing them to the rest of the guys and to their "mother."

Pearl's classic pickup story was that they (Pearl, Jim, Vu, and Bryner) were all American boys who had come to Vietnam with their mother (me) to learn Vietnamese. Either he was really convincing, or a lot of young women simply wanted to believe that four good-looking young Americans who could barely speak English would actually travel halfway around the world to learn Vietnamese. At any rate, something worked, because we were soon joined by those very attractive young women, all of whom professed a great desire to learn to speak English. The one with the glasses sat down next to me and immediately began practicing her English.

"Hello. How are you?" she asked. I assured her I was fine. She understood and told me that she, too, was absolutely fine.

"What is your name?" I asked, continuing our lesson. "How old are you? Where are you from?" By this time I'd been in Vietnam long enough to follow the drill. I was beginning to feel like a portable language guide. A conversational circuit rider whose chats often resembled units from a human (and, tonight, humid) "Learn the Language" textbook. I ascertained that her name was Thi and she was from Saigon and she was thirty-two years old. With those units out of the way, I knew it was time to move on to the big stuff.

"What is your job?" I asked politely, a nice smile on my face.

"I sleep with men."

"Oh. You—sleep with men?" I asked. My eyes may have widened, but my smile didn't slip.

"Oh, yes. I sleep with men every night."

"Why do you do that?" I asked. Honestly, I didn't mean to be so stupid. I was just so stunned. I really thought she was a secretary. Or a schoolteacher. Sometimes thirty years in a big city counts for nothing.

"I do it for money," she answered simply.

"Do you like your job?"

"Oh, no. I no like at all."

Oh, God. Now what do I do. I was in too deep, so I just kept going. "Why do you do it?"

"I very poor. My family very poor. Vietnam very poor. No job. Eight kids in my family. I do it for money. Every month I send money back to my family in Saigon."

"How much money?"

"Oh, about eighty dollars a month." In present-day Vietnam this was a small fortune.

Part of the Communists' anticorruption drive after Liberation in 1975 was to round up all the prostitutes and ship them off to reeducation camps to purge them of what they claimed was a noxious foreign (translation: American) influence. I once asked an official what happened to the women in those reeducation camps. "Oh," he replied, "it was very good for them. They learn many things." Like what. "Sewing." He said this with a very straight face. Who knows? Maybe they did.

"Do the police ever bother you?" I asked the young woman.

"Oh, yes. Sometimes they come and take us to jail."

"Then what happens?" I asked. Were there judges? More reeducation camps? Advanced tailoring?

"Oh, they just take all our money. Then let us go." She shrugged.

I looked around the disco. There were plenty of unattached men there, probably from the hotels around town. "Will you sleep with any of these men," I said, gesturing around the room.

She let out a little sigh, then smiled. "I suppose." Then she looked around the room. "But tonight it is very bad."

"Why?"

"These mens all from Philippines. No like Philippine mens. They are not nice. Sometimes they very bad." She didn't elaborate, I didn't ask. "Besides—they very cheap. No pay much money."

"What about Russian men?"

She laughed out loud at that. "You kidding? I no crazy. No take Russian men. They no have money!" I marveled at the sad state of affairs mighty Russia had gotten itself into when even hotel prostitutes wouldn't take them and their worthless money. Saigon had hundreds of Japanese businessmen in town at any one time, so I asked if they ever came to Vung Tau.

"Oh, yes. They the best. They very kind. You stay all night with them—you get ten dollars." She said this with amazement in her voice, as if $10 was a lot of money. But then, of course, to her it was.

By this time these young women knew for sure that all those good-looking American-looking guys at the table were not native-born Americans, much less paying customers, but that didn't seem to matter. They stayed with us for quite a while, laughing and talking and dancing with them. I have a picture of Pearl and the "secretary." They are doing the cha-cha and he has a big wide-open grin on his face, not because he is dancing with a prostitute but just because he is a happy-go-lucky kid who is also a good dancer. And he has found someone who can follow his intricate lead.

The cyclo ride back from the Palace Hotel was long but un-eventful. Jim and Pearl and Bryner said they were going down to the beach, so I acted like a chaperone and told them to be careful. Upstairs, the toilet was still stopped up, the air-conditioner was still broken, and the ceiling fan—ripped from its moorings—still didn't work. Fortunately the sun had gone down and people had stopped careening and thumping into one another on the roof outside our rooms, so at least it had quieted down. I fell into a light and un-comfortable slumber. I kept dreaming I was skidding and slipping. Then I realized I was sweating so much it made me feel as if I were sliding out of bed. I also kept hearing strange noises from one of the rooms. Lots of muffled voices and every once in a while Pearl's high-pitched giggle. I rolled over and tried to keep a grip on the bed. I felt like a housemother.

I couldn't take a second day of this. At least Saigon was cooler than Vung Tau. And if it wasn't, the Kim Do had a working ceiling fan to give me aid and comfort. Besides, it was Saturday and the weekend was full blown. If all those people had streamed to Vung Tau on a Friday I could just imagine how many people would descend on a Saturday. So I put it to a vote. (See: I don't give up on democracy so easily.) Linh and Vu opted to catch an early bus back to Saigon with me while Jim and Pearl and Bryner chose to stay on until late afternoon. I think for a brief moment I hated them for choosing the beach over a bus ride back to Saigon with me. Then I kicked myself and felt better. Linh and Vu and I went across the road to the hotel desk to check out. The cleaning woman shuffled across the road toward the rooms and about three minutes later she came flying back with the good news: I owed lots more money!

According to my sources (Linh and Vu), Jim and Pearl and Bryner had cleaned out all the courtesy fridges. There wasn't even an ice cube left. Moreover, they had somehow managed to carry their cleanup campaign into my room, probably last night before we went to the disco when I was doing battle with the communal shower (a bucket of water and a cup). That also explained the muffled talking and laughing that went on late last night and early this morning: they had met some girls on the beach and invited them back to the room, where they had promptly plied them with Cokes and bottled water and ice cubes. And stayed up until one o'clock in the morning.

Well, I lost it. I stood in that steaming hotel lobby with that obnoxious desk clerk waving a piece of paper under my nose telling me I owed extra money for Cokes and bottled water. The smell of that fetid toilet still lingered in my nose. The feel of that fiery hotel room still haunted me. The memory of that scalding day on the beach was burned into my brain. And my underpants were still wet. The desk clerk continued to wave a piece of paper under my nose that said I owed extra money for Cokes and bottled water.

So I killed her.

I strangled her. Then I shot her. Then I stabbed her thirty-seven times.

Oh, come on now. I did no such thing. Sometimes my self-restraint is overwhelming. I didn't even yell at anybody because I knew that the last American—a guy from Seattle, Washington—who had the nerve to complain about a hotel room had been "invited" (wink-wink, nudge-nudge) to leave the country. As for all that extra money I was being charged because Jim and Pearl and Bryner had done something without asking me—well, big deal. It was my fault for not setting the ground rules. Also, by that time I had stopped being a spoiled brat long enough to figure out the bill at the current exchange rate. That late-night hanky-panky of theirs would cost me an extra $6. At least I had the decency to be embarrassed by my own behavior. Before I left to go back to Saigon I even gave them a couple of dollars in case they wanted to have another grand fling while they were there.

*   *   *

The Great Kim Do Upgrade (Cont'd): Someone else had obviously been thinking about fire safety because when I got back to Saigon late in the afternoon there was a newly typed notice secured to my wall:

FIRE SECURITY
In the case of fire burning please follows these actions:

- Switch the main electricity current off. [Note: No one knew what that meant much less where it was. Miss Congeniality suggested maybe it meant turn off the fan.]
- Switch the air condition off. [Note: There was no air condition in my room at the Kim Do. There wasn't even an air-conditioner.]
- Fill out the bathtub with water and then soak the blinkits . . . into it for fire exiting wis. [Note: There was no bathtub in my room either.]
- Show the help signals as clothes, draps, paper . . . through the window. [Note: Huh?]
- In case of great burning fires, please do not run but crawl towards the rescue exit/ladder. [Note: Please be advised there was no rescue exit/ladder to crawl to. Unless, of course, they meant that twisting, winding firetrap of a wooden staircase that would turn me into toast if I was stupid enough to crawl anywhere near it.]

Over the next few days I watched as the tape used to stick the FIRE SECURITY notice to the wall gradually began to lift off the wall. First one corner, then another and another. Finally, after it had dangled precariously by one corner for a couple of days, it fell off the wall altogether. I watched, intrigued, powerless to put it back up myself as it gradually made its way around the room, pushed here and there against its will by the slap-happy cleaning women who came in every day just to agitate and irritate the dirt in my room. Finally, it came to rest under my bed, where it remained until the day I left. For all I know, it is still there.

13

A TRIP TO BIEN HOA

Cau was a Vietnamese citizen—
actually, he was Chinese—and he spoke almost perfect English. He
told me he had been in the South Vietnamese Air Force, stationed
most of the time at Tan Son Nhut Air Base just outside Saigon. Cau,
who was in his forties, had studied English in school long before
Liberation, but of course he felt he had perfected his English out at
Tan Son Nhut. I had met him one day out at the Amerasian Transit
Center when I still had permission to be there. He was visiting some
friends who were getting ready to leave Vietnam under the ODP
program. Bryner and Jim and Pearl all knew him, so they introduced us.

"He have Amerasian wife," they told me. "Name Trang. She
very beautiful." Cau and Trang also had a three-year-old daughter
named Kim.

We talked for a while and then Cau generously invited all of us
to come to his house for lunch. Right then. I hopped on the back of
his motorcycle. Bryner and Jim and Pearl loaded themselves into a
cyclo and off we went, stopping long enough to buy loaves of crusty
French bread at a bakery and some eggs at another stall. We buzzed
down some side streets, turned a lot of corners, until I was completely confused. Then I noticed the signs on the shops and stores.

I still couldn't read them but not because they were in Vietnamese. This time I couldn't read them because they were in Chinese. No wonder: we were in Cholon. Cholon is the Chinatown of Saigon, a cramped and tight-knit community that was settled hundreds of years before as a trading port by Chinese merchants on their periodic sweeps down from the North.

We twisted and turned down some more narrow streets and alleys, finally pulling up in front of a small shop selling hardware and paint from a display case perched on the narrow sidewalk. It was Cau's shop. He was a hard-working small businessman and that was his little hardware stall. He also fabricated—by hand—saw blades and other small tools. And, like many a small businessman, he lived over the shop, in a mildew-covered concrete box that rose a precarious two stories over a narrow street.

In total darkness we creaked up some rickety wooden steps to the top floor, kicked off our shoes, and went into the living portion of the house: one room with a tile floor and some extraordinarily frayed electrical wiring spilling from a hole in the ceiling, out of which blossomed a light bulb, a fan, a tiny old television set, a cassette player, and a radio. There was also a terrace, which doubled as the kitchen. Cau apologized that Trang was at work—she was a manicurist and worked in a small beauty shop—so I didn't get to meet her that day. Their daughter, Kim, was likewise away, visiting Trang's mother.

"Someday I want you to meet Trang's mother, Kelly. She's a good woman. You will like her a lot. She's terrific," Cau said, bustling around and fixing us a hearty lunch of fried eggs, fresh-baked French bread, and beer. Pearl had found an old windup toy that belonged to Cau's little girl, so he busied himself winding up that little dog and then laughing his head off as it wagged its tail and turned in circles. Bryner found an English grammar book and buried his nose in that for most of the time. After lunch, Cau insisted that he take me back to the Kim Do and further insisted that I come back for lunch the following Sunday so I could meet Trang and their daughter, who would be back from Bien Hoa by that time.

So I dutifully arrived the following Sunday to have lunch and to meet Trang. She was a stunning black Amerasian, model-thin, with exquisitely chiseled cheekbones and a jawline to match. And eyelashes to die for. Their daughter, Kim, was a curly-headed three-year-old, a complete charmer with a sunny personality. Trang cooked up a traditional feast for us out there on the terrace, over a one-burner kerosene stove. And after lunch she insisted on giving me a manicure and a pedicure. Kim crawled up in my lap and fell asleep, Cau poured me another beer, and Trang outfitted me with pink nails topped off by a Chinese character on each finger, which, if taken together, wished me a long life and much happiness. I figured I already had that and then some.

Cau had an interesting hobby: he played basketball. In an over-forty league. One night he loaded me onto the back of his motorcycle, threw a tarp over my head (it was raining), and took me to a basketball game. Trang came with some other friends of theirs, and we all ended up in an old gymnasium in Cholon. We walked through what had once been the lobby. It now held a collection of skinny Vietnamese body builders frantically pumping up under huge posters of Arnold Schwarzenegger.

The gym itself was wooden and creaky and old and terribly familiar. Then I realized: it looked—and smelled—a lot like my old sweat-stained high school gym back in Albion, Nebraska, actually the American Legion Hall on Main Street, which had been built in the early 1900s. Just like that old American Legion Hall, the gym in Saigon had rows of old wooden seats that banged when you flopped them down and squeaked when you sat in them. They encircled an all-purpose court that could be used for everything from basketball and volleyball to relay races and badminton. Instead of a digital scoreboard there was an actual scorekeeper, who meticulously changed the score by hand, hooking and unhooking the numbers as the tide of the game moved back and forth between the two teams.

I recognized a few of Cau's teammates, having met them at various times either at his house or at one of their homes. Before the game began they insisted on lining up for a team picture, and there I am—in the middle of the front row—squatting on the floor, holding the ball like a mascot.

The team's coach was an extremely tall man—a giant among Vietnamese men; he was well over six feet tall—who had been a very successful player before Liberation and had traveled throughout Asia representing South Vietnam. He lived with his wife, Huong, in what could only be described as an in-home basketball court: a huge corrugated-tin building, which contained, first and foremost, a full-size basketball practice court along with a pigsty and, almost as an afterthought, living quarters for them and their young daughter. (Huong was a thoroughly modern young woman, who worked as an English translator for a newspaper and was also studying computer programming, all the while resisting her husband's pleas to have another baby. "He just wants a son," she scoffed.)

Cau and Trang had taken me to visit them one night in that warehouse–basketball court home of theirs. We all sat around talking and drinking orange soda pop to the accompaniment of squealing pigs, a dog giving birth somewhere in the far reaches of that sports complex, and someone's three-year-old being toilet-trained. And presiding over it all, a Marv Albert basketball blooper tape playing over and over and over on the VCR.

Beyond basketball, Cau was anxious for me to meet his mother-in-law, Luong, and we started to make plans for that visit. But before we could finalize our plans, there was a problem here in Saigon: Bryner was about to be booted out on the street. He was still bunking with Linh but Linh's elderly landlady was fussing about having an extra person stuffed into her small and already-crowded room. Tensions were rising on all sides, so we all got into the act, trying to find Bryner a place to stay. Even Hung, my old cyclo driver from the Que Huong, volunteered his service.

I had stopped by one day for an iced coffee in the little sidewalk stall right next to the hotel and was catching up on the latest Que Huong gossip when Linh rode by on his bicycle, so he stopped and joined us. Then Bryner himself wandered by and our talk turned to his housing problems. There was a terrible housing shortage in Saigon as the population had surged over the years, with little or no housing being built at all. And the housing stock that was available was not only deteriorating but was itself overcrowded, with two and three families sharing single rooms. But Hung said he knew of a couple of rooms people might be willing to share, so they all took off. They spent days at it because the last thing any of us wanted was for Bryner to be back out on the street, living in Amerasian Park. They looked and looked but couldn't find anything. It all looked pretty hopeless until, once again, Jim provided the solution: "Talk to my mother."

So, after class one day, while the students were hanging around trying to sort through the complexities of "An American Kitchen" (they were having trouble figuring out whether you cooked chicken in a kitchen, or the other way around), I broached the subject of Bryner to Lan.

"Sure, Kelly. He can stay here. No problem. He a good boy."

It was the simplest thing I ever did over there. But Lan's generosity was only typical: if you had something, you shared it. She was already sharing her apartment with complete strangers—I never did see the people who lived in one of her front rooms—so to squeeze in an Amerasian friend of Jim's was no problem at all.

"What about rent?" I asked. Bryner's paperwork was moving through ODP so this would be no long-term thing. He would be leaving sooner rather than later, at least by the end of the year. But still I figured Lan should have something for sheltering him. Since Bryner, like most of the Amerasians, had no job and no money, I was more than willing to pay her a few dollars a month in rent.

"Oh, no, no." She waved her hand. "Kelly, I do this for him. I do this for you. It is no problem. He an American boy who needs a home. I give him a home." That was it. There was nothing more to be said. Once again, the great, expansive, all-inclusive Amerasian Mother Network had come through. I only wondered, if the situation were reversed, whether I would be so generous with my American home. Maybe. Maybe not.

Cau's mother-in-law lived in Bien Hoa, a town about sixteen miles northeast of Saigon. Long Binh Army Base, one of the largest American bases in Vietnam, had been located in Bien Hoa during the war. CBS correspondent Morley Safer did a straightforward report on Long Binh, which he called "Oh, What a Lovely War for Some" and in which he cataloged some of Long Binh's wonders. In 1970, at the time Safer did his report, Long Binh was nothing short of an American city of 26,000 support troops, complete with eight Olympic-sized swimming pools, archery ranges, skeet shooting, putting and driving ranges for any stray golfers who might have wandered into the combat zone, not to mention bowling alleys, basketball courts, and four football fields. At the height of its operations, Long Binh mushroomed to cover 25 square miles and boast an American population of some 43,000 people. Twenty-two thousand Vietnamese workers were brought in every day to support the troops based there. And one of them was Cau's mother-in-law, Luong.

But Long Binh Army Base is long gone. That bustling American city has disappeared without a trace. Nothing survives except some sturdy concrete foundations that no one has yet ripped up and recycled. And Bien Hoa itself is just another small, tired town on the Vietnamese map.

Bright and early one morning, Cau and Trang collected me at the Kim Do and we headed off to the bus station. I had actually gone past the bus station countless times and figured it was just a vacant lot where lots of buses had gone to die. Not at all. This was Vietnam's crack over-the-road fleet.

Now, GIs arriving in Vietnam in the late sixties were surprised to discover that the troop transports they were loaded onto at Tan Son Nhut Airport in Saigon had heavy wire mesh covering all the windows. That surprise quickly turned to shock and dismay when they discovered the mesh was there to deflect any grenades or other explosive devices lobbed their way by Vietcong supporters. Vietnam in general and Saigon in particular had turned uglier than usual in the late sixties as the war ground on to its eventual sad conclusion.

Many of those old wartime vehicles have survived the journey from war to the kind of depressing, frustrated peace the people of Vietnam now find themselves bogged down in. Three-quarter-ton U.S. Marine transports now serve as sturdy, tidy little buses running between villages. Additionally, most of the larger buses on the highways seem to be old diesel-fired DeSoto buses, held over from the war and held together by the ingenuity of their drivers and the mechanics who can—and must—fashion replacement parts out of practically nothing. As if for encouragement, those jerry-built buses are painted in bright colors and cheerfully spit smelly black smoke into the air, which trails them down the highway like a dirty wedding train.

We loaded ourselves into one of those old American leftovers and headed off for Bien Hoa to visit Trang's mother. In all the confusion at the bus station I guess I hadn't noticed the bus had no windows. It could also have been because at eight o'clock in the morning it was already so hot that the only thing imaginable, in this country without the luxury of air-conditioned transport, was making sure every possible opening on the bus was indeed open. Imagine my surprise about an hour later when it began to rain and the passengers hurriedly started pulling down heavy reinforced window grates. They were solid metal except for some round holes stamped out for—air holes? Gun barrels? We were quickly sealed in like merchandise in metal shrink wrap.

"Very old bus," Cau offered by way of explanation. Then he laughed. "But look at it this way, Kelly: no grenades!" Yeah, right.

Finally, after about two hours of being sealed in that metal box, we were dumped out at the bus station in Bien Hoa. It was a decrepit stucco affair presided over by a flock of furious chickens, who flew out of the building as soon as the bus pulled in and began screaming at the passengers as we debarked. The people paid absolutely no attention to them, except for one old woman, obviously fed up with this kind of attitude on the part of these chickens, who gave one a kick so powerful it flew across the courtyard. It lay there for a moment, dazed and bewildered. I imagined cartoon stars floating around its head. Finally it got up and wobbled back inside the building, perhaps to the safer haven of a stewpot.

We picked up our belongings and I told Cau I wanted to stop in a market before we got to Luong's house. I wanted to arrive with food but couldn't imagine carrying dead chickens—or live ones, for that matter—and heavy bottles of beer on a two-hour bus trip. So we slowly set out from the bus station, strolling briefly down the highway before turning onto a street that was obviously the main drag of Bien Hoa. It was narrow and filled with gaping holes and slabs of misplaced concrete. The sidewalks had long ago been broken into chunks and heaved here and there, obviously by repair crews going for a drainage pipe. At one point, they had been thrown in such a way as to form a barricade on the sidewalk. Someone had decorated that rampart with a few scoops of dirt, and now a scruffy dog had happily taken up residence on top of it. He was snoozing deeply. I couldn't figure out whether to walk in the street to avoid those gaping holes in the sidewalk or to walk on the sidewalk to avoid those gaping holes in the street. So we split the difference, doing an odd little dance down the main thoroughfare of Bien Hoa as we dodged back and forth between the holes in the street and the holes in the sidewalk.

We found a small market and did our shopping, and as I went back to dodging my way through the debris of the street, I heard Cau yelling at me. I turned to see what he was talking about and encountered a throng of people trailing after us.

"Good God, Cau! What's the matter?" I thought perhaps we had blundered into a funeral procession. I looked around to see if I could spot the black hearse and white-clad mourners that always filled the street behind it. There was no hearse. Just a startled American woman stumbling down the street holding two dead chickens and three bottles of warm beer.

"I think this is the first time an American has been in Bien Hoa since the war," Cau explained.

We finally turned off the main street and began heading down smaller and smaller streets, roads, and paths until finally we edged our way alongside a building and then stepped over an open sewer ditch. I ducked under a tree branch that was alongside a public well.

The woman hauling water up did a double take and spilled all the water.

We were in a little neighborhood tucked away in a corner of Bien Hoa. There were about a dozen huts fashioned out of odd bits and pieces of wood and bamboo. Some had thatched roofs, some were topped with rusted corrugated metal. Most had crude fences in front outlining bare spots of earth. We headed for a rather substantial-looking hut made out of some kind of thin pieces of pressed wood. This one was unusual because it appeared to have square corners and was also standing pretty much upright. Others had noticeable sags and bags to them. A rusty barbed-wire fence enclosed a poured-concrete porch. I remember thinking how grand that little touch was. A string hammock was slung along one side of the small porch.

Suddenly Cau and Trang's daughter, Kim, came running up to throw her arms around her father's legs, jumping excitedly the way three-year-olds everywhere do when confronted with their favorite things in the whole world. Then a rather tall woman with a shock of white hair came running toward us, wiping her hands on her black trousers. She took one look at the three of us, grabbed my hands in her damp ones, and promptly burst into tears.

"This is my mother-in-law," Cau said by way of introduction. "She very surprised to see you here."

"You didn't tell her we were coming?" I stammered.

"Kelly—how could I tell her we were coming?" Cau looked at me as if I had checked my brains at the city limits. Of course. Unless he had written a letter—which might or might not have gotten delivered for weeks—how could he possibly have told his mother-in-law that they were coming down to visit and, oh, by the way, we're bringing an American woman with us. The first American you will have seen for fifteen years. I thrust the two dead chickens and the three bottles of hot beer into her hands. Fortunately, Cau had remembered to get a chunk of ice.

"Come in, come in," she said in English with a definite French accent. "You come in. Sit down. Be comfortable." She opened the gate to the little porch, then hustled around and found a stool, found a pillow. "You hot. Wait here." She tore inside and returned about ten minutes later with a big glass of fresh lemonade. The beer could wait. Then she sat down on a stool, her eyes filling with tears once again.

"I so glad to see you," she said, taking one of my hands and stroking it. "Cau—he tell me about this American woman he know.

He say you come to his house, you meet my Trang, you meet my little Kim. He say you very good. He say they like you very much. But I never think to meet you." She shook her head again at her obvious good fortune. "You know—I never think to meet an American again. He say you love basketball." She patted my hand. She might have been overstating the basketball thing a bit but this was no time to argue the point.

Then I looked over and there, squatting in the doorway, was one of the loveliest young girls I had seen in Vietnam. She had brown curly hair and sparkling brown eyes. There were a few freckles on the pale skin of her turned-up nose. "This my daughter Hoc," Luong said, jumping up and putting her arms around that lovely Amerasian girl and leading her over to the tiny little table where we were squatting.

"How old is she?" I asked.

"She only fifteen," Luong said. She went on to tell me that Hoc's father had been a civilian from one of the many American companies that had done business in Vietnam during the war. Hoc had been born just before Liberation and that her father had left the country just as Vietnam was falling, leaving behind Luong and his lovely daughter. In the upheaval that followed Liberation, Luong had long ago lost and then forgotten his strange American name and his equally strange American address. "He try very hard to get us out," Luong insisted. "But things so difficult then. So difficult."

"She's very beautiful, Luong."

"She my baby. My American baby." Luong smiled but her eyes seemed to fill with tears. Then she reached over and hugged her daughter with a ferocity that startled me. "You know—I could sell Hoc. Make lots of money." I must have reacted to that because Luong nodded her head vehemently. "Yes. Yes. You no believe me but I could sell my baby. From 1980 on, people, they come to my door and they want to buy Hoc."

"Buy her? People wanted to buy her?" I was shocked to hear this. I could hardly believe that people would actually come knocking at women's doors wanting to buy their American kids like poultry or armloads of vegetables.

Luong nodded firmly again. "Yes. You bet. Last year I could sell her for two thousand dollars. I poor but I no sell. She my baby!" She grabbed her again as if to guard her from those outside forces.

Cau then explained the incredible black market in Amerasians. Overnight they had gone from being society's curse to being a family's blessing. From being the hated and despised half-breeds, the "dust of life," to being the "children of gold." Because Amerasians were now, quite simply, a person's ticket out of Vietnam. Under the Amerasian Homecoming Act, if an individual or a family had an Amerasian child, that entire family could be issued passports by the Vietnamese and processed out of the country and sent to America. After passage of the Homecoming Act there ensued a frantic search for Amerasians, with some people knocking on doors like Luong's and offering poor families money for their previously outcast children. As the Orderly Departure Program picked up steam and word got out to other cities and towns and villages, Amerasians from outside Saigon streamed into the city to start the paperwork to get out of the country. Some were orphans, homeless and unattached. These Amerasians were being approached on the streets of Saigon by Vietnamese families offering them homes and money to "marry" a family's son or daughter and thus provide that Vietnamese kid's ticket to a new life in America.

One of my students back in Saigon—an orphan and quite obviously an Amerasian, with his all-American features—had come from Danang and, when he first arrived, he had lived outside on the streets or in Amerasian Park. One day, a few months after I met him and a few months after Cau had explained the traffic in Amerasians to me, the young man was in the market buying rice when he was approached by a man and a woman who made him an offer: come live with us and "marry" our daughter and take her out of the country with you. In exchange for this, they promised to feed and shelter him and pay for a private tutor so he and their daughter could begin learning English. Oddly enough, I then became the icing on his cake: of all my students, he was the only one who now had a private tutor who came to his new home at night to teach English to him and his "bride." Meanwhile, he also came to my classes during the day for a chance to hear a real American speak real English and thus speed his progress and improve his pronunciation at the same time.

His new family even had me over for lunch one Sunday afternoon. Their house was quite grand compared to some I'd seen. It was on the second floor of an apartment complex. They had actual beds and a working TV set. The family was educated and charming and had obviously welcomed this young Amerasian. Their daughter was a beautiful young girl, and you could sense both the resignation and the conflict the parents felt: the sadness at eventually losing this lovely daughter of theirs; the realization that, at least for now, this was the best they could offer her in the way of a future.

I thought about all this as I sat there with them that Sunday afternoon. Of course it was lying and cheating and stealing. But was it so wrong to want the very best for your child and to discover a way to do it that would benefit both a homeless Amerasian and your own child as well? Did the means justify the ends? Ever?

I didn't know. How could I possibly know?

In the meantime, a huge press of people had collected around Luong's little hut there in Bien Hoa. Obviously the word had spread: there was an American in the vicinity. And she was sitting on the porch. Right out in plain sight. At first it was just little kids come to stare and giggle at the sight of this white-skinned, white-haired woman. I could hear Cau telling them I was an American. Oddly, it meant nothing to them.

"They don't know what an American is?" I was stunned. Politically, I was the enemy. Historically, I was representative of yet another in a long line of foreign imperialist bad guys. Weren't we even being denounced in the classrooms of Communist Vietnam? Obviously not. Over the course of the year I was there, I kept marveling at this: after all those years, all those reeducation camps, all those recriminations—and discrimination—the American presence in Vietnam during the 1960s and 1970s wasn't even being taught in the Communist schools anymore. With all the youngsters I met and talked to up and down Vietnam there was not a whisper of America the Bad. What kind of Communists were these people? To have hated us so much and now to be producing a generation who don't even know who we are? The inefficiency of it all was truly bewildering.

Suddenly, a young man pushed his way through that throng of children, pushed open the gate, and came up onto the porch. He dragged up a stool and sat down right in front of me, staring directly into my eyes.

"And now, American woman, I would like to talk to you about Jesus Christ."

I looked at him. "Jesus Christ?"

"Yes. Do you know him?"

"Well, not personally." Then I realized he was probably asking me if I was a Christian and had I heard of Jesus Christ, so I assured him that, yes indeed, I had heard of Jesus Christ. There was no Catholic school in Albion, Nebraska, when I was growing up but I had spent every Saturday afternoon during the school year sitting in the church attending catechism classes, taught from the old Baltimore Catechism. ("Who made you?" "God made me." "Why did God make you?" "To know him and love him and serve him in this world and in the next.") Then for two weeks every summer, the nuns from the church in Petersburg would come down and instruct us. There were even nuns in my family, including my aunt, Sister Placida. She was my dad's foster sister, an orphan from Chicago. She had been swept up by some charitable institution in the late 1800s and brought to Nebraska on one of the so-called "Orphan Trains," put together by charitable groups that rescued unwanted children from the streets and institutions of the big cities. They then brought them out to farm families in the Midwest who were willing to care for them. The Kelly family—huge and loving—had taken that little girl, who eventually grew up to become a Franciscan nun. She was assigned to Mundelein College back in Illinois, where she worked in the kitchen, cooking for the seminarians there. I adored her.

"Do you like Jesus Christ?" the young man persisted. "I like him very much. I believe in him very much. I think he is a good man. Every day I pray to Jesus Christ. And I think someday he will hear my prayers." Then he stood up and stuck out his hand. "Thank you very much. It has been a pleasure speaking to you about our friend Jesus Christ." Then he turned and left. I had slipped out of my own faith long ago, discarding it casually the way Americans discard so many other things in their lives. I wondered and marveled at his ability to keep and maintain his faith. Perhaps I was even a bit envious at that moment. To believe anything requires a certain amount of strength. To maintain it as he and others had done over the past fifteen years requires courage.

Luong's house was a typical Vietnamese structure: long and narrow, with the kitchen located in the back. Luong had divided it into two sleeping areas. As usual, she had people living with her I couldn't begin to identify since after a while everyone in Vietnam becomes your "mother" or your "sister" or your "aunt." She had elected to decorate her walls with bright-colored religious posters. Most of them were of Jesus Christ. Catholics would surely recognize the Sacred Heart of Jesus theme of some of the posters: Christ holding his right hand up in a blessing while in his left he held his stylized heart, encircled with thorns to symbolize the crown of thorns he wore to his crucifixion.

Cau, Luong's hard-working Chinese son-in-law, had financed the "renovation" of her house, which included that little concrete porch in the front, a concrete floor throughout the house, a new front door that actually closed, and a new corrugated tin roof.

"He very good to me," Luong whispered of her son-in-law. "He very good to Trang, too. I get along with him very well. I lucky woman to have him."

Cau had met Trang during a trip to Bien Hoa. He had gone there to sell things from his shop and met her on the bus when she was going up to Saigon to sell things in the market there. They ran into each other a few more times on their mutual "business trips."

"At first I no like him." Luong laughed, poking Cau in the ribs. "I think he too old for Trang." Indeed, Cau was about twenty years older. He had been married before and had three children, but his wife had died and he had raised his family by himself. He persisted in his courtship of Trang and eventually won the reluctant Luong over to his side. From the looks of things, it was a good marriage. Trang was as hard-working as she was gorgeous and Cau encouraged her every step of the way. Although she didn't speak any English, she was literate, unlike many Amerasians—and most black Amerasians, who had been hounded out of school by the color of their skin. In fact when the Bien Hoa–to–Saigon version of Literary Man got on the bus extolling the virtues of his stack of books, Trang immediately bought a copy and rode the rest of the way home with her nose stuck in a book.

Cau not only loved Trang but he was very proud of her.

"She is very smart, Kelly. It wasn't her fault she couldn't go to school. She tried but she was called *my den*—black American. So she left school. But she can read and write. Then she had to work very hard. You know, when she was eight years old, she sold ice cream from pole baskets. After the war, when Long Binh was closed down, Trang and Luong would go out to the base and dig things up to sell. My Trang, she didn't even have shoes to wear when she was a little girl. When I met her, she had big, terrible calluses on her feet from walking around barefoot all her life."

Since her marriage to Cau, Trang not only wears shoes but she has learned how to be a manicurist. When Trang expressed some interest in learning the fine art of hairdressing, Cau found a school for her to attend. By the time I left Saigon at the end of the year,

Trang had not only completed her hairdressing course but she was now instructing others.

"I hate VC!" Luong hissed at me after lunch when we were sitting around talking. "VC Number Ten!" she cried, labeling them with the worst number possible. Bo Derek notwithstanding, to be Number 1 was to be the best. To be Number 10 was the lowest of the low. And to Luong, the VC were "Number Ten! Number Ten!"

Somewhere along the way, Luong had lost her front teeth. The replacements were heavy, old-fashioned things that were held in place by thick metal prongs that fit around her other teeth. And now Luong was so angry her front teeth kept flopping up and down and periodically she would have to stop and suck them back into place. Luong had been dealing with the VC since 1947, when she was eighteen years old and living in the countryside with her family.

"In 1947 the VC come three times to get my brother to join them. To be Vietminh. That what they call them then. But he say no. He say no three times." She held up three fingers to emphasize her point. "Three times. But the third time they come for him and he say no—they cut his throat." She reaches up and makes a hard, slicing motion across her throat. "I see this. I see him die." The tears start flowing down her face. They form a silent river of anger. Luong's voice is low and firm. The tears keep coming. "Then the VC they come for me. I no want to go but I have to go. I so scared. They take me far away into the countryside. Basic training they call it. They make me crawl on glass." She held up her elbows. I could see deep, coarse scars from her encounters with that broken glass. They ringed her elbows like age lines on an ancient tree stump. "I no like to do this but they kill people. So I go." She shook her head. "But I never believe them. I never believe them. They lie all the time to the people. All the time."

I sat there, a privileged American woman who had witnessed the horrors and terrors of the Vietnam War from the safety of the Time-Life Building and the comfort of my living room. My teeth were bonded by an East Side New York dentist, and any cuts I might have received as a child or a young woman had been immediately dealt with in immaculate operating rooms by doctors wearing disposable gloves. I could only imagine what the Luongs of Vietnam had suffered. I held her hand tight if only to hold my own.

Cau had already told me how his mother-in-law had stood up to the Vietcong. Luong and her children had taken refuge in Bien Hoa after Liberation, hoping to escape any dangers that might have awaited them in Saigon. But the retaliations had followed them. Indeed, they probably met them head-on there in that small village. The Vietcong had rampaged through the countryside and were especially hard on villages like Bien Hoa, which had had such an obvious American presence. And which, after Liberation, still contained such an obvious American presence: hundreds and thousands of Amerasian children.

"After the war, the VC are all over," Luong said. "All over. They have meetings. They make us go. They say, 'Who hates America? Who hates Americans?' People are scared. Many hands go up. Not mine. I have my American babies, so I say, 'My family is American.' So now I am Number Ten." She thumps her small chest with her fist. "I tell those VC I have American babies. I don't care. 'You want kill me—you kill me! I no lie. Sure: I have black American baby. Sure I have white American baby. What you do to me? What you do to them?' " She was breathing heavily by this time, little short gasps of breath. She anchored her teeth and went on to say that during that tumultuous time, right after Liberation, when the Vietcong tore through Bien Hoa, one of their targets was the hospital with its South Vietnamese Army patients. "VC go to that hospital," Luong said. "They throw those soldiers out of their wheelchairs. Throw them out on the road. Then they go to the orphanage. Have many American babies there. Throw American babies out on the street. When the Vietcong leave, people go out and pick up those cripples and those American babies. They take them home with them. They take care of them."

She told me about one of her neighbors, a man who, to the Communists in 1975, had committed two flagrant sins: he had not only served in the South Vietnamese Army but he had married a woman with an Amerasian child. "They kill him," Luong said. "They take him out and kill him." She looked at me with such sadness mixed with such anger and, even, exhaustion it was if the mere thought of these decades of inhumanity had tired her to a point of despair.

Over the afternoon, as we talked, Luong had dug out some old photos from "before." I turned them over slowly, one by one, and had difficulty reconciling the beautiful woman I saw in some of the pictures with this still-lovely but tired white-haired woman sitting in front of me with her front teeth falling out of her mouth. There was one particularly poignant picture of a beautiful young woman wearing a brocaded *ao dai*. She was sitting in a restaurant. There were a crisp white tablecloth and two glasses of red wine on the table. I could see waiters wearing black pants and white shirts hovering in the background. With her left hand the young woman was lifting a fork to her mouth, while her right hand held the knife, French fashion. It was Luong captured in her beautiful, long-ago past as a young woman in Saigon.

I was squatting on a hard stool at a small table that had never seen a white cloth. We had just finished the fabulous meal she had cooked over a small charcoal stove with what we had picked up in the market on our way from the bus stop, and now we were all sitting around bloated from food, beer, lemonade, and tea. I was sitting there in my languid stupor thinking about Luong in her long-ago life as a young woman in Saigon. Then I realized I was sitting there alone while a hushed consultation went on back in the kitchen area among Luong and Trang and Cau. They had obviously come to a decision because they now approached me like a delegation.

"It time you go to the bathroom, Miss Katie," Luong announced formally, holding out her hand. I took it and rose like a queen to her lady-in-waiting, following her into the back of the house to the kitchen. She kicked a couple of chickens out of the kitchen, barred the back door with a stick slipped through a piece of notched wood. Then she draped a long cloth over a string hung across the corner of the room and indicated a hole in the corner of the kitchen. Finally, she handed me two pieces of toilet paper and silently left the room. A chicken wandered up from somewhere and stood watching me solemnly.

I peed all over my foot.

I washed up in a basin outside, and when I came back, Luong grabbed my hand and held it tightly. "You know, Miss Katie, when I lived in Saigon I had a real toilet." She leaned her head on my shoulder and sighed, a small, far-off sigh. "Imagine. A real toilet."

Obviously figuring I was exhausted after sitting around all day doing nothing and then stuffing myself with delicious food that had been cooked in my honor, Luong led me outside to the hammock and motioned for me to get in. "You rest now," she said solicitously. "You tired." She handed me a fan and then disappeared back into the house. A picture taken at that time reveals an American woman, her shoes and socks off, lying in a hammock fanning herself while a mural of children's faces stares at her through a rusty barbed-wire fence. She looks very happy indeed.

I put one bare foot on the concrete and began rocking myself back and forth in that hammock, slowly fanning myself. I must have dozed off because when I looked up I saw Hoc stepping off the porch. When I had arrived I had noticed an old Army helmet propped on one of the porch's support posts. Hoc now had that olive-drab helmet in her hand and was strolling back down the dusty path toward the well we had passed when we came into this little compound. I watched as she dipped the helmet into the well and hauled out some water. About that time Luong came out onto the porch to check up on me. She had a glass of fresh lemonade in her hand.

"How old is that?" I asked her, gesturing to the helmet Hoc had in her hand. I had seen old Army helmets in use all over Saigon. I never thought too much about them except vaguely to think, oh, how interesting. Sometimes they were empty and just propped up on a corner next to a bicycle pump, indicating that there was a vendor who would pump your tires up for a small fee. Once I even saw one of the night people around the Kim Do bathing her new baby out of an old helmet. From my disposable society, I just couldn't believe anything had lasted from the war. Luong assured me it was very old.

"Whose was it? Communist?" I asked. She looked at me as if I were very stupid indeed. I felt I had gone down a significant number of notches in her estimation.

"Oh, Miss Katie," she admonished me sternly. "That no Communist helmet. That American helmet." She pursed her lips like a customer in a specialty store demanding only the very best. "Those damned Communist helmets no good, Miss Katie. They only last few years. GI helmets—they Number One. Last a very long time."

The common perception of the women in Vietnam during the war—and particularly the women who had children by Americans—is that they were all bar girls, hookers, and whores who participated in the ultimate service economy. Some were. Most weren't. There are no facts or figures to back me up, but I would bet that most of the women who bore Amerasian children were hardworking women (as opposed to "working girls"). Many established long-term relationships with the Americans they lived with and certainly with the American children they bore and cared for long after those American fathers left. Against all odds, Luong had not only cared for one Amerasian child but two—one who was black, one who was white. Both of whom looked so American they were a constant reminder of the American presence in her life, in that country.

Luong had been a civilian worker at Long Binh Air Base in Bien

Hoa during the war. She was living in Saigon at the time and every day she and the hundreds of other Vietnamese workers it took to keep a base up to American standards would climb aboard buses and be driven to the base.

"What did you do there?" I asked her.

"I iron. I iron clothes for GIs. I iron for Trang's father. He see me, he like me. He say to me, 'You have husband?' I tell him no. He say, 'You no work no more. You stay home.' He good man. He take care of me." I had seen a picture of Joe as a handsome young soldier back at Cau and Trang's house, so I asked Luong if she thought Trang's father was handsome. She shrugged. "I no care handsome. He have a good heart, Kelly. That the most important thing." She looked over at her son-in-law. "Cau—he have good heart. I very glad my Trang marry this man."

As the conversation turned to Trang's father, Cau, who was sitting at the table with us, began quietly rummaging around in a brown plastic tote bag he always carried with him. He finally found what he was looking for: a set of photos carefully protected by plastic. Slowly, he turned the plastic pages and I saw Trang's little photographic history unfolding before me. There was a picture of Trang as a fat baby in 1967. And here was a studio picture of her daughter, Kim, an equally fat much-loved baby, looking very much as her mother, Trang, did. And there—a picture of Trang's father, a handsome black soldier wearing the familiar Army jungle fatigues. They were like family pictures everywhere. On my bedroom wall in New York was my baby picture, taken in 1937. I am six months old, a fat little thing, wearing a smile and a white dress. Right next to it is my mother's baby picture taken in 1893. We look exactly alike. We could be the same child, separated only by a few years from two different centuries. Katie and Maggie. Trang and Kim. Life goes on.

According to Cau, Trang's father had been a communications specialist at Long Binh Air Base. Cau then produced some letters that Joe had written to Luong after he had been shipped out of Vietnam. They indicated not only a desire to come back to Vietnam to Luong and their daughter but outlined his attempts to do so, including applying for jobs with various civilian companies. There was even a letter Joe had written to a buddy to see if he had any strings he could pull to get him back into the country. Joe, obviously a musician, even suggested that perhaps there was a band some-place that could use his services.

"Where'd you get this?" I asked, turning the friend's letter over in my hand.

"Joe send to his friend," Luong said, pointing to a man's name at the top of the page. "His friend come to visit me, bring letter. Give to me. I keep all these years." The postmark was 1970. And by that time, things were so tense in Vietnam—and at home—and our involvement was so complicated Joe didn't stand a chance at getting back into the country. Even as a saxophone player. Even as a father, worried about his daughter.

Trang's mother had somehow managed to hang on to those pictures and letters and, most important, Joe's American address. In 1987, when it was finally safe to do so, Trang had written to her father. Surprisingly, after twenty years, the old address was still valid. And Joe had not only gotten Trang's letter, he had replied. Cau reached back into his tote bag and produced the letter. In it, Joe had expressed surprise and apparently genuine delight at finally hearing from his daughter. He then went on to outline briefly his life in America: he ran a small upholstery business on the East Coast, he thought about his daughter a lot, and he closed by asking her to write back to him. He had enclosed a current picture of himself along with his business card complete with company name and phone numbers. All in all, it was a warm letter from a father to his daughter. Trang had immediately written back, but in the eighteen months that followed, she had never heard from her father again. I promised them that when I went back to America I would call Joe and send him some pictures.

"Trang doesn't want anything from her father," Cau assured me. "She just wants to know if he's O.K." Then he picked up their daughter and kissed her on her curly head. "And if he thinks Kim is beautiful."

When I got back to New York, I called Joe at his upholstery business. He was somewhat surprised to hear from someone who had met his daughter in Vietnam. He was cordial, but a bit distant. We talked for a while and I told him what a lovely daughter he had and what a wonderful, hard-working son-in-law he also had. Then I informed him he was a grandfather and told him I would send some pictures of Trang and her family to him, including his grand-daughter, Kim. After checking his address (it was the same) I sent the photographs off. Joe never contacted any of us again. But I kept my promise to Cau: I showed Joe how beautiful Kim was.

14

NEXT GENERATION

$\mathbf{B}$efore Liberation, Dong Khoi Street was the notorious Tu Do Street, a throbbing neon-lit stretch of bars and honky-tonks and whorehouses that stretched down from the cathedral—the Cathedral of Our Lady—to the Saigon River. Today that street is a quiet, tree-shaded boulevard, filled not with bars and whorehouses but with antique shops and stores filled with tourist knickknacks. And if those tourist shops are the definition of hastily produced schlock—godawful lacquerwork with thick, clumsy mother-of-pearl inlay that is a mockery of the exquisite inlay work of the past—the antique shops are merely sad. Desperate people are hauling out cherished family treasures—probably long hidden from the authorities—and selling them to finance yet another escape attempt, a child's education, a medical bill. Survival itself. You can practically see a family's history and a country's heritage diminishing and disappearing in the goods for sale: jade, lacquer, ceramic, carved wood. Musical instruments, opium pipes, water bowls, wedding boxes. Family pictures, people forever young staring solemnly out of ancient frames.

Late one afternoon I went out for my usual stroll. I headed up Dong Khoi Street in the general direction of the cathedral. I was aiming for Amerasian Park, but as I came to the cathedral, I wandered in and sat down. I had slipped away from the church a long time ago, but it still had a small hold on the edges of my heart and around the far corners of my beliefs. And I seldom passed up an opportunity to sneak inside a church, if only to revel in church architecture or listen to some beautiful music, especially if it was a high mass still being sung in Latin. In Nebraska, for kids of my generation, our culture began in the church: Victorian architecture, the decorative arts, classical music. It was there, during high mass at St. Michael's Church in Albion, Nebraska, that I first heard the magnificence of Bach, Beethoven, Haydn, and Mozart.

Saigon's cathedral, unlike some of the gaudy baroque churches of Italy or those overwrought rococo extravaganzas I had seen in South America, was quiet and subdued. Indeed, compared to those other productions, it was positively austere. Except for that red neon cross on the front altar. And that yellow neon halo encircling Holy Mother's head. Admittedly, they were a bit jarring. Beyond that, I was struck by the air of peace and serenity it had, very much like my old parish church back in Nebraska. They were actually very similar. St. Michael's was also of red brick and it, too, had a huge spire soaring heavenward. As you came into Albion, you could see it for quite a distance across the prairie. Like the cathedral, St. Michael's had rows of unyielding wooden pews marching down from the altar. But the two churches differed on the kneeling-bench question. Back in the mid-fifties, Father Crowley, who had been at St. Michael's forever, shocked the parish by installing padded kneeling benches. Saigon's cathedral had no such modern conveniences.

Sitting there in that cool, quiet cathedral in downtown Saigon—a stone's throw from Communist Party headquarters and a mental hairsbreadth away from that church of my childhood—I began to cry. It was just a gentle welling of emotion, perhaps brought on by all those universal qualities a Catholic church holds for all its old children whether they are faithful or not. The peace, the quiet, the dim quality of the light. The distant smell of incense. The sound of people dipping their fingers in holy water. Feet shuffling slightly as they make their way down the aisle. The clumsy fumbling as someone drops a kneeling bench with a thud that cracks the silence, then echoes off into an eternity of embarrassment.

I sat there in that dim old Saigon cathedral, in the twilight gleaming of Mary's neon halo, and had a good old-fashioned cry. Why was I crying? What—who—was I crying for? For all those poor, misbegotten Amerasians and their lost youth? Or, selfishly, just for my own. When I believed all this. I never knew why. But I could hear my Irish mother assuring me that some things are just a mystery, Kathryn Ann. So I blew my nose and left, dipping my fingers deep into the holy water. I never went back. I couldn't. I cry too easily.

After I left the cathedral, I headed on over to Amerasian Park—which was right behind the cathedral—to see what was going on. It was a Saturday afternoon, and since I kept strictly observed weekends, there were no classes, but I knew I would probably meet up with some of my students. Students who, quite honestly, baffled me. For kids who came armed with only four or five years of formal schooling, they seemed to me positively extraordinary and their progress remarkable. And for some—like Tom and Be—what they lacked in formal education they more than made up for in enthusiasm and just plain old effort. They were the Avis of second-language students: they tried harder. Only Tai was in turmoil. He would be my one failure. I just could not crack his illiteracy. And he just kept his head in the clouds, dreaming of an America consisting entirely of rock music and blue jeans.

As for the rest of us, we continued to storm the ramparts of present tense, past tense, and future tense. Winning the wars of colors and clothing and rooms and prepositions. And I was using any cheap means available to make things sink in.

My very first teaching job had been in a small high school in rural Nebraska. My students were mostly the sons and daughters of very well-to-do farmers, whose horizons extended only as far as the boundaries of their father's extensive cornfields. They weren't dumb, they just refused to read or study or see any practical use whatsoever for the likes of Beowulf or Shakespeare or Chaucer. I could understand that, so I improvised: we read *Sports Illustrated*. And *Road and Track* and *Field and Stream*. I even got a lot of mileage out of *Modern Romances* and *Photoplay*. Reading is reading and you have to start somewhere. By the end of the year, they were reading Edgar Allan Poe and they didn't even know what hit them.

And so it was with my Amerasian students in Saigon. We weren't quite up to even *Modern Romances* but the point was the same: Get real. Be practical. We did whole units on "Fruits and Vegetables" and then went to the market and put it into practice. And every day, after we finished eating, a different student got to "Pay the Bill." The trip to Vung Tau inspired "Going to the Beach," although once again the thing that really stopped us was the fact that they still wanted to hang out on "the bitch" instead of the beach. I suggested that when they got to America they simply ask to "go swimming" instead.

And like all that historical drama done by my fifth graders way back in Illinois, there was also great vocabulary drama in Saigon that year. "Do You Have a Girlfriend?" prompted this exchange between Tom and Bryner:

TOM: Do you have a girlfriend?
BRYNER: No, I don't have a girlfriend.
TOM: Why not?
BRYNER: I don't have a girlfriend because I'm poor.
TOM: I'm sorry you are poor. Why are you poor?
BRYNER: I am poor because I don't have a job.
TOM: Oh.

Once I suggested they do a conversation called "Do You Want a Haircut?" It came out something like this:

BE: Hair long. (He points to Pearl.)
PEARL: Yes, I know.
BE: Want haircut?
PEARL: No.
BE: (Looks over at me, helplessly. "Ask why not," I suggest.)
BE: Why not?
PEARL: I want to look like Michael Jackson.
BE: O.K.

Oh, well. I still thought we were on the right track.

"Buying Jeans and Shoes" was a favorite unit (it ranked right up there with "Ordering from a Menu") because, of course, we actually went out and did just that. Result: by the end of the unit everyone, including the girls, had new jeans and new shoes plus a load of exotic American words like "size" and "zipper" and "pocket" and "shoelaces."

There were a few people in the park that afternoon. As usual, Mary and her mother were at their little stall, and there was a small gathering of Amerasians just hanging out. As I walked toward the stall I heard someone say: "I want a *pair of socks!*"

I looked over and saw Bryner with a big grin on his face. I had recently taught the class a unit called "The Two Most Important

Things You Will Ever Have to Know." I know it sounded like the title of a Robert Fulghum book, but my students were as practical as I was and they were quite happy to add "I want" and "Do you have . . . ?" to their repertoire.

"What do you want?" I kept asking during class.

"I want . . . some rice!" Huong answered.

"I want . . . new shoes!" someone cried.

"I want chicken!"

"I want a chair."

"I want a *new car!*" It was Pearl who excitedly escalated things to the higher plane of an American TV game show. From there they took off, adding their new American words like charms on a vocabulary bracelet. They wanted a refrigerator, a television set, the contents of a house. I figured we had reached our peak when someone yelled, "*I want America!*" Made sense to me.

I looked over and saw Bryner, with a big grin on his face, asking for a pair of socks. Obviously that lesson took. Then I looked around and noticed that for once he was on his own, without Jim or Pearl. The three of them were so inseparable it was easy to think of them as a single person who one day got confused and split off into three different bodies. This was completely unfair to all three of them, however, since they were three of the most separate and distinct personalities I had ever met. Jim was the teenager, generally happy-go-lucky and eager to please. Pearl was outgoing and exuberant, with a lively personality. Bryner, on the other hand, was the quietest of the three. He was never without the small English-Vietnamese dictionary I had provided for each of the students, and periodically he would come in with lists of English words he had found in the dictionary. (I did the same thing when I was trying to learn Spanish: I hauled around lists of words and phrases and would study them endlessly. I became incredibly adept at ordering people to go get my luggage.) One day when we were sitting around doing nothing in particular, he handed me a little scrap of paper with some words written on it in his small, precise handwriting. It was his vocabulary list for the day, and he wanted me to help him with his pronunciation. On that scrap of paper he had written the words "depression, despair, desperation, hopeless, sad."

For a short time, Bryner had a crush on a pleasant but forgettable young Amerasian and would mention his "girlfriend" in soft and dreamy tones. She was there that day in the park, all round-faced and, well—nice.

"Teacher, you take our picture?" Bryner whispered to me, nodding over to the girl who was sitting quietly next to Mary. I agreed and he moved her into position. The photo shows Bryner and the young woman standing solemnly in Amerasian Park. The cathedral is in the background. Bryner has put his arm around her shoulders and there is a small smile on his face. She simply looks stricken.

Bryner spent the rest of the afternoon mooning over the girl. In the meantime Jim had wandered up from somewhere and joined us. A few other people had drifted over and I was sipping an orange soda and thinking how peaceful it all was.

A few days later, I was relaxing on the terrace at the Rex. Pretty soon Bryner drifted up. He was the first one to arrive but I knew the others would join us. When I gave him a copy of the photo I had taken in the park of him and his "girlfriend," he was thrilled. He immediately slipped it into his cheap plastic photo album and was looking at it, lost in thought, when Pearl arrived on a gust of good spirits. He had the girl in question on his arm.

Bryner was stunned. He looked as if he'd just taken a body blow. Then his face crumpled and fell. Like me, he would never be a good poker player. His emotions were raw, lying dormant right on the surface ready to break loose. I had long ago realized that Bryner was so much like me. And looking at him and his reaction to things was like looking in a mirror and seeing myself when I was his age: a skinny, driven kid full of self-doubt. I knew the pain he was going through and later I took him aside and tried to reassure him. I wanted to put my arms around him and hug him like I would a little kid but instead I patted him on the back like a teacher, a friend, an aunt. I tried to tell him things would be all right. That no matter how bad things looked, this was really not the end of the world, although it certainly felt like it to him. The words stuck in my mouth like mud. I felt like such a fraud, because of course it did absolutely no good. These are the kinds of things every kid in the world has to experience. The pain is real and overwhelming and awful. And there is neither any escaping that kind of pain nor is there any help for it at the time. Like Mount Everest—it's just there. And phony platitudes don't help at all. So I shut up. It was the best I could do.

Well, we all had to endure a few days of hurt feelings and pouting and sulking from everybody involved. It was as if the high school jock had muscled in on the president of the Honor Society. Mr. Personality taking on Most Likely to Succeed. Pearl and Bryner stopped speaking to each other except for periodic sharp outbursts from one or the other of them. Pearl would get so upset his face would turn red. Bryner would just get all silent and spend hours sulking. It took forever to get seated in a café or in the classroom, as they all had to shuffle around and accommodate this Amerasian version of the Hatfields and McCoys. These young men and women might have been nearing their mid-twenties but so much in them was stalled, hopelessly mired in those quicksilver emotions of childhood and adolescence that they had been forced to speed through, if only to survive. They had grown up so fast because they had to. They had had to double-time through their youth, and now they were constantly having to stop dead in their tracks and wait for part of them to catch up. The part we call, simply, growing up. They had never been allowed the leisure of doing that. Childhood. Such a luxury.

Fortunately, that crisis passed and the friendship was restored. Pearl moved on to other conquests and Bryner likewise lost interest. And I never saw the poor girl again. I don't even know if she ever knew of the upheaval she caused for a few days.

One night, after having my usual late-evening close encounter with those bats to get to my room, I did my usual evening chores—took a shower, sorted out the next day's lessons for my students, washed my clothes, wrote in my journal, and read a few pages in the latest issue of *Time*. (With reading material in short supply, I rationed those weekly copies of *Time* like drops of water in a desert. They were precious indeed. I always recycled the magazine, generally starting with Cau, who could—and did—read every word. Then it would make its way down the literary chain until it got to the likes of Tai, that California mall-rat wannabe who would simply soak up the various fashion statements he found in the ads.)

It felt as if I had just turned out the lights when I slowly became aware of some vague noise coming from somewhere. It was a fluttering, scratching sound. At first I couldn't figure out where it was coming from, much less what it was. I remember thinking perhaps it was a lost bat, and I wondered if tossing a rubber shower sandal at it would do any good. But as I slowly roused myself from what had obviously been a deep sleep, I realized it was someone at my door.

It was Lon, a young Amerasian I had met briefly in the park the day I took the photo of Bryner and his "girlfriend." He was standing outside with an absolutely dazed look on his face. The bats were wheeling in the background.

"What's wrong?" I asked stupidly. Not having Bryner or Jim

around to translate for me severely limited my ability to get to the bottom of this situation, but I kept trying. No use. His anxiety just seemed to get worse. Finally I gave up, got dressed, and followed him downstairs. (Funny. He walked right through those bats. It was like Charlton Heston parting the Red Sea. Fortunately, I had my cone hat and broom close at hand, so I was ready for them when they closed ranks around me.)

We rushed down the stairs and crept through the pitch dark of the old lobby (the new one was locked up tight). Fortunately all the motorbikes had gone home by that time, but I did crash into a glass display case and set a few dozen fake Rolexes rattling against one another. Lon finally roused the gatekeeper, who had let him in just moments before, and once again got him to unlock the solid roll-down metal gate that covered the entrance to the hotel. It went up with a series of shudders and screeches and we slipped through. We made it outside and there, in the dim street light, I could see a young woman standing on the sidewalk, clutching her stomach. It was his wife, Mai. She was likewise an Amerasian and I had also met her in the park. She was in labor. And they had come to me for help.

"Oh, my God. My God. My God." I kept repeating that over and over. This young woman was in labor. She's having a baby. What should I do? What can I do? What am I supposed to do? Mai let out a little sigh and I could see she was gritting her teeth. I think I was in a panic, so I began to do something really dumb: I started to walk in circles. And talk to myself. Oh, Kelly. Do something.

I ran to the corner and woke up a cyclo driver. Fortunately, it was one I knew and he looked at the two Amerasians and then at me and quickly assessed the situation.

"Oh, Kelly—you want hospital. Why you not say so?" He packed us all in his cyclo and pedaled furiously through the darkened streets.

Saigon after midnight is eerie. It is dead quiet. No motorbikes whining, no loud music booming out from competing loudspeakers, no buses rumbling. Nothing. Periodically a dog would bark somewhere, off in the distance. It was just us, rushing like wind through the dark night.

"O.K., Kelly. Here you are. You go. Have baby. I wait." The cyclo driver let us out, then wheeled his cyclo over near a wall, crawled into the seat, and promptly fell asleep. What efficiency.

Lon, meanwhile, woke somebody up, and before I knew it, we were being walked up a flight of steps and down a long corridor.

There were no bright lights, no wheelchairs, no admitting clerks taking down pertinent information while other people screamed, "Can't this wait? This woman's having a baby!" The next thing I knew, we were in what I guessed was a delivery room: it had a metal table with stirrups. The doctors shooed Lon back out into the hall, where he squatted on the floor looking absolutely dazed. By this time Mai was lying down on that metal delivery table moaning and groaning, while a smiling woman wearing a white coat and a white thing on her head that looked like a chef's hat shoved a chair under me. Like it or not, I had a front-row seat.

I looked around and saw that I was in a small, white room. It was fairly clean but there were enough smudges and chipped paint to make me uneasy. The overhead lights were dim and far-off. There was a gooseneck lamp—very much like an old student's lamp—that was positioned down near Mai's lower extremities. One by one I saw the doctors and nurses—all women—go to the rubber-glove tree and pluck off some freshly washed surgical gloves to wear during the birthing procedure. Everything in the room was old and scratched or bent or battered in some way. But it was oddly comforting, too. The women doctors were serene and reassuring as they calmly went about the business of bringing Mai's new baby into this world.

Now please know this: the closest I had been to childbirth was a long string of movies and TV shows about the subject. I reviewed them. Other than that, I had done nothing more than meet a lot of friends for dinner after their birthing classes and listen to them toss around technical terms like "inhale" and "exhale." All of which, of course, made me the world's biggest know-it-all on childbirth. A self-styled, secondhand, know-nothing expert in various breathing and relaxation techniques available to today's pregnant women. Which explains why, sitting on that chair in the delivery room of Tu Du Hospital in Saigon, I went into automatic Lamaze mode, wheezing and whistling and breathing so loudly people turned and stared.

"You O.K.?" a doctor asked anxiously. She came over to me and put her hands solicitously on my shoulder. She had a look of worry and concern on her face. "You need something?" She had left Mai dangling in midpush over on the delivery table.

No, no. I assured her I was fine and she should concentrate on the pregnant woman she had on the table. But I couldn't help myself. The more Mai pushed and gripped the edge of the delivery table, the more I wheezed and whistled. The more she grunted and groaned, the more I panted and sucked in air and blew it out again. I was making so much noise even Mai raised her head and looked at me with a puzzled look on her face.

Finally, things reached their normal crescendo. There was a last-minute rushing around, followed by a piercing shout, and then some excited confusion. The next thing I knew, there was a general air of jubilation in the room as the doctor held up a brand-new and apparently healthy baby boy, who proceeded to yell and turn red. I was as excited as everyone else at the sight of Mai's ecstatic face and that tiny baby boy. And as I took one look at them and at all the blood and mucus and all those other precious bodily fluids—I fainted dead away on the floor. Nature, which had taken its normal course with Mai, had taken its toll on me.

The last thing I remember was a section of the tile floor coming up to meet me. The next thing I knew I was being helped to my feet by an army of concerned health-care professionals. As my eyes focused, I could see Mai. She was stranded, alone and abandoned on that delivery cart. She held a newborn baby in one arm and with the other she was holding herself up so she could look at me. She had a look of absolute horror and disbelief on her face: I was being propped up on a stool in the corner, leaving Mai and her newborn baby alone to fend for themselves.

The Tu Du Women's Hospital is a 750-bed hospital run for women and almost entirely by women, a cheerful, dedicated bunch of doctors and nurses treating twentieth-century problems with equipment and supplies that should have been condemned and destroyed about twenty years ago.

"Just look at that!" Dr. Phuong Nguyen said as she walked me down a dim hallway. I had recovered enough from the rigors of childbirth to go back to the hospital the next day to visit Mai. She and the baby were doing wonderfully well. I was expected to make a full recovery sometime within my lifetime. After paying my respects to Mai, I caught up with some of the doctors who had gotten me through the night. Dr. Phuong Nguyen was the head of the Medical Department of Tu Du Hospital. That meant she was in charge of everything from training and research to supervising the delivery room, the gynecology ward, and the newborn ward. She had offered to take me on a tour, and we were walking through the neonatal unit in the pediatric ward. With an angry flick of her arm she was gesturing to a room overflowing with premature infants.

They were lying in incubators that looked as if they belonged in a museum.

"Look at those incubators!" she cried angrily. "They're thirty years old! I have nurses who aren't that old!" Some of those premature newborns were lying two and three to an incubator, stacked there like tiny dolls in a child's playroom. There were no lights on in the room and most of the incubators weren't even plugged in. They appeared to be there simply as storage bins. I looked more closely at those tiny, wizened infants. Their i.d. tags were little pieces of cloth tied to their birdlike wrists, their names scratched in with ballpoint pens. They were all wearing paper towels instead of diapers. I counted at least fifty babies in that premature nursery, while across the hall in intensive care there were at least fifty more. There were more further down the hall, but I had stopped counting by that time.

I was both appalled and moved by what I was seeing. "Why are there so many preemies?" I asked. "And all those babies in intensive care?"

"Kelly, we have terrible problems here in Vietnam," Dr. Phuong said. By this time we were sitting in a small room downstairs, drinking tea. "This country is broke. These women are so poor they don't get the proper care when they're pregnant so their babies are born early and they are born hungry. And, of course," she shrugged, "there are the drugs and prostitution."

Vietnam, for all its reeducation camps, has stamped out neither drug abuse nor prostitution. And detox centers are unheard of in Vietnam. Result: drug addicts, addicted babies, venereal disease, malnutrition, and premature births. And, as the doctor explained, malnutrition and undernutrition and abysmal prenatal care throughout the country mean thousands of premature infants flooding into hospitals that are absolutely not equipped to deal with them.

And now Vietnam was facing yet another health-care disaster: AIDS. AIDS is coming to Vietnam from Eastern European countries, to which Vietnam has been shipping "guest workers" whose labor works off Vietnam's enormous foreign-aid debts to those countries. Returning Vietnamese, coming home to visit, have also been bringing in the AIDS virus. Worse, Bangkok and Manila—two of the most sexually promiscuous cities in Asia—serve as the only two port-of-entry cities for Vietnam. Most people stop off in either one of these two cities to get over jet lag and pick up visas to enter

Vietnam. Often they pick up more than their visas: they pick up the AIDS virus and bring it into Vietnam. What happens then? In a country that hasn't stamped out polio. Where people still die of tuberculosis and malaria. I shut my eyes. I couldn't even imagine the pain and suffering that waited for these people.

The doctor gave me a "shopping list" when I left. It included everything from incubators to condoms.

"Oh, we have condoms here," she said, laughing. "They come from Russia. The men hate them. They tell me it's like wearing rubber boots."

I visited Mai and her baby in the hospital the next day, just before they were to be discharged. Besides this healthy new baby, there was another reason to celebrate: their paperwork to leave the country had been finished and now they were all just waiting to be put on a flight out of the country so this new baby of theirs would grow up in America.

"We thank you so much, Mama," Lon and Mai said as I loaded them into a cyclo. Minh, my regular cyclo driver, was back on duty and acting as interpreter. Then Mai held up her baby boy. "We call him your name," Lon said. Oh, my God. This poor kid is going to arrive in America with a name like Katie. That would make him worse than a boy named Sue. "We call him My."

My. Well, I was certainly relieved. And puzzled. I allowed as how that was a very pretty name but still I was confused.

"Him name My. It mean 'American'."

Yes, it was a very pretty name.

GOODBYE, VIETNAM!

Saigon is my ghost city, a memory that rises up out of my past like a mist. I feel a choking sensation as I walk through Saigon, for I am walking through my own memories. The sight of the old American Embassy turns grainy, like an old piece of documentary film. It's 1968, the Tet Offensive. I stand on the outside of the action, horrified, watching the blazing firefight as the Vietcong breaks through its defenses and storms the embassy. Emotionally and philosophically, America started going home that day. I fast forward to 1975 and see the choppers making frantic last-minute rescues from the roof of that embassy. A few blocks away from the embassy is the presidential palace, built in the ugliest of 1960s styles: flat, squat, boring. It looks like a big Kleenex box. If I squint my eyes I can see all the way back to April 30, 1975. A North Vietnamese tank crashes through the ornamental front gate. The tank sticks there, impaled on the wrought iron, stuck in my mind.

Slowly, standing in front of the palace in this dreamscape of my own making, I turn my head. I can see the cathedral. It is big and red and brick, vaguely Gothic, vaguely Romanesque, completely European. As I stand in front of it, the pictures in the hallway of my mind reorganize themselves, a series of black-and-white photographs hanging by the thread of memory. I see a parade of haughty Vietnamese presidents standing in front of that cathedral: Diem, Thieu, Ky. It is a study in arrogance and corruption. I turn back to the palace and then, standing in front of that now-repaired gate, I shed the skin of my memories and confront Saigon head-on.

"American!" It is both a statement and a signal. I turn to see a plump, smiling woman wearing a bright blue dress. She is astride a huge motorcycle. "I'm going to Kansas!" she cries jubilantly as she waves and zooms off into traffic, headed toward the cathedral and down Dong Khoi Street.

It was time for me to leave, too. Sometimes you feel it in your bones. Sometimes you smell it in the air. I could see it: the Amerasians were disappearing. Or just about.

By early fall most of the Amerasians I knew had their paperwork done. They had trudged through the minefields of two bureaucracies—the Vietnamese (who had to approve them for their exit permits to leave Vietnam) and the Americans (who had to approve them for visas to enter America)—and after picking out the official shrapnel from both sides, they were ready to move on. Some of them had already gone: Kim, Cong, Raymond, Vu. Many more had been issued all the necessary papers and were now just waiting for the next most important document: that precious plane ticket out of Vietnam. To their new life. A new life that would start with a six-month stint in a refugee camp in the Philippines for a crash course in English and a cultural-orientation program on the American way of life. Everything from "Introduction to a Flush Toilet" and "How to Use the American Steam Iron" to "Opening a Checking Account" and "Applying for a Job." In the refugee camp they would be assigned sponsors, usually church groups, like Catholic Charities or Church World Service, or individuals who volunteered to help the newly arrived refugees. The sponsors would meet them at the airport and help them through those first few weeks in their new country: finding a place to live, enrolling in more language training courses, maybe finding entry-level jobs.

As for me, the timing was perfect. I had given myself a year in Saigon, figuring I could renegotiate with myself at the end of a year and, if need be, re-up. That decade-plus in television—with the binding ties of a series of long-term contracts—had taught me that I was really George Washington: I wanted no more entangling alliances. No more long-term commitments. Forever was much too long. I had long ago decided that this self-imposed early retirement of mine was simply a work-release program of my own making. From now on I would take life one day at a time. The fact that most of my students—my friends—were likewise leaving Vietnam simply justified that decision.

And so I began to look homeward. And that really made me stop dead in my tracks and think about these kids. My homeland would soon be theirs. And what in the world would happen to them there? I could only imagine the complicated and uncertain future these young people would face in America. The bottom line was, despite all their efforts to "become" Americans, to the American world around them they would be Vietnamese. Despite their very American features, despite their hard work at establishing and then defiantly celebrating their American selves, by this late date these kids were simply American wannabes. And, for a terrible time at least, they would not fit in anywhere. Not into mainstream America, not into any established Vietnamese community. As one Vietnamese man put it to me much later: we didn't help them in Vietnam, why should we help them in America?

I knew deep down in my heart of hearts that Bryner and Jim and Pearl and Tai and Kim and all the rest were cruising for some sort of bruising. They were headed for America and a new life that would bring great joy and success to some of them—probably most of them—but somewhere along the line they would all face a terrible, sad combination of disaster and despair. And a series of clichés: because things would indeed get worse before they got better. There would indeed be no place to go but up because when they arrived in America and fell off their recently achieved pedestal—after all, they were getting out—they would land with a thud. Call it what you will—culture shock? homesickness? anger? all of the above?—it was bound to happen. And it would be a rude, crude shock.

Most of these kids were completely unprepared for America. The only thing they had any experience in was survival—living from one day to the next. They were uneducated and unskilled. And, equally as bad, they didn't know *how* to be educated. Most had never learned how to sit in a classroom, take notes, do homework, read a book, write an essay. None had learned how to organize themselves the way American kids learn from the very beginning: organize their time, organize their money, make appointments, keep appointments. I could see how a lifetime on the run for some of these young people would affect the way they approached things: if something didn't work out, you abandoned it. Before it could abandon you.

As for their new country, that country they had dreamed of for so long? Well, sad to say, that America probably did not exist. Nothing could be that good. It simply would not, could not live up to their dreams. For their dreams were fantasies. America is not an easy country because democracy is not easy. Freedom is not easy. And our own experiment in democracy was still young, still in an infancy experiencing terrible, awful growing pains that left us reeling and bewildered. We sometimes forgot that we were a nation of immigrants. A nation of people who had, for nearly three centuries now, shoved our personal hopes and dreams into a series of burlap bags and steamer trunks and plastic tote bags and backpacks and set off for the Promised Land. It was a land that, by its very nature, didn't know what it was doing—because nobody had ever done this before. We were making it up as we went along. And we were making terrible mistakes in the process. I could only hope that their dreamland did not turn out to be their worst nightmare. These days, we all seem to be at each other's foreign, tribal throats.

And once here, these young people—who try so desperately to be Americans—will be thought of not so much as Americans who were born in Vietnam, but as Vietnamese who don't speak English very well. And then I had to admit, with terrible sadness, that I am part of their problem. To be an Amerasian in Vietnam these past few years was to be very special indeed. Americans—like me, like those veterans I met—came over and fussed over these young Amerasians. We were overwhelmed by our encounters with these kids because in a sense they were all our children. Their Amerasian faces might be the ticket to their future, but those same faces were our past. For these were our special, spiritual children haunting us by holding our past up to us, reminding us where we'd been, what we had done. By being who they are, they reminded us of who we were.

So we hung out with them, taught them English, bought them things, took their pictures, took them shopping, took them to Vung Tau. Were we really taking them for a ride? Leading them down a narrow cultural path that would only dead-end in some ghetto of bigotry in the land of the free and the home of the brave? No wonder these kids thought all of America was good and kind and had just been standing around waiting for them for the past fifteen years. Waiting to welcome them, waiting to continue making them feel special. Get real. We barely welcome our own relatives to the national trough.

Meanwhile, after years of discrimination or outright rejection (how much more rejected can you be when first your American father disappears and then, in some cases, your Vietnamese mother likewise abandons you to an orphanage or a grandmother or a neighbor), Amerasians were now in a very enviable position. They were getting out. In Vietnam, that's real power. If you were Amerasian, you now held incredible power right in the palm of your own hand—your own white or black or light-brown hand, your American hand—to take others out with you. Mothers, stepfathers, half brothers and sisters. Husbands, wives, and children. Entire families could come out, that parade of people being led by a single Amerasian. Imagine their surprise when they get to America and discover they are nothing special whatsoever. Just kids with a language problem. And no education. And no marketable job skills. So what else is new? Next.

I was concerned about all of my students, my special friends. Fortunately most of them would have their mothers and a load of siblings with them to help ease their way. But I was especially concerned about the unattached kids, particularly Bryner. I had gotten to know him so well over the year and had grown very fond of him. And I worried about him and his introduction to our fast-paced American life. Who would sponsor him? Help him over those cultural rough spots? Get him into a school that would respect his lack of formal education but encourage his natural abilities? He was such a bright young man that it would be a shame to waste his inherent talents and curiosity.

So here we have it: a mass movement of paperwork that was leading these Amerasian students, friends of mine, directly to the airport and eventually to America. It was just a matter of weeks or months for most of them. Tai's paperwork was being held up because of a medical problem but it did not seem insurmountable. Oddly enough, Jim, who had been interviewed long before anyone else, was still on hold. That troubled me, so with Jim in tow I buttonholed an ODP interviewer one day and was reassured, in English, that there was a medical problem with one of his sisters and when that was straightened out the whole family would be quickly processed.

I took all this as my signal to wrap things up and get out of town. I knew there were projects and programs in America to help these new Americans adapt to their adopted country and I wanted to be part of them. I wanted to be part of their future, not just their past.

Besides, despite the speed with which most of the cases were being processed, there were enough serious snags and hitches with some of my friends to make it quite apparent that I could now do more good back in America than here in Saigon. And for that I needed three things I did not have here: my Rolodex, my word processor, and a telephone that worked. I figured if I had any left-over clout at all, it certainly needed tossing around. And that would work only back in the U.S. of A.

Cau had come to me in great distress one day. He and Trang and their family—their daughter Kim plus Trang's mother, Luong, and Trang's Amerasian half sister, Hoc—had gone for their interview with the Americans who came to Saigon each month to process people wanting to leave under the Orderly Departure Program. I had known the interview was coming up and had not given it a second thought, figuring this family would make it through in a breeze. I had seen all their documents and everything appeared to be in perfect order. They were a family. Who could turn them down?

The Americans, that's who. ODP turned this family down flat.

Actually, the ODP interview team hadn't turned the entire family down. They had approved Trang and her daughter, Kim, and her Amerasian half sister, Hoc. For some inexplicable reason they had denied permission to both Cau and Luong. If the Americans had held a high-level meeting to decide what was the worst thing they could possibly do to this family, they couldn't have screwed it up any better. They denied permission to the two people who could speak English (Cau and Luong). They denied permission to the two people who had spent their lives fighting against Communists. They denied permission to the two people tough enough and sophisticated enough to have even a halfway decent chance to help this family survive in America. Both Trang and Hoc had grown up in that small village. But at least Trang had moved out and learned to cope with Saigon. Hoc was still a shy, naïve, bewildered village girl who walked around barefoot and hauled water from a well in an old GI helmet. Neither one spoke a word of English. And the news got even worse: Trang was pregnant again.

I was stunned. And bewildered. And mad as hell.

"My God, Cau! This is terrible!" I shouted. We were sitting in a little sidewalk café, ironically very near the office where the interviews were generally held. Cau was shaken. He handed me some papers that had just arrived. They were Vietnamese on one side, English on the other, so I had no difficulty seeing the judgment that had just been rendered by the American interview team. Cau had been denied. Luong had been denied. "What reason did they give you?"

Cau explained that while they were being interviewed he had sensed the interviewer did not believe he and Trang were actually married. "She thinks we are a false couple."

"A false couple? What does that mean?"

He shook his head. He was in despair. "She thinks we are not really married. She thinks I have arranged this so I can get out of the country." He shook his head again. "Trang is my wife, Kelly. I love her. I love her very much. Kim. Little Kim. Kim is my daughter. My baby. What would Kim do without me? I am her daddy. What would Trang do without me? She cannot speak English."

I shook his marriage certificate under his nose. "What the hell do they think this is?"

Cau took the paper from me and smoothed it out. "They think this paper is false," he explained patiently. "They looked at me and said, 'You are an old man. This is a young Amerasian. How can this young Amerasian be married to such an old man?' "

I checked the birthdates again. O.K., so Cau was forty-six and Trang was twenty-four. Big deal. So what. Hadn't those ODP people ever heard of Cary Grant and Dyan Cannon? Supreme Court Justice William O. Douglas? Senator Strom Thurmond? My parents? Jim Kelly married Maggie Doyle when she was thirty-eight and he was forty-six. Not quite the same but I suppose by ODP standards they would have been rejected, too.

I thought back to all the times I had been with this family, in Saigon and during all those trips of mine up to Bien Hoa. Unlike many men—Vietnamese or American—Cau was a completely involved family man. Trang and Kim were the small center of his universe. He adored them. I remember being at their house for lunch one hot day, and while we were sitting around afterward, I started goofing around. Luong had come up from Bien Hoa and had worn her cone hat, so I grabbed the hat and put it on and began sweeping the floor with a short little Vietnamese broom. Everybody thought this was a big joke and started laughing out loud at the crazy American woman sweeping the floor. Even the neighbors stopped to see what we were having so much fun with. Then tiny three-year-old Kim grabbed a broom, which completely overwhelmed her, and began sweeping furiously. A photograph shows the two of us laughing and being silly. And after all that silliness it was Cau who calmed Kim down for her nap. It was Cau who took her in his arms and laid her down. I have a photograph of him cradling his daughter in his arms, wiping her damp hair back from her forehead with one hand. With the other hand he is fanning her with an old paper fan. His fake Converse basketball shoes loom large over the edge of the bed. The photo doesn't record it, but Cau is talking and singing softly to his daughter until she is eventually lulled to sleep by the softness of his voice. This is the man—the husband, the father—the American interviewer does not want in our country? A man wearing basketball shoes and singing his daughter to sleep? What a crazy world.

And that still left Luong in the lurch. Luong, the mother of not one but two Amerasian daughters. A woman who had defiantly stood up to the Vietcong, local Communist officials, and baby buyers to keep her American children. There never was an explanation for the rejection of this brave, bold woman. As far as I was concerned, the American government should be paying people like Cau Luong and to come to America: good parents, people who loved America. Who could ask for anything more?

I caught up with an ODP worker in the bar of the Cuu Long Hotel early one evening. Over a couple of Heinekens I confronted him with this case and asked if he knew anything about it. He said he had heard something about it. He didn't seem to be concerned. "Don't worry about it. You know, these people—they lie about everything." These people? *These people?* These people were my friends. These people were good people. I kept fussing until finally the exasperated man looked at me and said: "Look. You don't understand how it is. These people arrive with documents that are so new they're still wet. And we're supposed to believe it's a birth certificate from 1967? A wedding certificate from 1985? These people are so desperate to get out of this country they'll do anything. I have people come in with marriage certificates who don't even know their partner's first name."

"But, but, but . . ." I tried to plead Cau's and Trang's cases. I pointed out I'd been to their home. I knew their child. I had been to Bien Hoa, met Trang's mother. Didn't any of that count for anything.

"Look. Sure this is frustrating. Sometimes it gets so confusing we just sit there and say, O.K.—you and you and you have permission to leave. You and you and you don't have permission to leave. Sometimes that's the best we can do."

I was appalled. Somebody had made just such a whimsical decision concerning Cau and Trang because they couldn't believe a man of Cau's age could have such a beautiful young Amerasian wife. O.K., you and you and you can go to America. The rest of you can't. Result: a husband would be separated from his wife and child. A mother would be separated from the two daughters she had fought so hard to save from the Communists.

And the hits kept coming. Direct hits on many of my closest friends in Saigon. Kim had gotten out months before, taking with her most of her Vietnamese siblings, and leaving behind her grief-stricken mother. The mother who had sheltered her and protected her through all those years when the Americans were leaving, when the Communists came. Made a home for her on the streets, in a work camp, and finally in one half of one room. Kim's mother, my good friend Nguyet, had elected to make one last sacrifice for her other Amerasian daughter, Roan-na: she would stay behind with Roan-na while her paperwork got straightened out. In the months that I was there, Kim not only had left Vietnam but she had completed her stay in the refugee camp in the Philippines and had gone on to be reunited with her American father in North Carolina. She left behind a sorrowful mother who nonetheless had to keep going, if only to get her other Amerasian daughter out of the country.

During all that time, Nguyet and Roan-na—and sometimes I—had trooped from one office to another trying to stay afloat in the bureaucratic backwash that threatened to drown them both. I don't know how they did it. I would have been a raving maniac. While I had been convinced that our encounter with the American psychiatrist at the mental-health clinic all those weeks ago had clinched the deal, I was wrong. Dead wrong. Among other things, somewhere along the line, the Americans had changed the rules. Again. And Nguyet literally had to start all over. Again. This was really nuts. Yet another reason to leave Saigon. I figured I'd just go home and write a few letters on the matter.

One day in July, Pearl came moping into our midst confessing he had done a terrible thing. Indeed he had. I could not believe what he had done, the trouble he had caused, the mess he had made. He was now reaping the whirlwind and was devastated by it. It seems that when Pearl went for his initial interview with the Vietnamese authorities to start the paperwork to eventually get his exit visa, he had lied. And it was a whopper.

Now Saigon has always been a city of rumors. Saigon runs on rumors. It is the fuel that keeps it going, especially now without even the pretense of a free press. And Pearl had listened to a rumor that proved to be disastrous. He had heard—and believed—that if you were an unattached Amerasian, you got priority treatment in getting out of the country. So Pearl, who had one of the most fiercely loyal mothers I had ever met, lied. He lied big. And he lied bad. He told the Vietnamese authorities he was an orphan. And that is what all his paperwork showed. So by the time he had worked his way through the Vietnamese side and had gotten to the Americans, he was in deep trouble. And when he took his mother with him and tried to straighten it out with the Americans, guess what? They didn't believe him. To the Americans, he was just an unattached Amerasian trying to sneak some Vietnamese woman out of the country with him.

Oh, Pearl. What have you done?

So here he was: through with his paperwork, armed with an exit visa, and manifested out of the country. He even had a date to go pick up his airline ticket. And now he came to me, asking for help as the enormity of what he had done finally hit him squarely between the eyes.

Pearl and I went to his mother, Dung, in her corrugated tin shack hooked onto a friend's house. She was in tears. The single most important thing in her life was now about to be taken from her. She was overcome with sadness. I spent an afternoon with her. The tears never stopped. Then it began to rain. It was a horrible storm. The thunder rolled in like a bombardment. The water came down in grim, steely gray plates. It pounded and thudded and beat down on that shack so hard I could feel it roaring inside me. But none of that compared to the tears of Pearl's mother. Her face seemed to dissolve behind her veil of tears. We sat there, in that ramshackle lean-to, while the rain tore the air around us. I held her hand for a long time, then I went and stood in the doorway while she wiped her face. I was weeping, too.

"Get out all your papers," I demanded. I was like an emergency-room nurse. Why not? This woman was about to die of a broken heart. A broken heart caused by carelessness. Caused by a kid so desperate to get out of a country he hated so much he had selfishly sacrificed the one thing that was important to him: his own mother.

Dung burst off the bed like a woman possessed. She became a fury, pulling out boxes and plastic bags and going through a lifetime of papers. She and Pearl kept up an excited chatter as she directed him through the papers that began building up on her wooden pallet.

"Here!" she cried, triumphantly putting a pile of papers in my hands.

"Is it all here?" I demanded. I was fired up. She nodded firmly. "I want everything, everything, everything."

"You got everything," she agreed firmly. We were co-conspirators. By the end of the afternoon, I was convinced I had the paper history of Pearl and his mother: birth certificates, housing registrations, permits. I even had Pearl's grammar school report cards.

"See, Miss Kelly. See how smart he is!" Dung said, pointing to that report card. "Look. Here. He even get good grades for being good boy." Not these days, he wouldn't. I told Dung not to worry but I was taking it all with me. She'd get it back the next day. My plan was to put Pearl and his mother through a photocopy machine. About that time, the neighborhood manicurist wandered by and I had to sit and have my fingernails and toenails done again. When the last butterfly was finally transferred to my big toe, I took off, clutching that precious paper trail. It took over an hour, sitting on a stool at the photocopy kiosk across from the Kim Do, but I finally had four complete sets of their documents: one for Pearl (to take with him to the Philippines and try to get something done), one for his mother (in case she needed an extra set here in Saigon), one for me (to take back to America to start bugging the bureaucracy there with), and one for my secret plan.

Now listen up: I did not spend nearly twenty-five years working in and around the high-powered New York media for nothing. Those were not wasted years. I did not sit on my can, totally unaware of my surroundings. Of course not. I observed. I saw things. Think of it: all those press releases! All those press kits! Yes: I made up a press kit for Pearl and his mother. It wasn't quite as glossy as the ones announcing the arrival of Ringling Brothers Circus to Madison Square Garden. Not quite as glitzy as the one that arrived one Christmas from the local public broadcasting station, which came attached to a huge tin tub containing three kinds of popcorn—plain, spicy, and caramel. No. Mine was by necessity simple. But it had all the basics: a covering letter introducing Pearl and his mother and explaining the problem and pleading their case. It also had a full set of their documents, including Pearl's grammar school report cards. And my *pièce de résistance:* two photos of Pearl and his mother.

One photo, black-and-white, was a copy of one taken in 1968 when Pearl was about six months old. It shows a pretty, solemn young woman wearing a sleeveless blouse and a pair of 1960s slacks that—in the style of the day—stopped tight just above the ankle. She is sitting on a stone bench in a park, and cradled in the crook of her arm is her very American-looking baby. He, too, is very solemn in a little baby baseball cap and a white shirt with a little baby bow tie.

The second picture I included in my photo essay was one I took of Pearl and his mother out at their house. Again, it shows a very American-looking kid, only this time he is wearing a T-shirt and a pair of jeans. And this time their roles are reversed: the child has his arm around the mother, an older, somewhat thicker version of that solemn young woman from 1968. But there is no doubt they are the same two people.

I organized all this material and put it into a shiny black presentation folder that had somehow found its way into my luggage. The next day I walked over to the Cuu Long Hotel, where the American interviewers from the Orderly Departure Program were staying and dropped it off. I suppose the desk clerk thought I had real "mental health" when I solemnly kissed the package and raised my eyes to heaven before handing it to her. I also had the fingers of my right hand crossed.

A few weeks later, when I was getting ready to leave Saigon, I ran into an Orderly Departure representative at the Givral and brought up Pearl's case. He knew immediately what I was talking about. "Oh, yeah, right," he said with a smile, acknowledging that they had not only gotten the packet but it had actually made its way to Bangkok for review. "The woman with the kid who looked like Charlie McCarthy." I wanted to smack him. My Pearl didn't look like a ventriloquist's dummy. You dummy. But it was one more reason to get back home: keep the pressure on ODP to get Pearl's mother processed and out of the country.

The lobby of the Kim Do was packed. There were so many people there to say goodbye to me you couldn't even see the yellow linoleum upholstery on the furniture. Even Miss Congeniality looked a little sad. Well, maybe "sad" is too strong a word. Bewildered? Nguyet had found a pair of high-heeled shoes to wear. Roan-na had on a skirt and blouse. Cau and Trang arrived with their little daughter Kim, who was wearing pink eye shadow. Trang wanted to give me a fresh manicure, right there in the chaos of the lobby. Somehow I managed to weasel out of it. Even the basketball coach and his wife and little girl were there. The only person missing was Linh. But he was missing with a purpose: he and Thanh, his Amerasian half sister, had finally been scheduled for their first interviews to get out of the country. In typical fashion, though, he had organized everything: when my tote bag had broken, he had taken it off and had it repaired. When I had needed string to tie up some packages, he had found it for me. He had even organized my transportation to the airport.

I had given some cash gifts to the kids in my class, telling them firmly it was to buy things for their stay in the Philippines. The guys all arrived wearing new black pants (with belts, what a treat) and white T-shirts. The girls had invested in new sandals made out of gold plastic. After I had packed and locked my bags, I told the gang to go up and get my stuff and clean out my room while they were there. They came down armed with everything from jigsaw puzzles and paperback spy thrillers to empty file folders and marking pens.

It took three cars to get us all to the airport. Like a corpse at her own burial, I was graciously loaded into the lead car, a vintage 1965 Ford Fairlane.

It was the usual mess at the airport, and while we were sorting ourselves out I stood the crowd to one last round of Coca-Cola. Pearl had somehow dug up a guitar, and as I sat there on my duffel bag sweating and drinking a Coke, they started to sing their favorite American songs for me. I thought back over the year. My stay in Saigon was a catalog of contradictions. I had laughed all day (live chickens during an eye exam? hotel prostitutes? fried birds? a head injury?) then cried myself to sleep at night over homeless kids, a beautiful young girl living under a staircase, Vietnamese mothers who were ostracized, American fathers who disappeared. I shook my head and climbed off my duffel bag. It was time to go.

I lined everybody up and began fussing over them. Bryner, don't break your new teeth. Pearl, take care of your mother. Jim, stop smoking. Tom, work on your past tense. I was dithering. Marking time. Wandering around like a lost cause looking for some way to distract myself so I wouldn't have a complete emotional meltdown. I would save that for later. This parting was bittersweet: a truly wonderful and exhilarating year was about to end. I was leaving fine and wonderful friends. I would see most of them again. But still, that didn't ease the sadness.

I took one last picture of everyone, made sure my papers were in order, clutched the most precious thing in the world—my American passport—and then hugged everyone for the last time. They were crying, I was crying. "I love New York!" somebody yelled. I laughed. A little.

Then Pearl began playing the guitar again and they all started to sing. As I gathered up my bags and walked away from them I could hear them singing their favorite American song for me. Maybe no one else could understand the words, but as for me, I have never heard a more beautiful version of "We Are the World."

I cried until my nose ran.

EPILOGUE

Park Avenue, New York City. There was already a crowd of well-appointed types milling around on the street in front of the Waldorf-Astoria, that snazzy East Side hotel. A fleet of likewise well-appointed buses was parked nearby, idling in the cold New York night as people boarded them. It was time for my reentry into New York night life: Frank Sinatra's seventy-fifth birthday bash. We would board those buses and be whisked out to a concert at the Meadowlands Arena in New Jersey, then whisked back to the Waldorf-Astoria for a sit-down dinner. Pat Kennedy Lawford climbed on the bus with me. She locked herself in the toilet on the way out. Harry Connick, Jr., and his drop-dead gorgeous model girlfriend sat in front of me. They exchanged very long, damp kisses on the way to the concert and back again. I shared the rest of the evening with the likes of Liza Minnelli, Joe Piscopo, New York Mayor David Dinkins, Roger Moore, R. J. Wagner, and gossip columnist Liz Smith. Obviously, I didn't get to this big-time bash on my own. My long-time good friend Cliff Jahr, at the time researching Barbara Sinatra's autobiography, took me to this fancy do.

And after a year in Saigon, it wasn't easy.

*   *   *

I was back. But I wasn't really back. My heart and mind had been captured by all those people I was now separated from. And my reentry to the American way of life was difficult indeed. It was much harder to settle back onto my American life and lifestyle than it had ever been for me to settle into Saigon. I just couldn't find my niche. I was sent reeling by everything from wearing pantyhose to hot water on demand. The shelves in my local supermarket stunned me. Do we really need fifteen different kinds of breakfast flakes? Even garbage depressed me. All that waste. All those things— thrown away. Leftover food being scraped off plates in restaurants drove me nuts. I became sour and judgmental, a loony old lady stomping around the neighborhood glaring at limousines, designer water, and Donna Karan ads, demanding to know: WHO BUYS THIS STUFF? Then I took my cat to his kitty dentist and had the plaque removed from his teeth. That straightened me out but good. Life does go on and I got going.

I had promised Cau and Trang and Luong to see what I could do about their case. They were frantic when I left Saigon and so was I. So I took advantage of what I left Vietnam for: my Rolodex, my word processor, and the telephone. I bombarded my congressional representatives—from both New York and Nebraska—with regular letters on their behalf. Every week I sent another letter to the Orderly Departure office in Bangkok, outlining the situation and becoming an airmail character witness for Cau and his family. Everyone from Congressman Mrazek, who wrote the Amerasian Homecoming Act, to Senator Daniel Moynihan, Senator Al D'Amato, and Senator Bob Kerrey wrote letters on their behalf. Bangkok didn't know what hit them. It took a few weeks but then I had word: Cau and his family had been reinterviewed in Saigon and they had all been approved to leave Vietnam and come to America. By May they were in the refugee camp in the Philippines where Cau and Trang's daughter Mai was born. Late in 1991 they arrived in Hartford, Connecticut. Shortly after that, Cau and Trang and their daughters had a brief reunion with Trang's father in Maryland. They hope to see more of him in the future.

KIM, that lovely Amerasian who actually got me going on all this, arrived in America in the fall of 1990. She is living with her American father in Fayetteville, North Carolina, and going to school. She is almost completely fluent now and we talk often on the phone, and her future plans include going to college. Her mother and half sister were still in Vietnam when I left. The confusion surrounding their case was bewildering, and Nguyet, generally so optimistic and cheerful, seemed despondent. I was unable to get any sensible answers to questions about her case. She just seemed to be caught in a twilight zone of bureaucratic confusion. I came home and had a sad letter from Nguyet saying she felt in her heart she was going to be in Vietnam forever. "Maybe I die here," she said.

Dr. Judy Ladinsky from the University of Wisconsin, who heads a joint U.S.-Vietnamese scientific exchange program, had met Nguyet and her family in Saigon. We talked back and forth a few times and I was reassured that Dr. Ladinsky was not only interested in Nguyet but was also on the case. I continued to write letters on Nguyet's behalf and made some phone calls. Then, one night in July of last year, I had a phone call from Kim. With lightning speed, Nguyet and Roan-na had not only gotten out of Vietnam but had come immediately to America.

"Yes, they are here. In America. I was so happy to see my mother and my sister again," Kim told me on the phone in her by-now almost flawless English. "She got off the plane, I cried, she cried. Roan-na smiled. It was very good." Nguyet and Roan-na are now living in Charlotte, North Carolina, with the rest of Nguyet's children. There Nguyet can work on her English and, hopefully, Roan-na will find a program to deal with her problems.

Meanwhile, the forward momentum of the Orderly Departure Program continues to propel most of the rest of my students and friends on toward their final destination. Without fail, every month brings good news as those Amerasians slowly make it out of Vietnam, through the six-month educational and processing program in the refugee camp in the Philippines, and finally to America:

PEARL was sponsored by John Pritchard, the Vietnam vet we all met on the roof of the Rex Hotel in downtown Saigon. Pearl now lives in Rochester, Minnesota, where he immediately began attending high school. Three months after he arrived, John and Pearl both came to New York to visit me. Pearl's English was astonishing and, I am happy to report, he never shut up. Among other achievements, Pearl now has his driver's license and has bought his first car, all within six months of his arrival. He also helped form a youth organization in Rochester dedicated to helping new immigrants and refugees from Vietnam, particularly Amerasians. As for Pearl's mother, it took longer than I thought it should, but on September 30 of 1991 she left Vietnam headed for that refugee camp in the Philippines.

HUONG and her mother, who once lived under that staircase in downtown Saigon, now have an apartment of their own in Lacey, Washington, near Olympia. The building has an elevator. Huong is attending high school and her mother goes to adult English classes.

Vu and his grandmother are in western Ohio, just outside Dayton. Vu, who knew only one word of English when I met him ("Good! Good!"), is nearly fluent now. We talk regularly on the phone and he speaks with hardly an accent. He is also in school, looking forward to getting a job soon.

Tai and his mother are in Atlanta, Georgia. They were held up in Vietnam because it was discovered Tai had TB, but once that was cleared up, thanks to a steady treatment with American-supplied miracle drugs, they went to the refugee camp in the Philippines. Because of his illiteracy, Tai had a great deal of difficulty with the educational programs in the refugee camp, which don't deal very well with illiteracy among these Amerasians coming out of Vietnam. Through his sponsoring agency Tai did get a low-level job, but unless he gets into a top-notch literacy program in Atlanta, Tai will be one of this generation's lost boys.

Tom ended up in Memphis, Tennessee. A friend of mine looked him up and reported he was living in a rundown apartment in a rather depressed area but seemed to be doing well. There were other Vietnamese nearby, and he got a job almost immediately working in a warehouse. I was disappointed to hear he likewise was not continuing with any school.

Cong, the actor who threw such a farewell party for himself, plunged into politics in the refugee camp. The camp was divided into neighborhoods and in a program designed not only to bring a bit of self-government to the camp but also to introduce the refugees to the concepts and workings of democracy, Cong successfully ran for a seat on his neighborhood's governing body. Early in 1990 he was resettled in Camden, New Jersey.

Bieu and her family are now in Hawaii. Be and his mother and three brothers and sisters are in Chicago. Huy, the young Amerasian cyclo driver, and Mary, who ran a refreshment stand with her mother in Amerasian Park, were both relocated to Rochester, New York. Even the smugglers—Tho and Ky—and their family made it to America. They now live in Louisiana, where all three of their children were mainstreamed directly into an American school. Ky got a job as an assistant painter on offshore oil rigs and has since been given two promotions.

Jim continues to be the hardest case of all. Despite that reassurance of the ODP officer in Saigon, by early 1992 Jim and his family still were not out of Vietnam.

Meanwhile, through some of the nuns I had met while serving Thanksgiving dinners at St. Malachy's Church in Times Square, I discovered St. Rita's Asian Center in the Bronx. This is a resettlement agency working primarily with Vietnamese refugees being settled in the New York City area. And among those Vietnamese refugees are dozens of Amerasians. Sister Jean Marshall, who runs St. Rita's with both compassion and composure, has put together an all-purpose agency to serve the needs of these refugees. St. Rita's has an alternative high school for older Amerasians, a series of adult English classes for their mothers and stepfathers, plus advanced classes for refugees able to work toward their GEDs, General Educational Development for high school equivalency diplomas. There are a job-training program and a job-placement program and a computer training lab. There is even a clothing bank for those in need of emergency clothing. There are Vietnamese caseworkers to help the newcomers through the bewildering maze of paperwork involved with this fresh start they are making. As for me, three days a week I catch the D train and go up to help tutor the Amerasian students in English and, from time to time, organize field trips.

Then I made a momentous decision: to sponsor one of my Amerasian students from Saigon. After a grueling thirty-hour flight from the refugee camp in the Philippines, Bryner arrived in New York City on April 11, 1991. I met him at the airport and, typically, our cabdriver was from Laos and our route from the airport to Manhattan took us through Chinatown and Little Italy. Ten minutes after he got into the house, still dazed from that transpacific flight that hurtled him through time and place, he asked when he could start going to school. Within a week he was in an adult English class at the local YMCA. Three months later he got his first job, as a porter at the local movie theatre. He started typing—in English—four months after he arrived. He wants to graduate from high school and learn a skill so he can get a good job. Even before Bryner's arrival I had written to his father and enclosed a picture I had taken of his son in Saigon. Bryner himself wrote to his father after he arrived in New York. John Pritchard even called and spoke to him one night. John reported that Bryner's father seemed interested, even concerned—but so far he has not contacted his son.

Then I agreed to sponsor Linh and his Amerasian half sister, Thanh. They arrived six weeks after Bryner and took up their positions in my New York brownstone. They, too, were immediately enrolled in English classes at the Y. Thanh, who left both Vietnam and the refugee camp completely illiterate, went into a literacy class. She worked hard both at school and at home on the dining-room table. Her proudest moment came when she could actually write her name—on her brand-new American Social Security card.

Linh and Thanh stayed most of the summer, then moved on to Worcester, Massachusetts, to be with friends. Back in Vietnam, where residents needed police permits to live "officially" in a chosen city or town, we had often talked about freedom of movement in America. Thus they learned their first big lesson in freedom: if you have the price of a bus ticket, you can go anywhere you want.

"I knew it, Mama. I knew America would be wonderful," Linh marvels.

I suppose I went to Vietnam as much for myself as for any high-flown ideas of goodness and mercy. Unlike the veterans who suffered first the horrors of war in Vietnam and then returned to scorn and contempt here in America, I had no demons to exorcise. No ghosts to banish. But I was so shocked and saddened at the sight of all those Amerasians roaming the streets of Saigon that I wanted to go back and do some little bit of good. The American Dream had paid off for me and I just wanted to put back some of my own good fortune. But, as usually happens in cases like this, I got back a lot more than I gave. Perhaps even more than I deserved. I may have taught a bunch of Amerasian kids the difference between a shoe and a chicken leg but they and their families and all the rest of the people I met up and down Vietnam taught me about forgiveness and generosity. To us, the past is prologue. To them, the past is over. Finished. Life goes on. In America that's the name of a TV series. In Vietnam, it is something to live by. A credo. A doctrine of faith. They have a philosophy; we often have only attitude. In Vietnam I saw both the strength of will and the grace of spirit that allowed people to continue to celebrate the most precious belief of all—the belief in the goodness of life. And it was their everlasting gift to me.